Betraying Big Brother

T0286743

Also by Leta Hong Fincher

Leftover Women: The Resurgence of Gender Inequality in China

Betraying Big Brother

The Feminist Awakening in China

Leta Hong Fincher

VERSO
London • New York

This paperback edition published by Verso 2021
First published by Verso 2018
© Leta Hong Fincher 2018, 2021

1 3 5 7 9 10 8 6 4 2

Verso

UK: 6 Meard Street, London W1F 0EG
US: 20 Jay Street, Suite 1010, Brooklyn, NY 11201
versobooks.com

Verso is the imprint of New Left Books

ISBN-13: 978-1-78663-365-1
ISBN-13: 978-1-78663-366-8 (UK EBK)
ISBN-13: 978-1-78663-367-5 (US EBK)

British Library Cataloguing in Publication Data
A catalogue record for this book is available from the British Library

The Library of Congress Has Cataloged the Hardback Edition As Follows:
Names: Hong Fincher, Leta, author.
Title: Betraying Big Brother : the feminist awakening in China / Leta Hong
  Fincher.
Description: London ; New York : Verso, 2018. | Includes bibliographical
  references and index. |
Identifiers: LCCN 2018016225 (print) | LCCN 2018016960 (ebook) | ISBN
  9781786633668 (United Kingdom) | ISBN 9781786633675 (United States) |
  ISBN 9781786633644
Subjects: LCSH: Feminism—China. | Women—Political activity—China. |
  Social media—Political aspects—China.
Classification: LCC HQ1767 (ebook) | LCC HQ1767 .H648 2018 (print) | DDC
  305.420951—dc23
LC record available at lccn.loc.gov/2018016225

Typeset in Fournier by MJ & N Gavan, Truro, Cornwall
Printed and bound by CPI Group (UK) Ltd, Croydon, CR0 4YY

For Aidan and Liam
And for my sisters resisting around the world

Chinese women will throw off their shackles and stand up with passion; they will all become heroines. They will ascend the stage of the new world, where the heavens have mandated that they reconsolidate the nation.

—Qiu Jin, *Stones of the Jingwei Bird* (1905–1907)

Contents

Introduction

The recording begins with the bell-like soprano voice of a young woman singing a cappella in Chinese. Her melody is from *Les Miserables*' "Do You Hear the People Sing?" but her lyrics are about women's rights:

> Are you the same as me?
> We believe in a world with equality
> This is a song of freedom and dignity
> A song for all women!

Twenty-five-year-old feminist activist Li Maizi circulated "A Song for All Women" to feminist chat groups on China's popular messaging app, WeChat, in mid-April 2015. She had just been released from more than a month of detention, along with four other feminist activists: Wu Rongrong, Zheng Churan, Wei Tingting, and Wang Man. Her song—which has become the anthem of China's feminist movement—announced to the Chinese government that despite constant threats and rounds of interrogation during her incarceration, she was unbroken.

Chinese authorities had jailed the five feminist activists for planning to commemorate International Women's Day, March 8, by handing out stickers against sexual harassment on subways and buses. At the time of their arrest, the five women were almost completely unknown. Had they not been jailed, their activities likely would not have attracted much attention. In cracking down on these largely anonymous women, however, the Chinese government sparked the creation of a powerful new symbol of dissent against the patriarchal, authoritarian state: the "Feminist Five."

If China's leaders thought they could crush a nascent feminist movement by detaining five young women in Beijing and two other cities, they were sorely mistaken. News of the arrest of the Feminist Five spread swiftly around the world through social media. Protesters marched in support of the five feminists in the United States, the UK, Hong Kong, South Korea, India, Poland and Australia. Many of the world's mainstream news organizations reported on the women's detention.

The jailing of the five feminists coincided with preparations for Chinese president Xi Jinping to cohost a United Nations summit on women's rights in New York to mark the twentieth anniversary of Beijing's World Conference on Women, sparking an international outcry from rights organizations and world leaders. Hillary Clinton—then considered the frontrunner to become the next US president—tweeted, "Xi hosting a meeting on women's rights at the UN while persecuting feminists? Shameless." The US secretary of state and government representatives from the European Union, the UK, Canada, and elsewhere called on China to release the detained feminists. US vice president Joe Biden—using a Twitter hashtag adopted by US government officials to refer to the run-up to the UN women's summit—tweeted, "Rights of women and girls should never be suppressed. We urge Chinese leaders to show respect for women's rights and #FreeBeijing20Five." The US ambassador to the UN, Samantha Power, tweeted, "In China speaking out against sexual harassment is 'creating a disturbance.' Disturbance is restricting NGOs [nongovernmental organizations] fighting for universal rights." Faced with tremendous global diplomatic and social-media pressure, Chinese authorities released the women after holding them at a detention center for thirty-seven days. But today they remain criminal suspects, subject to constant surveillance by the state.

The Chinese government's detention of the Feminist Five marked an important turning point in the history of women's rights in China, showing the world that a relatively small group of young feminists was capable of posing what the Chinese Communist Party perceived to be a serious challenge to its rule. Inside China, feminist activists, university students, lawyers, workers and scholars were galvanized by anger and shock over the injustice. Even male workers who had benefited from the feminists' labor rights advocacy showed their solidarity with the Feminist Five on social media. One male worker posted a photo of himself naked from the waist up on Weibo—the Chinese version of Twitter—with his bare back turned to the camera, showing off large red characters written on his body: "Giant Rabbit (the nickname for Zheng Churan), always proud of you! The proletariat supports you!"

Ever more young women—some of them only in high school—began signing up as volunteers for the fledgling but growing feminist movement. Some women who had previously avoided political discussions now decided to identify themselves publicly as feminists on social media, forcing the government's internet censors to work even more aggressively to shut down online expressions of solidarity with the Feminist Five. The term "feminist" (*nüquan zhuyi zhe*) suddenly became a politically sensitive keyword, subject to waves of censorship. One of the Feminist Five activists, Wei Tingting, wrote an account called "Prison Notes," which she posted on WeChat (under a pseudonym), about her "joy in betraying Big Brother" during her 2015 detention, and it is from her that I draw the title of this book.

~

Betraying Big Brother is about the conflict between the Chinese government's unprecedented crackdown on young feminist activists and the emergence of a broader feminist awakening that is beginning to transform women in cities across China. The outcome of this conflict between the patriarchal, authoritarian state and ordinary women who are increasingly fed up with the sexism in their daily lives could have far-reaching consequences for China—the world's second largest economy—and the rest of the world.

Nearly one out of every five women in the world lives in China—more than 650 million women in total. Any major demographic shift as a result of women choosing to reject marriage and children—or perhaps even to rise up collectively against the Communist Party's oppression—will inevitably reverberate throughout the global economy.

Under President Xi Jinping, China's strongman authoritarianism has taken an alarming turn for the worse. On March 11, 2018, China's legislature abolished presidential term limits, allowing Xi to remain China's paramount ruler for the rest of his life. There are many reasons that China's Communist regime has survived for almost seventy years, in spite of the collapse of communism in the Soviet Union and elsewhere in Eastern Europe. But it is impossible to understand the longevity of China's Communist Party without recognizing the patriarchal underpinnings of its authoritarianism. In short, China's ultimate strongman, Xi, like other autocrats around the world, views *patriarchal* authoritarianism as critical for the survival of the Communist Party.

The Chinese government aggressively perpetuates traditional gender norms and reduces women to their roles as dutiful wives, mothers and baby breeders in the home, in order to minimize social unrest and give birth to future generations of skilled workers. The government is also carrying out a sweeping crackdown on feminist activists because China's all-male rulers seem to think that the entire security state would collapse were it not for the subjugation of women. As a result, the #MeToo hashtag against sexual harassment has been the target of frequent censorship, posing yet another extreme challenge for Chinese feminist activists, who have made sexual violence one of their central causes.

Outside China, the #MeToo campaign (created by the African-American civil rights activist Tarana Burke) went viral in more than eighty-five countries in 2017, in some cases ending the careers of extremely powerful men found to have engaged in sexual harassment or assault, from Harvey Weinstein in Hollywood and Matt Lauer in TV news to several prominent US politicians. Merriam-Webster announced that its word of the year for 2017 was *feminism*, citing a 70 percent increase in lookups for the word over 2016.

Yet, in China, heavy online censorship and the extensive security apparatus may have stopped a large-scale, nationwide #MeToo campaign from taking off. In November 2017, authorities forced three feminist activists to move out of their homes in the southern city of Guangzhou in retaliation for planning to hand out anti–sexual harassment placards for women to wear on the streets. That same month, censors deleted a #MeToo–like essay from a woman in Shanghai who complained on her phone messaging app, WeChat, about a serial molester in her neighborhood who had groped her and other women repeatedly on the street. Her post received more than a million views and almost ten thousand comments, but within two days WeChat authorities deleted it, saying that her post "violated regulations." When the woman posted about the incident on the social media platform Weibo, she was deluged with misogynistic comments from other users, who blamed her for "overreacting" to being groped and dressing too "revealingly."

In January 2018, thousands of students and alumni in China—women as well as men—signed Me Too petitions at dozens of universities across China, demanding action against sexual harassment. But many of the petitions were deleted by censors soon after being posted on social media. Then late on the night of March

8, 2018, International Women's Day, Weibo banned the most influential feminist social media account, *Feminist Voices*, because it "posted sensitive and illegal information." The following day, WeChat deleted their account as well. At the time the ban was imposed, *Feminist Voices* had over 180,000 followers on Weibo and over 70,000 followers on WeChat.

The shrinking public space for discussing women's rights in China makes it even more extraordinary that a feminist movement is able to survive at all. The Party-state's ongoing crackdown on women's rights activists is particularly ironic, given the central importance of gender equality during the Communist revolution and the early Mao era, following the founding of the People's Republic of China in 1949. From the 1950s through the 1970s, the Chinese government publicly celebrated gender equality and boasted the biggest female workforce in the world (a strategy it employed to boost the nation's productivity). But in the 1990s, gender inequality deepened as China accelerated economic reforms, dismantling the Party-mandated system of equal employment for women and men. In 1990, for example, the average annual salary of an urban woman was 77.5 percent that of a man, but by 2010, urban women's average income had fallen to just 67.3 percent that of men, according to government data.

In my first book, *Leftover Women: The Resurgence of Gender Inequality*, I described how Chinese women—from poor, rural women to middle-class, urban women—largely missed out on arguably the biggest accumulation of residential property wealth in history, worth around 3.3 times China's gross domestic product—GDP—according to a report by HSBC Bank. That amounted to around US $43 trillion at the end of 2017. I analyzed how gendered factors following China's privatization of housing, such as pressure on women to leave their names off property deeds and new regulatory barriers to women's property ownership, have created a giant gender wealth gap.

The reform-era media has also aggressively promoted

traditional gender norms. As I argued in *Leftover Women*, the Chinese government began a crass campaign in 2007 to stigmatize single, professional women in their late twenties, mocking them as "leftover" women to push them into marrying and having babies for the good of the nation. But with record numbers of Chinese women attending university, both at home and abroad, they are beginning to challenge widespread sexism and unequal treatment, and more and more have identified as feminists.

Far too often the role of women in resistance movements is overlooked, but it is critical that we bear witness to the persecution of feminist activists resisting authoritarian repression in China. The stories of these women show us why China's male rulers feel so threatened by the prospect of a large-scale feminist movement. While prominent male human-rights activists have emerged over the years (most notably, the Nobel Peace Prize laureate Liu Xiaobo, who died in custody in 2017), very few ordinary Chinese citizens knew about them or could relate to their abstract goals. The feminist resistance may yet have the potential to become China's most transformative movement in the long run—provided that any social movement is allowed to exist.

In 2012, around a hundred feminist activists were regularly participating in performance art and direct action across the country, to denounce growing gender inequality driven by market reforms. They took up domestic violence (China had no anti–domestic violence law in effect until 2016), sexual harassment, gender discrimination in employment and university admissions, and insufficient toilets for women—issues chosen because they were not overly politically sensitive, but relevant enough to spark public debate. Since then, Chinese feminist activists have cultivated a networked community of supporters numbering into the thousands, revolving around university students and graduates. Some have become highly effective organizers. These feminist activists arguably pose a larger, more complicated challenge to the Communist regime than the male activists who preceded them.

7

"The feminist movement is about women's everyday concerns and building a community, rather than just having one or two famous individuals who can enlighten everybody else," says Lü Pin, founding editor of *Feminist Voices*. "Chinese women feel very unequal every day of their lives, and the government cannot make women oblivious to the deep injustice they feel."

By 2016, social media had already played an important role in promoting greater feminist consciousness among Chinese women. Even as the government cracked down on feminist organizing, ordinary women were increasingly sharing information and voicing their anger about sexism on the internet. Sometimes, they even succeeded in pressuring the government to retract its sexist propaganda. In an authoritarian state where citizens do not have freedom of assembly or freedom of the press, such a critical mass is remarkable.

Consider the propaganda faux pas shortly after the May 2016 inauguration of Taiwan's first female president, Tsai Ing-wen, when a Communist Party–linked newspaper published an op-ed calling her an excessively "emotional" single woman without family or children and therefore prone to take "extreme" political positions. The op-ed was widely ridiculed by both women and men on social media. Within a day of its publication, all Chinese media outlets were ordered to delete it because it was "inappropriate" and had a "bad influence on public opinion," according to a leaked censorship directive.

When I heard about the detention of the Feminist Five, I was shocked and deeply worried. I had reported on China for many years as a journalist before doing my PhD in sociology at Tsinghua University in Beijing, so I was very familiar with the country's egregious record of human rights abuses. I also had a personal connection with one of the jailed women. I had met Li Maizi (whose birth name is Li Tingting) in 2013, at a party at the *Feminist Voices* office in Beijing, celebrating a landmark Chinese court ruling granting an American, Kim Lee, a divorce from her abusive celebrity husband, Li Yang, on the grounds of domestic violence. Li Maizi had stood outside Kim Lee's courtroom during the legal proceedings, wearing a wedding dress stained with theatrical blood and holding up a sign saying, "Shame on You, Perpetrator Li Yang!" This legal victory—including the first-ever restraining order issued by a Beijing court—was a milestone in paving the way for China's new anti–domestic violence law, which was enacted in 2016.

Over the following years, I personally interviewed all of the Feminist Five and some key actors in the feminist movement in Beijing, Guangzhou, Shenzhen, Hangzhou, Hong Kong, Shanghai and New York, including Xiao Meili, who walked two thousand kilometers across China to raise awareness about sexual abuse and reclaim public space for women; Zhang Leilei, who walked around Guangzhou every day wearing a large sign against sexual harassment, until the police threatened to kick her out of town; Huang Yizhi, a feminist lawyer who won her client a landmark settlement of thirty thousand renminbi (around US$4,500) in what is believed to be China's first gender-discrimination lawsuit; and Lü Pin, the founder of *Feminist Voices*, who has lived in self-exile in New York since 2015. I also interviewed dozens of labor rights activists, university students, and women's rights lawyers.

I was struck by the passionate intensity, unwavering commitment, and resilience of feminist activists in China. Despite constant police surveillance and occasional eviction by landlords who were themselves threatened by police, almost none of the women I interviewed wanted to give up their activist work. They were extremely unlikely to realize their dreams of justice or see an end to authoritarian repression anytime in the years to come. Yet their personal commitment to the fight for women's rights had only deepened since the government crackdown began.

Although they lived in different parts of China and the world, these women had formed close bonds of solidarity. Several core members of the feminist movement relocated to Guangzhou after 2015 to live close to each other, looking out for each other's safety and keeping track of when the police were harassing their fellow activists. Feminists in other cities kept up constant communication and met for morale-boosting meals whenever they were in the same city.

These women were all engaged in a fierce battle against a misogynistic society and an authoritarian state—often with no support from their own families. Some had survived or witnessed abuse as they were growing up, such as frequent, brutal beatings from their own fathers; violent misogynistic and homophobic bullying at school; or sexual assault and sexual harassment in their early years. They often described their feminist awakenings as deeply transformative experiences, through which they realized for the first time that their lives actually mattered, that they deserved to live in dignity, and that they could raise the consciousness of other women as well.

During the alternately inspiring and excruciating process of writing this book, I too experienced a profound personal transformation. As I listened to the harrowing stories of feminist activists, my own deeply repressed memories surfaced of a sexual assault by several attackers when I was fifteen, a mixed Chinese-American girl in Australia. I felt on a visceral level how the struggles of women in a repressive police state were connected to patriarchal oppression everywhere. Although our life experiences were radically different, I recognized in the accounts of these brave Chinese women the same pain I had endured and the shame that had silenced me afterward. Instead of remaining a detached, academic observer, I came to believe that it was critically important to forge deeper bonds of feminist solidarity with women around the world. Those of us with immense privilege, like me—a middle-class American citizen—have much to learn from our persecuted feminist sisters in China. We are all fighting in different ways against a common enemy: patriarchy.

~

Since the founding of the People's Republic of China almost seventy years ago, the Communist Party has required all major women's rights activities to be affiliated in some way with the official state women's agency, the All-China Women's Federation. Only since 2012 have well-organized, feminist activists independent of the Communist Party begun to develop a following among young women in multiple cities. The government has responded by aggressively shutting down some nongovernmental organizations working on women's rights (in particular, organizations receiving foreign funding), dispatching police to monitor and harass feminist activists, tightening ideological controls on gender and women's studies programs at universities, and cracking down on feminist social-media accounts. I interviewed far more people than I was able to include in the book, but with only one exception, everyone portrayed here asked to be identified by their real name or a commonly used nickname.

Chapter 1 gives a narrative account of the coordinated arrests of feminist activists on March 6 and 7, 2015, in Beijing, Guangzhou, and Hangzhou. Although Chinese authorities conducted a sweeping round of arrests and interrogations during those two days, I focus here on the women who became known as the Feminist Five, some of whom are also deeply involved in the LGBTQ rights movement.

Chapter 2 explains how the evolution of China's internet was closely linked with the growing rights awareness among many Chinese women in recent years—despite the government's intrusive censorship and interference in online communications. It depicts the birth and rising influence of *Feminist Voices* and shows how the government made *feminism* a politically sensitive term, launching a harsh crackdown on feminist social-media content in 2017 and 2018. Against all odds, a #MeToo movement in China caught on in early 2018, as thousands of students at different universities demanded greater protections against sexual harassment and assault, in one of the largest displays of coordinated student action since the pro-democracy movement of 1989.

Chapter 3 describes some of the experiences of the Feminist Five in detention. They suffered psychological and sometimes physical mistreatment while incarcerated, but still found ways to communicate and lift each other up. Some of them also had terrifying encounters with security agents after their highly publicized release from detention in April 2015. Chinese state security agents penetrated deep into the family networks of the detained feminists in an attempt to wipe out the movement's leaders, with a brutal efficiency reminiscent of the Stasi in Communist-ruled East Germany.

Chapter 4 delves into some of the most important issues of the feminist movement: sexual harassment, sexual assault and violence against women. It shows how some of the feminist activists' early experiences with abuse made them even more determined to fight for women's rights. In addition to enduring prolonged mistreatment by state security agents, the feminists had to face entrenched misogyny and even sexual harassment from some men in the human rights movement.

Chapter 5 shows how China's feminist movement today fits within a historical tradition of feminism dating back to the turn of the twentieth century, when feminist revolutionaries such as the cross-dressing Qiu Jin wrote *Stones of the Jingwei Bird* about Chinese women's struggle against patriarchal domination. Qiu Jin was beheaded for conspiring to overthrow the Qing empire, but the liberation of women continued to be a rallying cry for revolutionaries in the early days after the founding of the Chinese Communist Party in 1921. By the end of the 1920s, male Communists had denounced "bourgeois feminism" and declared that the fight against class oppression must take precedence over all else, including the struggle for women's rights. Following the

Communist revolution of 1949, the "equality of women and men" was enshrined in the Constitution of the People's Republic of China and the new government introduced ambitious initiatives to put women to work in building the new Communist nation. With the onset of market reforms and the dismantling of the planned economy in the 1980s and 1990s, however, gender inequality came roaring back, leading to the rise of the contemporary feminist movement.

Chapter 6 explores how feminist perspectives have begun to permeate the related social movements of labor rights and rights law in China, as some middle-class feminist activists began collaborating with working-class women involved in labor disputes. It shows how landmark legal cases in 2013 involving the sexual abuse of girls at school began to threaten the Communist Party, which feared that feminists, lawyers, and workers might come together to create a powerful force of opposition.

Chapter 7 shows how China's paternalistic patriarch, Xi Jinping, has positioned himself as a strongman and father of the nation, presiding over a "family-state under heaven (*jiaguo tianxia*)." The Chinese government's warning in 2017 that "foreign hostile forces" were using "Western feminism" to interfere in China's affairs was just one manifestation of China's patriarchal authoritarianism. The government's pro-natalist propaganda aimed at college-educated, Han Chinese women is only getting more intense, since policymakers continue to view women primarily as reproductive tools to realize the nation's development goals. I argue that sexism and misogyny lie at the very heart of China's authoritarian control of the population and the battle for Communist Party survival.

In the concluding chapter, I describe how the persecution of feminist activists in China is increasing just as more and more corporations are recognizing the mass-market appeal of consumer feminism. Looking to the future, China's feminist movement is beginning to globalize as key feminist activists start building new "battlegrounds" outside China, just as many reformers did in exile during the revolutionary period over a century ago.

As Xi intensifies his hypermasculine personality cult and strongman rule in China, the crackdown on feminism and women's rights—indeed on all of civil society—may well escalate. This trend is very dangerous for the rest of the world as well, since it is already happening in other authoritarian countries such as Russia, Iran, the Philippines, Hungary and Turkey, with misogynistic autocrats who are rolling back women's rights as an integral part of their authoritarian repression. We see it even in the United States, with rising authoritarianism and the undermining of long-established democratic norms wrapped up in a backlash against feminism.

Although *Betraying Big Brother* focuses on China, the experiences of the Feminist Five and other courageous women involved in the Chinese feminist movement are a lesson for all of us. Through their stories, I have tried to provide a window into the government's unprecedented crackdown on women's rights activists and show why anyone concerned about rising authoritarianism globally needs to pay attention to what is happening in China. I hope that these women's voices serve as a source of inspiration and a call to arms for people around the world.

1

China's Feminist Five

When Chinese authorities arrested feminist activist Wei Tingting in Beijing on March 6, 2015—just before International Women's Day—they confiscated her glasses so she could no longer see. Severely visually impaired, Wei was only able to tell people apart by their voices. State security agents took away her cellphone and laptop and demanded her passwords. They led her to a dimly lit, underground area of a police station, took her warm snow boots and put her in a small, unheated room about five square meters wide, as the temperature outside fell to below freezing.

Then the interrogations began.

"Why are you engaged in subversive activities about sexual harassment?"

"Who is collaborating with you in your women's rights activism?"

"Which foreign agencies are funding your actions?"

Wei told the blurry figures in front of her that she wanted to call a lawyer before answering any questions.

"You can't call a lawyer now. Don't you get it? Don't you understand the law?"

Wei made it through one round of interrogations and thought

it would be over, but in the middle of the night—she had no idea what time it was because she had no watch—the agents took her out for another interrogation. This time, someone videotaped her as she spoke. Even when she went to the toilet, a female agent observed her.

For the first time in her life, Wei Tingting—just twenty-six years old at the time of her detention—began to think about escaping abroad. She felt disoriented and overwhelmed by a mounting sense of powerlessness. Then she heard some indistinct murmurs seeping through from outside and put her ear up against the wall of her cell to listen more closely. With astonishment, she recognized the voice of one of her feminist sisters, Wang Man, who had taken part in some activist campaigns with her, in the adjacent room.

My God! Wang Man is in here too! she thought. Wei yelled out to a guard that she was thirsty and needed a drink of water, then put her ear up against the wall to listen again. She made out the voices of other feminist activists who had been arrested along with her: besides Wang Man she could hear Li Maizi; Li's girlfriend, Teresa Xu; and several other university students who had volunteered for feminist campaigns in the past.

Wei later described how she overcame her feeling of helplessness in an online essay (later deleted) she called "Prison Notes," which she posted on WeChat under a pseudonym. "I decided I must resist this feeling of sorrow and take action, so I started to do a lot of different things: my room was freezing and I was only allowed to wear slippers, so I began doing leg exercises, such as kicks and squats; then I did deep meditation exercises; other people before me had scratched words onto the old walls, so I squinted my eyes up close to the walls to examine them; then I spun around in circles, singing songs," she wrote.

Wei sang out loud, both to cheer herself up and to let the other detained women hear her voice and know that they were not alone—that she, too, was in there with them. Li Maizi also sang back "A Song for All Women," the anthem of China's feminist movement:

> Protect my rights, don't keep me down
> Why must I lose my freedom?
> Let's break free from our heavy shackles
> And reclaim our power as women!

Her spirits buoyed, Wei Tingting writes, she recovered her sense of defiance: "Even as I heard two guards walking back and forth, making clanking noises outside, I felt a kind of joy in betraying Big Brother."

The women jailed in Beijing that night and for the subsequent thirty-seven days have come to be known as the Feminist Five, but the movement they are part of is much larger.

Zheng Churan, at twenty-five, was one of the younger activists. A recent university graduate, she still lived with her parents in Guangzhou, the major port and manufacturing hub located in southern China. While the parents of many other Chinese feminists were openly antagonistic toward their daughters' work, Zheng's parents respected her independence. She was very close to them and talked with them about everything, including her feminist activism. Although they did not always agree with her, they supported her efforts to bring about social change and she did not want them to get hurt.

Zheng had been deeply involved in feminist activism since she was a student in sociology and archival science at the prestigious Sun Yat-sen University in Guangzhou. It was there that she became interested in feminism and LGBTQ rights and adopted the nickname Da Tu (Giant Rabbit). She made friends with some lesbians (*lala*) at university and joined an LGBTQ student group. Zheng identified as queer; though she also dated men, she found women to be much more fun.

Then she realized that her LGBTQ group was sexist. "The male organizers looked down on us, even though they gave lip service to gender equality, and they never gave any funding to women in the group," says Zheng, who believed that any LGBTQ rights group must have a feminist perspective. So she, her lesbian friend Liang Xiaowen, and other *lalas* decided to split off from the main LGBTQ group and form their own queer feminist group, called Sinner-B (*b* for *bitch*). Its members, mostly students, collaborated on acts of feminist performance art.

They joined up with the Gender Equality Work Group run by the activist Wu Rongrong and affiliated with the more established nongovernmental civil rights organization Yirenping (meaning "public interest, humanity, and equality") in 2012. The Gender Equality Work Group was planning its Occupy Men's Toilets protest, calling for more public toilets for women. There Zheng met other activists—including Li Maizi—who were to become prominent figures in the feminist movement. They took over a men's public lavatory in downtown Guangzhou and invited women into the vacated stalls to shorten their typically long wait.

The feminist activists chose to focus on gender parity in public toilets because they believed it was a campaign that could not be seen as politically sensitive or even remotely opposed to the Communist Party. Everyone could easily relate to the overly long lines for women using public toilets, so they were able to win widespread support for their cause. They used it to highlight the underlying problem of systemic sexism and the constant devaluation of women's lives in Chinese society. Their campaign even received media attention from official Chinese news outlets, including Xinhua News Agency and *People's Daily*. Members of the public quoted in state media reports expressed support for the action, and Guangdong provincial officials later promised to provide more toilets for women.

In 2012, Zheng Churan worked on the "Bloody Brides" Valentine's Day action against domestic violence, in which activists Li

Maizi, Wei Tingting, and Xiao Meili paraded down a Beijing street wearing white wedding gowns smeared with faux red blood. They carried signs with slogans like "Love is No Excuse for Violence" in a visually shocking protest against the absence of a nationwide law against domestic violence in China. (China subsequently enacted its first such law in 2016.) They also shaved their heads in public in their "Bald Sisters" action in Guangzhou to protest blatant discrimination against women in university admissions: many programs require women to score higher than men on their entrance exams to be accepted. (After Lü Pin and feminist lawyer Huang Yizhi wrote a formal letter of complaint to the Ministry of Education, they received a response saying that the policies—basically affirmative action for men—had been introduced "to protect the national interest.")

When Zheng graduated from university, she began working for the Gender Equality Work Group in Guangzhou. Shortly before International Women's Day in 2015, she thought that it would be a good idea to highlight the pernicious problem of sexual harassment on public transportation. The Chinese government does not release reliable statistics on sexual assault; this lack of transparency disguises the true extent of sexual violence. But sexual harassment on public transportation is seen as less politically sensitive and one survey by the state-run *China Youth Daily* in August 2017 found rampant harassment, with over 53 percent of female respondents reporting they had personally been sexually harassed while taking the subway.

Zheng received a small grant from the Swedish embassy to print and distribute colorful stickers against sexual harassment to be handed out on subways and buses on International Women's Day. One sticker showed a cartoon of a woman screaming, with blurbs on either side: "If you are sexually harassed, SCREAM!" and "Fight lechers!" Another, with pictures of police caps, said, "Catch sexual harassers. Police, go get them!"

Zheng's idea was appealing, and volunteers—many of them university students—signed up in multiple cities, including

Guangzhou and Xiamen in the southeast, the capital Beijing, the eastern city of Hangzhou, Nanjing, Wuhan, and the southwestern city of Kunming. She arranged for a store to print out the stickers and send them by express mail to the cities where volunteers had signed up to take part. "All of our actions are pretty fast and spontaneous," Zheng says. "In each city, we only needed a small number of volunteers: mainly one person to show off the stickers and one person to take pictures. Then you sent out a press release and the whole event would be over."

But late on the night of March 6, 2015, just after Zheng finished her shower and was relaxing in front of the TV with her parents, a loud knock came at her door. Zheng told her parents not to get up. She looked through the peephole and was startled to see a large group of around eight men in her crowded stairwell, with some standing on the stairs as well. Only the man knocking wore a police uniform.

"What is it?" Zheng asked through the closed door.

"We're checking your household registration," said one of the men.

"If you're checking my registration, there's no need to come inside, please just tell me what you want right here."

Silence.

After a few seconds with no reply, Zheng knew that she was in trouble. She went back inside to tell her parents to go into their bedroom; she would take care of the men at their door. She quickly used her hands-free phone to dial her friend Liang Xiaowen and left the phone on without saying anything, so Liang could hear everything that happened next.

"Open the door," demanded the men outside, as they started banging loudly.

"I'm not opening the door unless you have a search warrant," said Zheng.

"If you won't let us in, we have to take you with us to the police station."

The men had no search warrant or other forms of identification and refused to say why they were there, so Zheng argued with them for a while, but finally agreed to go with them because she did not want them to enter her parents' home. In the predawn hours of March 7, Zheng found herself being interrogated at a Guangzhou police station. After several hours, agents took her home to print out all her emails related to the anti–sexual harassment activity, as well as her agreement with the Swedish embassy. Then they brought her back to the police station and interrogated her again until dawn, before holding her at a hotel for the rest of the day. Around eight in the evening on March 7, the agents drove her to yet another police station, handcuffed her and made her stand as they read out a formal notice of her criminal detention on the charge of "picking quarrels and provoking trouble"—an all-encompassing charge increasingly being leveled at critics of the Chinese government. On March 8, the agents flew her to Beijing to begin her formal detention.

By that time, news of the arrests had already spread through China's network of feminists. Wu Rongrong was visiting Shenzhen, the southern city that links Hong Kong to the rest of China, when she received a call at around eleven at night on March 6 from Liang Xiaowen, who described what she had heard over the phone. This was not the first call Wu had received that day. A state security agent had already sent her a message earlier that afternoon, telling her to cancel their International Women's Day activity.

Late that same night, Li Maizi texted Wu from Beijing: "Damn, they're knocking at my door." Wu called her back immediately but got no response. Then she received several WeChat messages saying that security agents had detained other colleagues and university students who had volunteered to hand out stickers against sexual harassment.

Wu Rongrong, at thirty, was something of a veteran in the feminist movement: before founding the Weizhiming Women's

Center in Hangzhou, she had worked for many years on women's rights at Yirenping in Beijing and elsewhere. Initially, she wasn't worried: she had been called in for questioning multiple times over the years. She expected the others to be released by the following morning. But after the missives from Li Maizi and Liang Xiaowen, Wu became anxious and couldn't sleep. At three in the morning she called a security agent she knew in Guangzhou. Zheng Churan had been taken for questioning, he said, and would be released very soon. But at four, Liang Xiaowen called again to say that security agents had taken Zheng home briefly to pick up some work files and were going to keep her at a hotel for the rest of the night.

As dawn broke, the women had still not been released, and Wu Rongrong discussed what to do with a colleague on the phone: return to Hangzhou, which her colleagues thought was unsafe, or stay in Shenzhen—just a short train ride across the border to safety in Hong Kong—until the situation calmed down? (The former British colony of Hong Kong returned to Chinese control in 1997 and is now a "special administrative region" with more freedoms than anywhere else in China, although those freedoms are being eroded.) Wu felt very conflicted. She had personally recruited Zheng Churan and Li Maizi for the Occupy Men's Toilets action. Wei Tingting and Wang Man, in Beijing, were not even working full-time on women's rights issues; they had just volunteered to hand out stickers on sexual harassment. If anyone should be held responsible, Wu thought, it should be her. She had been a feminist activist longer than any of them. She decided to fly back to Hangzhou. "I was so naïve. I thought if I could only get a chance to explain the whole situation to state security agents, I could clear up this misunderstanding and they would release the other women," she said later.

Wu Rongrong grew up in a poor village in Shanxi Province, China's coal country, where young girls were considered worthless and often forced to quit school and work while their brothers continued studying. At age six, she began plowing the fields with her father, since her mother was too sick to do farm work. As a teenager, Wu was diagnosed with chronic hepatitis B, and the doctor told her she would likely not become ill until she was twenty-eight. "I took this to mean that I had only ten more years to live, so from then on, I made a habit of trying to live each day to the fullest, and make sure each day was meaningful," she writes.

Many of her relatives and fellow villagers tried to dissuade her from going to university and urged her to get married instead, but Wu was determined to break out of her stifling home environment. She moved to Beijing to study social work at China Women's University. There she volunteered for public-interest nonprofit groups, working on issues such as poverty alleviation and HIV/AIDS as well as women's rights.

When Wu applied for scholarships, she needed to obtain proof of residence from officials in her home village. Many of her village officials exploited her vulnerability and sexually harassed her. She had no one to turn to for support and felt powerless to speak out. "Had I tried to speak up for myself, it would have resulted in humiliating gossip and innuendo and made me unable to show my face in the village," she says.

Another frightening incident happened when Wu was nineteen and looking for a job in Beijing over the Lunar New Year holiday. A man posing as an employer lured her into a car to the distant suburb of Shunyi and started to sexually assault her. She managed to escape, but the experience was terrifying and shook her profoundly. "I began to understand just how helpless I was ... Like me, several of my female friends encountered harassment when looking for full-time or part-time work," writes Wu. "As eighteen- or nineteen-year-old girls, all we could think of was buying a fruit knife for self-defense."

These experiences left a deep impression on Wu. When she graduated with a B.A. in social work in 2007, she was eager to work on women's rights and other social justice programs. She found jobs with the HIV/AIDS NGO Beijing Aizhixing Institute and with Yirenping on women's and children's rights. In 2009, Wu organized Yirenping's first high-profile women's rights campaign around the case of Deng Yujiao, a twenty-one-year-old woman working at a karaoke and entertainment center, who had stabbed a government official in Hubei Province while he was sexually assaulting her. According to Deng's statement, published in the *Southern Metropolis Daily*, the official had stripped her from the waist down and forced her onto a couch as he cursed and slapped her on her face and shoulders with a wad of cash. Deng stabbed the official in the neck with a pocketknife, killing him in self-defense.

Although the incident took place just before the establishment of Weibo, Deng's case became a hot topic on the internet. Foreshadowing the raw emotions of the Me Too campaign, Chinese citizens inundated blogs and online comments sections with millions of impassioned posts, expressing sympathy for the young woman and anger at corrupt, abusive officials who faced no consequences for their sexual violence against women.

"Why was she even in court in the first place? They tried to rape her ... Any woman would defend herself if she were threatened with rape," wrote one commenter on the *China Daily* website.

"How do these government officials get so much money? During the dispute, [the official] was hitting Deng with a wad of cash. How could a public servant on a regular salary have so much money without any trace of compassion? Was he using public funds or embezzled money?" wrote a blogger for the *People's Daily* website, People.com.cn.

"[From] the bottom of my heart, she will always be innocent because I believe there's no such thing as excessive force when you fight against rape and for your dignity," wrote the women's rights activist Ye Haiyan.

To demonstrate solidarity with Deng Yujiao, university students in Beijing staged a provocative act of performance art. They carried a gagged woman bound up in white sheets and laid her on the ground, surrounded by the words "We Could All Be

Deng Yujiao." Wu also joined with the prominent women's rights lawyer Guo Jianmei to hold a public discussion on how Deng's case revealed the severe problem of government officials sexually assaulting women with impunity. As part of the campaign, dozens of female students signed a petition calling for understanding of Deng Yujiao's plight and respect for women's rights. In a legal victory, a court exonerated Deng and ordered her to be released in June 2009, saying that she suffered from "mood disorders" and had turned herself over to the police voluntarily.

In subsequent years, Wu expanded her women's rights work beyond sexual assault to include issues such as domestic violence. She helped organize the "Bloody Brides" parade in Beijing, as well as a petition drive against domestic violence in 2012 with ten thousand signatures. She and her team initiated programs to fight gender discrimination in hiring and performance-art protests against mandatory gynecological exams for women applying to join China's civil service. As part of their job applications, women were required to undergo tests for sexually transmitted diseases and were also asked invasive questions about their menstrual cycles, while men were exempt.

This history of activism turned out to be what security agents were interested in when, on March 7, a tall, uniformed policeman boarded Wu's flight the moment it landed in Hangzhou. He walked down the aisle until he reached Wu's seat and showed her his identification badge. "We are from the Public Security Bureau. You need to come with us now."

As Wu exited the plane, the officer leading her by the arm, she was stunned to see a convoy of police cars with their sirens blasting and lights flashing on the tarmac. A crowd of people stood waiting beside the police cars and several security agents surrounded her to guide her toward the cars. Police photographers snapped pictures of her and videotaped her as she walked. It was like a reality TV show where a massive police sting busts up a criminal gang.

Wu began to feel sick. She had just spent almost two weeks in the hospital, receiving treatment for complications from her hepatitis B, and was very thirsty.

"Could I have a sip of water, please?" she asked.

"You'd better behave!" an officer yelled at her.

At the Hangzhou police station, security agents ignored her request for water and began interrogating her about her feminist activism as though it were a major crime. "Who organized the anti–sexual harassment activity? Who are the donors behind your women's center?"

It was the feminists' strategy to decline to identify the organizers of any of their activist campaigns, in case the government fabricated criminal charges. Wu said at first that she did not know who the organizers were, but once the agents started asking about donor funding, she began to worry that they were building a serious criminal case. She wanted to deflect blame.

"You want to capture the head of the organization, right? Well, you've got me, I'm here, the founder of the Weizhiming Women's Center," Wu said. "The other women you detained were just volunteers." Maybe the agents would let the other feminists go.

The interrogation continued. Wu kept asking for water and saying she felt ill—she needed to hydrate and take her hepatitis B medication—but the agents kept ignoring her request, all the while yelling and cursing. "I realized I couldn't continue to speak to these people being so hostile and treating me like the enemy," she says. So she stopped talking and stayed silent as they yelled at her. Eventually, they took her to the Weizhiming Women's Center, searched it thoroughly (they never once showed her a search warrant or a permit for her arrest), confiscated all the computers and cellphones, and then took her to another detention center for the remainder of the night.

Later, she learned that security agents had also searched her home and interrogated her husband about her activities. But because her four-year-old son's toys were strewn everywhere, the

26

agents only managed to take some of Wu's USB drives and other material. Wu's son asked where his mother had gone. "Mama had to go far away to another country on a business trip," his father told him.

By the following day—International Women's Day—Wu felt so sick, hungry, and dazed from lack of medication that she can no longer remember details of how the agents took her out of Hangzhou. But sometime that day they put her on a train to Beijing to be criminally detained on the charge of "picking quarrels and provoking trouble."

Here Wu Rongrong was reunited with her activist sisters, even though they were placed into separate cells and locked behind bars. In one cell was Zheng Churan and in another Wei Tingting, both deprived of their glasses and seeing the world as a blur.

Li Maizi, who had texted Wu two days earlier, was also there. The police had begun banging on her door in Beijing just as she and her girlfriend Teresa Xu were getting ready for bed, but Li had not been too worried. The police had already called the twenty-five-year-old in for questioning numerous times, and she thought that if she stayed quiet, perhaps they would eventually go away. They didn't. When Teresa accidentally flushed the toilet, the officers began prying open the lock, and Li opened the door. Half a dozen men—some uniformed police, some plainclothes agents—barged in, grabbed Li's cellphone from her hand, and began searching the apartment to confiscate her electronic devices. Teresa was only in her underwear.

"How can you little girls be so indecent?" barked out one of the agents.

"Who are you calling indecent?" Li yelled back. They could insult her and dismiss her as a "little girl," but not her girlfriend. "This is our home! Of course we're in our underwear!"

Despite her protests, the agents brought them both to the police station. It was here that she realized this was not a routine questioning. Station attendants drew her blood, tested her urine, and took her fingerprints and palm prints. After making her take off her down coat and snow boots, they put her alone in an unheated interrogation room. The two men interrogating her did not identify themselves, wear uniforms, or explain the charges against her. They kept asking about foreign funding for her employer, Yirenping, and she concluded that they must be state security agents. Yet she still refused to cooperate.

"Those men acted like they had just won some glorious battle," Li later said with contempt. In an effort to get her to talk, one agent took her outside the room to "look at the big picture." He proudly showed her that they had arrested so many young feminists that night, there weren't enough interrogation rooms for all of them. Li recognized some feminist sisters—Wei Tingting, Wang Man, and other volunteers—although they were not permitted to speak to each other. But she knew she had an advantage: all of the other arrested feminists were nearsighted and, with their glasses confiscated, were—as Li joked—"blind." But Li had perfect vision, and this gave her a huge psychological edge. "The good thing about not being blind is that you can see the interrogators' faces," she said later. "That's a kind of threat, because they're afraid you'll remember them."

One of the agents interrogating Li boasted to her that he had two university degrees. The ever-pugnacious Li couldn't resist taunting him. "So I guess you're allowed to leave the country, then?" she asked.

He looked momentarily dejected. "That isn't possible, but even if I can't leave China, it's still very good here," said the agent.

"Really?" she teased. "You just dream on."

Eventually, Li realized her tough act wasn't working, so she opted for another strategy: she burst into tears. "That's better!" the agent said, and softened the tone of his interrogations. What Li did not realize was that one of the walls of her interrogation room was a one-way mirror: agents had put Teresa in the adjacent room.

Teresa was also visually impaired—like the others, her glasses had been confiscated—but she was still able to make out Li's blurry image.

"You're nothing but a little hooligan!" an agent yelled at Teresa. "Tell us who you know in this group of women! Do you think we're going to release you after twenty-four hours? You'd only make it to Beijing's fourth ring road and we'd just capture you and bring you back again."

Through it all, Teresa remained silent and stared at him. The following day the agents released her—because she was still a student, doing a master's degree in social science, they said—but not before making her sign a statement: "I fervently love my country. I fervently love the Communist Party. I support the Communist Party's work. I promise to stay far away from non-governmental organizations. I promise to stay far away from the Beijing Yirenping nongovernmental organization."

Li was not so lucky. She had not even contemplated the possibility that she might be detained for more than a day for planning to hand out stickers against sexual harassment. Because she and her fellow activists had done nothing to oppose the Communist Party, she simply told herself, *Just make it through the next twenty-four hours. Then you'll be released.*

Twenty-four hours later, the agents told her to gather her belongings and walk with them through the underground passage. More agents joined them, some in front, some behind. "I sensed that the people behind me were very afraid that I would escape," she said. "At that moment, I knew there was no way they were letting me go home." She emerged from underground to see a minivan waiting for her on the street, with Wei Tingting and Wang Man already on board, security agents seated on either side of them, to transport them to the Haidian District Detention Center.

~

The fifth woman to be jailed, Wang Man, had been a lively, rebellious child, and her parents and teachers had been disappointed by her lack of obedience. "How can a girl behave this way?" they had scolded. By puberty, their scolding took effect and she threw herself into quiet study. But she discovered that even with a master's degree in international relations and experience studying abroad in Kyoto, Japan, she could not escape blatant gender discrimination in the workplace. In her first job, teaching English at a prestigious high school in Tianjin, women were required to have a master's degree when men only needed a BA to qualify for the same position. Wang despised the double standard and quit. Then, when she turned twenty-seven, Wang—like most urban women in their late twenties in China—began to feel intense pressure to get married and avoid the stigma of being labeled a "leftover" woman (*sheng nü*). She did not like any of the men she had dated and began to feel that there must be something terribly wrong with her.

"I had always been told that I was too stubborn, too extreme, too abnormal, just *too* much, so that's why I was considered a failure at finding a marriage partner," she says. "As a woman almost thirty years old, I was told that it was my important duty to get married, and if I wasn't able to marry, I was either letting everyone around me down or letting myself down." In 2010, Wang received an offer to work in Beijing for an NGO that focused on poverty alleviation. Soon she met several feminist activists who showed her the limitations of her perspective. "My God, all these problems in my life that I thought were caused by my personal character flaws were actually the result of systemic gender inequality—it was a huge revelation!" she says.

Before long, she was volunteering for feminist campaigns, including the Occupy Men's Toilets action in Guangzhou, and writing articles about the uses of feminist street activism in China—which later came back to haunt her. During her detention, security agents often read her writing back to her as though it were criminal evidence of "betraying" China and allowing herself to be used as a tool of "hostile foreign forces" (a term generally used to refer to countries such as the United States or Great Britain).

On the night of March 6, 2015, security agents led Wang, who was thirty-three at the time, to an underground area of Beijing's Haidian police station—the same area where Li Maizi and the other activists now known as the Feminist Five were held—and confiscated her glasses. No longer able to see her captors or surroundings with clarity, she felt a creeping sense of terror.

The interrogations began. Agents repeatedly asked her about European Union research funding for her poverty alleviation group. After a long interrogation, she thought she was finally going home but was led back to an isolation room instead. She tried to sleep, but she was too cold and hungry—she had barely been given any food. It was winter, but an air-conditioning vent blew freezing air through wooden slats onto the only bench in the room. Though she had not taken medication in several years, Wang had a congenital heart condition, and she suddenly felt vulnerable and frightened about her health. Sometime that night—she had no idea what time it was—she began to feel she could no longer bear the terror of uncertainty.

Then she heard Wei Tingting's voice outside her locked cell door.

"I'm thirsty! I need some water!" Wei yelled, and began to sing out loud the traditional Chinese folk song "Moli Hua" (Jasmine Flower).

> Beautiful jasmine flower ...
> Let me pick you
> To share with another
> Jasmine flower, oh, jasmine flower.

Wang listened to Wei's singing voice and was overcome with gratitude, knowing that her activist sister was just on the other side of the wall.

2

The Internet and Feminist Awakening

The day after the jailing of the "Feminist Five Sisters" (*nüquan wu jiemei*), other feminist activists began staging solidarity campaigns on the social media platforms Weibo and WeChat. While global outrage spread through the hashtag #FreeTheFive on Twitter, Facebook, and Instagram—all banned in China— domestic activists posted pictures of women wearing masks with the faces of the Feminist Five and moving freely through public spaces.

"We chose public places full of the flavor of ordinary life for our photos, showing the women as though they were free, eating at a restaurant or shopping at a street market," explains Xiao Meili, a feminist organizer who in 2013 and 2014 had trekked from Beijing to Guangzhou, more than 2,000 kilometers (1,200 miles), to protest sexual abuse and reclaim public space for women.

The first photo they posted featured five women walking across a pedestrian crosswalk modeled on the Beatles' *Abbey Road* album cover, wearing the masks of Li Maizi, Wu Rongrong, Zheng Churan, Wei Tingting and Wang Man. The caption read, "March 7: Feminist Activists Arrested—Day One." The photo from Day Two showed five women wearing the masks of the Feminist Five outside a public toilet, recalling the Occupy Men's Toilets action.

On yet another day, a photo showed the five masked women waiting at a subway station, each holding a cup of tea, symbolizing the common police practice of contacting activists to "invite them to tea"—a euphemism for interrogating perceived troublemakers. Each day, a new photo appeared, marking the passage of their time in detention. "You can't arrest us all!" read one of the captions.

The activists also called for other people across China to post their own pictures of solidarity with the five feminists on Weibo and WeChat. In Beijing, police and plainclothes security agents were aggressively hunting down feminist activists for interrogation, so groups of five women posed for photos in public, then photoshopped masks of the detained feminists onto the pictures before posting. In Guangzhou, where the security was more lax at the time, feminist activists held up real masks of the Feminist Five as they took photos in lively public spaces such as shopping centers and busy street intersections. These activists remained mostly anonymous to avoid getting caught in the security dragnet, while others outside China—like Lü Pin of the famed *Feminist Voices* account—posted under their own names.

China's internet is heavily censored and monitored, shut off from the rest of the world by the "Great Firewall." Internet censors are embedded in virtually all tech companies, which are required to delete any social-media posts that might be considered offensive to the Communist Party or "disturb the social order." In a practice described by digital-rights expert Rebecca MacKinnon as "networked authoritarianism," internet companies routinely hand over the personal information of any user wanted for questioning by the police. The army of censors deleted many posts and news reports explicitly mentioning the arrest of the Feminist Five but stopped short of imposing a total ban on feminist social-media posts, so some messages and pictures of solidarity from students, workers, scholars, and rights activists (including men) continued to circulate. A female factory worker posted a photo of herself saying, "We can fight sexual harassment! Don't harass us! Support

34

[the Feminist Five]—Chinese woman worker." A male worker in Xiamen took a photo of himself holding a sign saying, "Xiamen workers support Wu Rongrong, Li Tingting, Wang Man, Zheng Churan, Wei Tingting." (Although censors deleted these pictures, Zheng Churan's boyfriend and later husband, labor rights activist Wei Zhili, compiled and wrote about some of them for Libcom.org.)

Many of the people who had received help through women's rights campaigns over the years now wanted to show their solidarity with the feminists. Some had met Zheng Churan (Giant Rabbit) through her campaigns for labor rights for working-class women and men. One petition attracted over 1,100 signatures—despite the great risk to anyone openly signing their name. Organizers mailed the petition to the Haidian District Detention Center in Beijing, where the women were being held, as well as the Haidian Public Security Bureau, municipal prosecutors' offices, and the All-China Women's Federation.

Another petition was signed by a group of feminist lawyers, the Public Interest Collaborative Network for Women Lawyers in China, and yet another by around a hundred human rights lawyers. Several months later, the Chinese government began cracking down on these and other human rights lawyers, rounding up and detaining hundreds of them—including Wang Yu, the lawyer for one of the Feminist Five (see Chapter 6).

That these solidarity campaigns circulated on the internet is significant. Despite intrusive censorship, the rise of China's new generation of feminist activists was inextricably linked to the explosion of Weibo in 2010 and WeChat in 2011. As record numbers of Chinese women attended university, both at home and abroad, they went online and began to challenge widespread sexism and unequal treatment, even if they did not explicitly identify themselves as feminist. The internet provided space for them to explore ideas with more freedom than many of their workplaces and homes, and also allowed like-minded women throughout the country to find one another. Given the extensive monitoring by state security, the outpouring of support for the detained women demonstrated how they had been able to connect with and mobilize a broad base of supporters across the country.

Even some of Weibo's "Big V" (verified account) stars have experienced something of a feminist awakening, thanks in part to the work of the feminist movement and the galvanizing force of the Feminist Five arrests. Li Yuan, as managing editor of the *Wall Street Journal*'s Chinese website, was one of the first women to become a "Big V" celebrity on Weibo, with around 2.5 million followers. Her experience illustrates the critical importance of social media to the growing feminist consciousness of Chinese women.

Li Yuan grew up in Yinchuan, the capital of the western province of Ningxia, and worked as a foreign correspondent for Xinhua News for several years in Afghanistan, Thailand and Laos before moving to the United States for graduate studies. She received two master's degrees, one from George Washington University in international relations and one from Columbia University in journalism, then became a tech reporter for the *Wall Street Journal* in New York. In 2008, she moved to Beijing to revamp the *Journal*'s Chinese-language website, hiring more translators and developing Chinese content.

Twitter and Facebook were still accessible to ordinary Chinese citizens then, as well as the main domestic microblogging platform at the time, Fanfou. In June 2009, the Chinese government temporarily shut down Twitter and other online services for the twentieth anniversary of the Tiananmen massacre, in anticipation of a torrent of politically sensitive news reports and tweets.

Then on July 6, 2009, large riots broke out in the northwestern region of Xinjiang between the Muslim Uyghur residents and the majority Han Chinese, killing 156 people and wounding more than a thousand. It was one of the deadliest incidents of civil unrest in China since Tiananmen. Hundreds of Uyghurs had been protesting at a large plaza in Xinjiang's capital, Urumqi, demanding a government investigation into a brawl between Uyghur and Han Chinese workers at a factory in Guangzhou, which left two Uyghurs dead. Many Uyghurs in Xinjiang are deeply resentful of the intrusion of the Han Chinese–dominated Communist Party into their private lives and religious customs, as well as the heavy policing of their neighborhoods by Han Chinese armed forces.

The central government realized that it had to control the fallout. Authorities launched a massive security clampdown and shut down internet service in Urumqi and other parts of Xinjiang to stop information from spreading about the massive unrest. At first the clampdown appeared to be confined to Xinjiang, but the central government quickly blocked access to Twitter and Facebook across all of China. To this day, the ban on Twitter and Facebook has not been lifted.

That same month, a former journalist turned tech executive, Charles Chao, who had been working on a new Chinese version of Twitter, saw a huge business opportunity and pounced. In August 2009, a few weeks after Twitter and Facebook were permanently banned, Chao launched Sina Weibo, a domestic social-media platform, complete with a complex internal system of human and software censorship. Since Weibo was brand new, it had to aggressively recruit people it considered social influencers—such as movie stars, well-known businesspeople, and media personalities —to set up accounts. In early 2010, a Sina executive urged Li Yuan to set up a Weibo account. She was reluctant at first because she was a journalist and did not want to share her personal opinions with the public, but she agreed. By October 2010—a little over a year after its launch—Weibo had 50 million users. Since then, usage has skyrocketed to 392 million monthly active users in December 2017—more than the total number of monthly active users on Twitter around the world.

"At first, it was very intimidating to use Weibo because after posting an article, I never wanted to look at the comments people made about me," says Li Yuan. People would often write, "Why are you so opinionated? Why are you speaking up so much? You're a woman!" "As a woman, you're supposed to be submissive," she says. Li Yuan initially did not feel comfortable with this level of visibility. Yet she started diving enthusiastically into Weibo debates soon after the Arab Spring began in early 2011, while she was spending Lunar New Year at home with her parents in Ningxia Province. She stayed up late into the night, posting about revolutionary events in Tunisia and Egypt.

"My parents didn't know that I was leading a double life," says Li Yuan. "During the day, I would hang out, eating and chatting with them at home. Then, at night, when things got really tense with [Egyptian president Hosni] Mubarak, I just started posting for hours and didn't go to sleep until two or three every morning."

Li Yuan describes this early period as a "Weibo Spring": many people in China were excited about the possibilities of a new, open forum for serious discussions of social problems and spent hours every day debating each other online. "Everyone was so involved in Weibo then and asking ourselves, 'How can we use this platform to shape China, to move it in the right direction?'" she says. "China is going through so many huge changes that no country in the world has ever experienced. There are so many issues that people need to think through—social, political, economic—and it just felt very empowering to have these public debates. We all got into these online fights and some of them were not pleasant, but it was all so interesting—this big clash of ideas."

Li Yuan saw a meteoric rise in her Weibo followers by 2012, and before she knew it she had become a "Big V" celebrity with more than 2 million followers. As her following grew, she became even more keen to expose systemic problems in China, such as the country's vast inequality and lack of rights—including women's rights. Meanwhile, the Chinese website of the *Wall Street Journal* had also become extremely popular.

Li Yuan approached me at the end of 2011 about publishing a Chinese translation of my op-ed for *Ms.* magazine, "China's 'Leftover' Women," in which I argue that the Chinese government deliberately created a sexist propaganda campaign to shame educated single women and push them into marriage. When the article appeared (uncensored) on the Chinese *Wall Street Journal* site, it became their top-rated news story for that day in China, with tens of thousands of pageviews on the first day alone—attracting exponentially more attention than my original article in English.

Even though Li Yuan did not publicly identify herself as feminist for years, her comments on Weibo challenged the sexism endemic in Chinese society and propaganda. For example, the *People's Daily* Weibo account posted an elaborate photo spread in 2016 of all the intricately prepared meals a young wife made each morning for her husband before he left home to go to work. "So much variety—every day a different dish for over three months!" gushed the captions, saying that the wife was such a good cook that her husband never wanted to go out to eat. Li Yuan posted the piece with a snide comment: "Why can't the man make breakfast for the woman instead?"

Another time, she posted a picture of a meeting of male world leaders and commented, "If we had more women leaders ... like Hillary Clinton or Angela Merkel, then I really believe this world would be more stable and peaceful." She often posted about how women should not succumb to the omnipresent marriage pressure in China: "Being single is nothing to fear. Don't rush into marriage just because you're afraid to be 'leftover.' Spending your entire life satisfying the demands of other people is a betrayal of yourself." Although censors often deleted Li Yuan's posts, her account was never "disappeared" altogether, unlike those of some of the sharpest government critics.

Li Yuan shared many details and photos from her personal life on Weibo. She had married in her early twenties without thinking much about it, then divorced a few years later and did not want to marry again or have children. She was very vocal about how much she enjoyed her life as a single woman, especially traveling alone. She often posted pictures from her exciting solo travel adventures in places like India and Thailand. "Freedom is very important to me and I don't want to be constrained by anything," she says.

In 2013, Li Yuan was ranked one of Weibo's "top 100 influential users" and featured in a BBC report entitled "Who Are China's Weibo Superstars?" Young women approached her and thanked her for showing them that they could lead a happy life without getting married, saying things like, "I follow you on Weibo and I think you're right, I shouldn't let my parents push me into marriage and it's fine for me to be single."

As Li Yuan's following increased, so too did the misogynistic online abuse. She tried not to let it bother her too much. (When I set up my own Weibo account in 2011, she advised me, "Don't pay attention to all the nasty comments.") Once, when she posted that she did not like to cook, a man she knew replied, "No wonder you can't find a husband!" People also accused her of being a "traitor" to China and of having an American passport (she is a Chinese citizen) because they thought the articles she posted were too critical. They drew up enemy lists of objectionable people on Weibo; several named her as an "agitator on the sidelines."

Many of the abusive messages were sexist plays on her work-assigned Weibo handle, @YuanLiWSJ, an abbreviation for *Wall Street Journal* that could also be read as shorthand for the Chinese word *weishengjin*, meaning "sanitary pad." Trolls often adopted the term. "People would attach pictures of bloody sanitary pads and tell me, 'What you are saying is not logical because you're just a woman,'" says Li Yuan. She believes that some of the misogynistic abuse online was from people paid or implicitly encouraged by the government to try to influence public opinion on the internet—known as the "fifty-cent party" (*wumao dang*), after the state-run *Global Times* wrote that online commenters were paid fifty Chinese cents for each pro-government post (although this is just an expression and not a literal amount).

"For a while, the 'fifty-centers' were especially nasty. When I said how much I enjoyed my trip in India, dozens of them posted that they wished I would be gang-raped there," said Li Yuan. "It lasted for days. There just seemed to be so many of them, obviously organized because their comments were very similar."

Li Yuan has blocked hundreds of people so that her family members will not see the worst of the threats, but it is, of course, impossible to block all the trolls. Even her young niece noticed the hostile comments she received and asked her, "Auntie, why do so many people scold you on the internet?" (I too have received gang-rape threats after posting about women's rights on Weibo, as have many other women who post anything identifying themselves as feminist.) After Chinese president Xi Jinping assumed office in 2012, Li Yuan and many other influential Weibo personalities who had been hopeful about the possibilities of social media became disillusioned.

In 2013, the government started warning "Big V" commentators to be vigilant about what they said on Weibo. One of the biggest opinion leaders, Chinese-American investor Charles Xue (also known as Xue Manzi)—with 12 million followers—was arrested in August 2013 and accused of having sex with a prostitute. He later appeared on China's state television, wearing a prison jumpsuit and handcuffs, and confessed to "spreading irresponsible posts online." Xue, who grew up in China but is a US citizen, was jailed, then released in 2014 for "health reasons." Xinhua News said that Xue's incarceration "sounded a warning bell about the law to all Big Vs on the internet." Some of Li Yuan's friends were also arrested for their social media posts, then later released. "They were forced to make confessions for crimes they did or did not do, even though they would never be prosecuted, but the crackdown on online dissent was very systematic," she says.

Li Yuan began having frequent trouble reading the Weibo posts of her friends. Some of their new posts were not visible from her account, although the posts had not been deleted, so it was almost impossible to detect the censorship. Other people often told her that they could not read her new posts either, even though the posts appeared normal on her own timeline. As soon as her followers reached 2.4 million around 2013, they were "capped" by Weibo and have remained at exactly the same number since. Li Yuan knows other people who have had their followers capped as well. "I asked a senior Weibo executive about this, and he admitted that people like me 'aren't the type of influencers they're after now,'" she says. In November 2013, censors blocked the Chinese *Wall Street Journal* altogether, along with Reuters, for unspecified politically sensitive reports. (The Chinese websites of other foreign news organizations, such as the *New York Times* and *Bloomberg News*, had already been blocked in 2012 because of investigative reports on the family wealth of China's top leaders.)

After the Feminist Five were arrested, Li Yuan joined many others to post her outrage on Weibo and began using the term *feminist* to describe herself. "I wasn't comfortable with the term for a few years while I was living in China from 2008 to 2015 because I was like a textbook feminist: single, childfree and too intimidating for most men," she says. She says the term *feminist* had so many negative connotations in China and was often thrown at her by misogynistic trolls after she had written a column, say, about sexism in the Chinese venture capital world or in the technology industry. "All these men in China think women are very powerful already. They say, 'There's no prejudice against women in China! Why do you still think you haven't achieved equality?'" says Li Yuan.

"There's a term in Chinese, *da nanzi zhuyi* [male chauvinist], and men would call me a female chauvinist," she says. When she moved to Hong Kong to take up a new job as China tech columnist, she reflected that by not publicly calling herself feminist for a long time, perhaps she was trying to protect herself. "Then so many things happened and some of my friends ended up in jail. I decided that I am a feminist and that's one label I should wear proudly," says Li Yuan. In April 2018, she was hired as the inaugural Asia technology columnist for the *New York Times*. She continues to post regularly on Weibo, but no longer sees the platform as a major force for social change.

Even with increasingly sophisticated, high-tech internet censorship and surveillance, feminist activists have continued to find new ways to keep the movement alive and burgeoning, both on and off the internet. Lü Pin, the founding editor of China's most prominent feminist social-media platform, *Feminist Voices* (*Nüquan zhi Sheng*), says it is no coincidence that more young women in China began identifying as feminists around the same time that *Feminist Voices* began vigorously posting feminist articles on Weibo in 2011 (censors banned the *Feminist Voices* account in 2018).

Lü Pin had just received her master's degree in Chinese language and classical literature from Shandong University when she moved to Beijing in 1994. She began working as a journalist for *China Women's News* (*Zhongguo Funü Bao*) just before the 1995 UN World Conference on Women. This credential gave her privileged access to the women's conference sessions, which the government had relegated to the remote district of Huairou, far away from downtown Beijing. At the time, she did not yet consider herself a feminist.

"There was no internet in China then, so the public had very little awareness of what was going on," says Lü Pin. "The UN Women's Conference was a good opportunity for some, but it was only open to a very small number of people in China," largely government officials and senior professionals affiliated with the All-China Women's Federation. Lü Pin describes *China Women's News* as "the Communist Party's bridge to women." She and fellow reporters wrote pieces trying to draw attention to the needs of women, but they also had to fulfill their duty to spread Communist Party propaganda—"two very contradictory goals," she says. For example, if they wrote an article about rural women living in poverty, they were expected to outline how the Communist Party was helping women to overcome their hardship.

These professional experiences also coincided with a personal awakening. Though she had to toe the Party line in *China Women's News*, Lü Pin began reading feminist theory extensively. Meanwhile, she moved in with her boyfriend and lived with him for several years. "At first, I thought I was just like other people and wanted to get married," she says. But as she and her boyfriend encountered problems in their relationship, she also reflected more deeply on how to combine her political commitment to feminism with her personal lifestyle and found herself increasingly resistant to marriage—not to her boyfriend alone, but any man. "Over time, I realized I'm actually not like other people and I have no desire to marry at all." They broke off their engagement and Lü Pin decided to renounce the institution of marriage altogether. She believed that it oppressed women by turning them into unpaid laborers—particularly in China, where married women's legal rights are frequently violated.

Lü Pin left *China Women's News* in 2004 to join the NGO Media Monitor for Women Network, where she could work more directly on highlighting gender discrimination in the media. Around the time that Weibo was established in 2009, Lü Pin founded the alternative media platform *Feminist Voices* (initially called *Women's Voices Journal*, or *Nü Sheng Bao*), which covered a wide range of stories, including the lack of support for domestic violence victims, workplace discrimination against women, and sexual harassment. At first, *Feminist Voices* generated very little interest from the public. They set up a Weibo account in 2010 but it remained largely dormant, with only several hundred followers, until mid-2011, when Lü Pin and her colleagues decided to make a concerted push to increase their following by posting much more frequently about women's rights.

Their moment came in August 2011, when China's Supreme People's Court announced its new judicial interpretation of the Marriage Law, essentially reversing a cornerstone of the Communist revolution: the notion of common marital property. Whereas the original Marriage Law of 1950 granted women equal rights to property and other rights such as the freedom to divorce, the new, vaguely worded judicial interpretation of 2011 essentially specified that, unless legally contested, marital property would belong by default to the person whose name was on the property deed—usually a man.

Feminist Voices posted a steady stream of detailed legal critiques of the interpretation, arguing that it was a severe setback for married women's property rights. Feminist attorney Li Ying, for example, called the new version of the Marriage Law "a man's law," because most property deeds are in men's names, meaning that men would generally be awarded ownership of marital property in the event of a divorce. *Feminist Voices* also posted outraged comments from married women panicked about losing marital property rights they had previously taken for granted.

The *Feminist Voices* Weibo account constantly posted photos, commentary and articles about women's rights, as feminist activists carried out street actions—including the 2012 "Bald Sisters" action in Guangzhou protesting gender discrimination in university admissions and Xiao Meili's "Beautiful Feminist Walk" from Beijing to Guangzhou to raise awareness about sexual abuse in 2013 and 2014. Eventually, Lü Pin's team built up a following of over 180,000 users on Weibo and over 70,000 users on WeChat, signaling a burgeoning interest in feminist ideas (before *Feminist Voices* was banned in 2018). Given the Communist Party's stigmatization of the term *feminist*, these numbers were very respectable, though nowhere near the stratospheric numbers for China's biggest Weibo personalities.

The largest online response in the immediate aftermath of the detention of the Feminist Five in 2015 came from Chinese university students. A group of students from Sun Yat-sen University in Guangzhou—Zheng Churan's alma mater—bravely signed their full names to an open petition in support of the detained feminists. The petition was initially posted on Weibo and WeChat; when it was deleted by censors, the students circulated it through encrypted channels.

> Online discussion groups about feminism and gender discrimination have sprung up everywhere. Although feminism has not yet become a hot topic for every member of society, these discussions have been inspiring and heartening … Given our society's widespread gender discrimination and objectification of women, the efforts of Zheng Churan and her friends are full of positive energy and reflect social progress. Sun Yat-sen University should take great pride in producing such an idealistic and passionate student.

It garnered almost a hundred signatures from Sun Yat-sen University students and alumni alone before the university disciplined the students who had signed, often by putting demerits on their academic records.

Petitions also spread to many more universities in China, until administrators began conducting internal investigations of all the students who had signed. The student affairs office of a Guangzhou university released a notice on Chinese social media: "There are reports that students at ten universities have signed a petition. Please ensure all institutes quickly hold activities to deeply penetrate student and classroom circles, investigate, and do educational and dissuasive work."

Students in Guangzhou who had signed petitions were summoned for "guidance" meetings with university officials, who warned them that they would receive a "bad mark" in their personal files, damaging their prospects for future education and jobs, according to Didi Kirsten Tatlow of the *New York Times*. Police and state security agents deployed to campuses across China to interrogate and intimidate students who had posted messages of support for the Feminist Five or volunteered for feminist campaigns.

Zhu Xixi, a doctoral student at Zhejiang University in Hangzhou, did not anticipate being a target of state security agents. When she heard that Hangzhou authorities had detained Wu Rongrong of the Feminist Five, Zhu offered to hide a box of International Women's Day stickers against sexual harassment at her university dorm room. Then, on March 7, 2015, Zhu received a call from a security agent saying that he wanted to meet with her. Zhu made an excuse, then shut off her phone and decided that she had to go into hiding temporarily, along with many other feminist activists in different cities.

Zhu, who was twenty-seven at the time, had been a passionate women's rights activist since 2012, when she was an MA student in Wuhan majoring in political economy. That year, she demonstrated against mandatory gynecological exams for women applying to join China's civil service.

Zhu and a group of young women staged a performance-art protest, standing in front of the local government's human resources office wearing large paper underpants, with the character for "examination" crossed out in a large red X over their crotches. The women held up signs saying things like "No pelvic exams!" and "No questions on menstrual periods!" They said the medical exams for women were sexist and violated laws against gender discrimination in employment.

Since then, Zhu had moved to Hangzhou to start her PhD in public administration at Zhejiang University. There she became good friends with Wu Rongrong, often volunteering at the Weizhiming Women's Center, which Wu had founded. After hiding outside Hangzhou for about a week, Zhu thought she would try returning to her university to see if security agents would leave her alone. Since she was a full-time student rather than a formal employee of a women's rights organization, she figured that she would be given more leeway.

Yet the moment she arrived back in Hangzhou and turned her phone on, she received a call from her Communist Party advisor. (Most university students in China have a Party advisor to monitor "political behavior"; this person is different from the student's academic advisor.) The advisor summoned her to his office on campus and had clearly been given instructions from state security to be very stern with her.

"Why did you leave the campus this whole week? Which of your acquaintances have gone missing? Who organized the activity on sexual harassment?"

Zhu politely feigned ignorance. After a while, the advisor let her go. Then Zhu received a call directly from a state security agent asking to see her on campus, and she agreed. The agent came to her Communist Party advisor's office, bringing with him a pile of anti–sexual harassment stickers and other pamphlets on gender discrimination, which agents had confiscated from the Weizhiming Women's Center on the night they arrested Wu Rongrong. He laid out the material before him as though it were evidence from a crime scene.

The agent was particularly interested in one picture of the protest in Wuhan against gynecological exams, in which Zhu stood at the front with her arms crossed. He told her to look carefully at the picture. "Is this you in the picture? Who organized this activity in Wuhan? Who are all the other women here?" The security agent ordered Zhu to sign a written confession stating that twelve women had taken part. Zhu said there were not that many women involved and refused to sign until they reduced the number of participants and toned down the inflammatory language. He agreed, then made her sign a revised statement before releasing her.

Zhu called around and discovered to her dismay that state security agents and Communist Party advisors were interrogating virtually every student who had volunteered for any feminist activity in the last few years. She was suddenly afraid that she would be called for another interrogation and that her testimony might be used as evidence to prosecute the five detained women on criminal charges, so she decided she had to flee Hangzhou again.

In early April, after the Feminist Five had been detained for a full month, Zhu's academic advisor contacted her and urged her to return to campus or she might "encounter problems" with her PhD program. He said that so far, her extracurricular feminist activities would not affect her academic record, but that she needed to "watch herself." Zhu returned to campus and the Communist Party advisor ordered her to meet with him in his office. This time he gave her an ultimatum: "If you don't cooperate fully with state security, the university may be forced to expel you." When Zhu showed up to her Communist Party advisor's office, the state security agent who had made her sign the written confession was there too.

The agent started interrogating Zhu again about her feminist activism and her PhD dissertation topic, domestic violence in China: "Why did you choose domestic violence as your research focus? Does your research have anything to do with your participation in anti–domestic violence activities?" This time, Zhu refused to be intimidated. There was no way she would ever agree to change her dissertation topic just because of pressure from a male chauvinist security agent, she thought.

In June 2017, the Communist Party's discipline watchdog, the Central Commission for Discipline Inspection, criticized Zhejiang University for being one of fourteen top universities that were "too weak in their political work," according to the *South China Morning Post*. Zhejiang University issued a notice in September exhorting its students and academics to write online content that showed "core socialist values" and influenced public opinion with "correct thinking," adding that content that promoted socialism and was widely circulated on the internet would receive the same amount of academic credit as a paper published in a peer-reviewed scholarly journal. Zhejiang University's Communist Party propaganda chief, Ying Biao, said the new policy on internet content would further President Xi Jinping's goal of making universities the "strongholds of the Party's leadership."

Even as the Chinese government tightened ideological controls on university campuses across the country, more and more young women were starting feminist social-media accounts. And the online debates about women's rights were not confined to Han Chinese women. Young Tibetan women were increasingly speaking out on WeChat about their unique burdens as an ethnic minority oppressed by the Han Chinese–dominated Communist government and by men within their own communities.

For example, the scholar Séagh Kehoe analyzed a heated WeChat discussion among Tibetan women in 2016 about the loss of "plateau redness," referring to the red cheeks common among people who live at high altitudes, because of the new beauty aesthetic of fair skin associated with the Han Chinese. "In this era of unitary standards of beauty, many young Tibetan women chose to apply whitening products, matching it up with bright red lips, and constantly engaging in endless cycles of weight loss programs that leave them exhausted," wrote a young Tibetan woman in an essay translated by Kehoe. "For those few who still have the plateau redness, this culture gives way to feelings of embarrassment and insecurity around this natural look." Kehoe argued that the women's WeChat discussions about the cosmetics and "plateau redness removal" industry in Tibet reflected "internal dilemmas and conflicts experienced by Tibetans living in the shadows of the dominant Han culture and state."

Uyghur women have also developed lively discussion groups on WeChat, focusing particularly on mothers, according to the scholar Dilnur Reyhan, who writes that Uyghur women barred men from joining their discussion groups in order to minimize the appearance of political organizing. The women's debates covered provocative topics such as "secularism and religion to homosexuality ... minority politics in other countries and the future of Uyghur identity," writes Reyhan. One Uyghur internet personality, Umun, started a "Liberal Youths" group advocating greater support for feminism and LGBTQ communities. But a new, hardline Communist Party Secretary for Xinjiang installed in 2016, Chen Quanguo, began a crackdown on Uyghur cyberspace and the Uyghur discussion groups on WeChat were shut down.

By March 2016, the one-year anniversary of the arrest of the Feminist Five, so many women had started calling themselves feminists on social media that Weibo banned new account names containing the term for several months. Feminist chat groups created through WeChat messaging apps received anonymous warnings to be "careful" about their activities. Feminist activist Zhang Leilei in Guangzhou teamed up with a lawyer to sue Weibo for deleting several feminist accounts, but courts in both Beijing and Guangzhou refused to accept her lawsuit. After several months, Weibo quietly allowed the accounts to be activated again.

Then, in February 2017, censors banned the *Feminist Voices* Weibo account for thirty days. Ostensibly, the suspension was related to an article it had posted about a planned women's strike in the United States protesting President Donald Trump on March 8, International Women's Day. Chinese feminists circulated the notice from Weibo: "Hello, because content you recently posted violates national laws and regulations, your account will be banned for thirty days." *Feminist Voices* founder Lü Pin believes Weibo was using the article as a pretext to send a warning to the growing number of vocal Chinese feminists online. She says the fact that the Chinese government felt the need to crack down so harshly on feminist social-media accounts was a sign of just how successful the feminists had been in tapping into the urgent needs of women across China and striking a nerve with the mainstream public.

"Once women experience a feminist awakening and stop believing Communist Party propaganda, they can never go back," says Lü Pin. Before *Feminist Voices* was banned in March 2018, she believed that China's feminist movement might become the most powerful social movement in decades because of its networked, flexible and fervently committed community. "Most [exiled or jailed] Chinese human rights activists don't have a large community of supporters to begin with, so they are basically independent, isolated activists and they lose their ability to mobilize people inside China," she adds. "The feminist movement is different because we are a large community and there is a huge demand for our message."

Feminist activists today no longer have to take the lead in calling out misogyny in the Chinese state media, because over the past several years, ordinary women—and men—have become emboldened to criticize sexism and sexual violence on their own. In April 2016, for instance, surveillance cameras caught a man grabbing a woman by the neck and hair in the Yitel Hotel in Beijing, then dragging her down the hallway until she finally escaped. The woman, who called herself "Wanwan," posted the video on Weibo and the video-sharing site Youku, where it received millions of views and a torrent of angry comments. The social outcry over the woman's assault put pressure on Beijing police to capture the perpetrator; the hotel later apologized for its lax security and customer service.

In September 2016, a student at Beijing Normal University, which has a majority female student body, published a 13,000-word report on Weibo detailing the times, locations, and frequency of at least sixty instances of sexual assault and harassment at the university over the past decade. One of the cases involved an assistant dean, who drugged female students and sexually abused them. And, in a #MeToo–like action in May 2017, one of China's top investment banks, China International Capital Corporation, suspended a senior analyst for sexually harassing female interns after an anonymous Weibo user posted screenshots of his salacious text messages to women.

Yet the feminist message can only continue to get out to a broader audience if the internet is not too tightly controlled. In the United States, the #MeToo movement started by Tarana Burke went viral in 2017 after the *New York Times* and *New Yorker* published in-depth investigative reports on the sexually predatory behavior of powerful Hollywood producer Harvey Weinstein, but in China the lack of press freedom combined with internet censorship prevents news media from conducting similar investigations.

Nevertheless, in January 2018, China's version of the #MeToo movement gained traction, demonstrating the extraordinary resilience of a feminist movement that has posed a unique challenge to China's all-male rulers in an era of global connectivity. Feminist activists and thousands of students at dozens of Chinese universities defied heavy internet censorship and seized on the global momentum of #MeToo to demand an end to sexual harassment on campus.

The swift mobilization of over 8000 students and alumni at around 70 universities in the Me Too petition movement showed that China's young generation was "enraged by the prevalence of gender inequality and repression," wrote Lü Pin in a short essay for the Asia Society's China File. "This networked guerrilla movement was much more effective than a centrally planned and executed campaign would have been at addressing censorship concerns and at allowing members to exercise individual initiative," she wrote.

Feminist activist Xiao Meili was just one of many who launched a Me Too petition addressed to her alma mater: "Given the severity of sexual harassment at institutions, we feel obliged to be vocal. It's imperative that Chinese colleges construct a mechanism to prevent sexual harassment on campus," said her petition to Beijing's Communication University of China. Xiao's petition was deleted by censors almost immediately after she posted it on

Weibo and WeChat. Then several women who signed it said that a Communist Party advisor from their alma mater had placed pressure on their former professor about the petition. The professor, in turn, contacted them to ask whether their Me Too petition was influenced by "hostile foreign forces."

This line of questioning has become increasingly common ever since May 2017, when the website of the *People's Daily*—the official mouthpiece of the Chinese Communist Party—warned that "Western hostile forces" were using "Western feminism" to interfere in China's handling of women's affairs. The vice president of the All-China Women's Federation, Song Xiuyan, was quoted as saying that Party officials working on women's issues were in the midst of a "serious political struggle" and urgently needed to follow President Xi Jinping's instruction to guard against Western ideological infiltration.

In spite of all the obstacles, online calls for an end to sexual harassment began to expand beyond China's university-educated women to factory women. An anonymous female assembly-line worker who was routinely sexually harassed by co-workers at Foxconn, Apple's main supplier for Asia, published an essay in late January 2018 on the women's labor rights website *Jianjiao buluo*, "I am a Woman Worker at Foxconn and I Demand a System that Opposes Sexual Harassment." The woman said that she was inspired by news about other women in China standing up against sexual harassment and wanted to "oppose this unjust and infeasible system." She demanded that her employer set up proper channels of recourse for victims like herself. "We call for more men to pay attention to the situation of their sisters," she wrote.

As censorship of the Me Too hashtag increased, Chinese feminist activist Qiqi came up with the idea of using emojis for "rice" 🍚 (*mi*) and "rabbit" 🐰 (*tu*), making the hashtag #RiceBunny 🍚 🐰 (*mitu*)—which sounds like "Me Too" in Chinese—to evade the internet monitors.

Then Weibo took the drastic step of deleting the *Feminist Voices* social media account after celebrations for International Women's Day ended late at night, March 8, 2018. The following day, WeChat deleted the group messaging account for *Feminist Voices*. The deletion of *Feminist Voices* also coincided with the three-year anniversary of the arrest of the Feminist Five. Not only was the Weibo account shut down, but WeChat erased many essays readers had written demanding that the *Feminist Voices* Weibo account be reopened. While Weibo announced in 2017 that it would only ban *Feminist Voices* for one month, the 2018 ban appeared to be permanent as this book went to press.

Censors had already deleted the Weibo account of Feminist Five activist Li Maizi for posting a candle emoji to mourn the death of Nobel peace laureate Liu Xiaobo, who died of advanced liver cancer in government custody on July 13, 2017, after being deprived of medical treatment. (Li Maizi later started another Weibo account.) And by 2018, China had adopted what is believed to be the world's most cutting-edge surveillance technology—including facial-recognition technology and iris scans—dramatically expanding the reach of its security apparatus deep into the private lives of its citizens to build a "digital dictatorship" on a massive scale.

In April 2018, tenacious students at several different Chinese universities continued to circulate Me Too petitions, demanding that university officials stop whitewashing charges of sexual harassment and assault.

At Peking University—China's most renowned academic institution—a group of eight students submitted a freedom of information request about the case of Gao Yan, a literature student who killed herself in 1998 after she told friends and family she was raped by a professor, Shen Yang. Shen had left Peking University by then and denied the accusations, but the university admitted that it had given the professor a warning in 1998 over his "inappropriate student-teacher relations."

One of the students who submitted the information request, Yue Xin, said that her advisor brought her deeply upset mother to her dorm room at Peking University's School of Foreign Languages late on the night of April 22 to warn her to stop speaking out about the twenty-year-old rape case. Yue was sent home with her mother, but she posted a widely circulated online statement about the intimidation she had experienced. "At 1 a.m., my advisor abruptly came to my dormitory with my mother, woke me up, and demanded that I delete all data related to the freedom of information request from my phone and computer," Yue wrote.

The advisor warned Yue that her activism might be seen as "subversive" and that she could face criminal charges due to her involvement with "foreign forces." Yue wrote that her mother had been so frightened by the encounter with university officials that she had threatened to kill herself.

Other Peking University students, enraged by the unjust treatment of their classmate, posted large, handwritten "big-character" posters (*dazibao*) on a campus bulletin board in solidarity with Yue Xin. The students wrote, "We ask you gentlemen in charge of the school, what are you actually afraid of?" and said their classmate was acting in the spirit of the historic May Fourth movement of 1919 (see Chapter 5). Their actions evoked memories of the Democracy Wall movement of 1978–79 and the student-led, pro-democracy uprising of 1989, which was crushed by the Tiananmen massacre. Campus security guards quickly removed the student posters and the following day, Peking University installed new surveillance cameras pointing at the location where the "big-character posters" had appeared.

Authorities warned the Chinese media, "Do not report on the Peking University open letter incident … Content expressing so-called solidarity must not be shared from personal social media accounts," according to a leaked censorship directive. But online supporters continued to defy internet censors by posting images of the student statements sideways and upside-down, even encoding them in the blockchain technology used for cryptocurrency.

Given the increasing barriers to communication, Lü Pin believes that the Chinese feminist movement needs a dedicated presence outside China, so she is focusing on "opening a new front" free from government interference. She decided that she could make more of a difference for the beleaguered movement in self-imposed exile, so after the detention of the Feminist Five in 2015 she became a visiting scholar with Columbia University in New York, then pursued a master's degree in gender studies at the State University of New York at Albany. Meanwhile, she and several partners started the first Chinese women's rights group to be based in the United States, the Chinese Feminist Collective.

"Even though in the past we never openly said that we were opposed to the Communist Party, we know what the Party thinks of us now ... We have entered the confrontational stage of the movement," says Lü Pin, who uses her new base in the United States to speak more freely than she ever could under the close monitoring of authorities in China. She hopes that the Chinese feminist diaspora can become a valuable resource for uncensored Chinese-language information on women's rights for feminists inside China, as well as a vehicle for recruiting new activists to sustain the movement. Although many activists lose their ability to tap into domestic Chinese networks once they are exiled, the internet (so far at least) has made it much easier to stay connected to communities inside China—particularly the large Chinese feminist community, which has an unusual degree of transnational cooperation through various social media and encrypted messaging platforms.

"If we don't set up this group in the US, China's feminist movement will become too passive," says Lü Pin. "The position of our core activists is extremely fragile, and we don't know when the police will come and arrest someone again—it could be today or tomorrow."

3

Detention and Release

On International Women's Day in 2015, the members of the Feminist Five were formally incarcerated at the Haidian District Detention Center in Beijing. Wu Rongrong had first been arrested and detained in Hangzhou, where she was given a medical examination before being flown to Beijing the next day. She had been hospitalized several weeks earlier for complications from her chronic hepatitis B, so when the medical exam showed abnormal results, agents at Haidian took her to a public security hospital, forcing her to wear heavy ankle shackles to keep her from escaping. They insisted that Wu be admitted, but the medical staff said there were no free hospital beds. "Now we've wasted all our time bringing the prisoner here when you didn't even make the proper arrangements!" the security agents shouted at the hospital staff. They took Wu back to Haidian, where the guard overseeing her cell assumed Wu had been turned away from the hospital because she was a troublemaker. "She's a political prisoner—don't talk to her," the guard told Wu's cellmates.

Guards removed Wu's ankle shackles, but they confiscated her glasses and forced her to sleep on the floor. Security agents interrogated Wu up to three times a day, with the last session always in the middle of the night. She kept reminding the agents that she had hepatitis B, so she needed medication and uninterrupted sleep at night, but they would not stop waking her up for interrogations, nor would they give her any medical treatment.

Many of her interrogations were videotaped and some of the male agents screamed insults at her to unnerve her just before pressing the record button.

"If it weren't for you demanding women's rights in China, poisoning the minds of our little girls, we'd still be able to have three or four wives like we did in the past!"

Sometimes they threatened her directly.

"If you don't confess, we'll put you in the men's section and let them gang rape you!"

Wu was sickened by the men interrogating her and she did not even care about her own well-being anymore. But when security agents realized that their threats of gang rape were not effective against her, they switched tactics and started bringing up her family members.

They terrified her by saying things about her four-year-old son that she did not wish to print.

This was too much for Wu to bear. She started sobbing uncontrollably and could not speak. After breaking her emotionally, the agents took her back to her cell. That night, Wu could not sleep at all. Her body was failing her and her nerves were shattered.

She thought of the activist Cao Shunli, a woman who had been detained by authorities in September 2013 after organizing a protest outside the Foreign Ministry to demand public participation in the country's human rights review. Cao was charged with "picking quarrels and provoking trouble" (the same language used to justify the arrest of the Feminist Five) and deprived of medication for her liver disease and tuberculosis. After falling into a coma in March 2014, she had been rushed to the hospital and died days later. *I don't have any medicine. I don't have a doctor*, thought Wu Rongrong. *I'm going to die here, just like Cao Shunli.*

Before long, Wu was spitting up blood, but no one heeded her requests for medical help until she was permitted to meet with her lawyer on March 16.

Another of the Feminist Five, Wang Man, was also denied medical treatment in spite of her congenital heart problem. When Wang arrived at the detention center, security agents interrogated her about everything she had saved on her computer and her emails, which they had thoroughly searched.

"Confess! You were being used by foreign forces!" they yelled, accusing her of being a spy because her nongovernmental organization had received European Union funding.

Later, Wang Man, an only child, learned that agents were also harassing her mother while she was in detention. One agent even videotaped her mother urging Wang to drop her lawyer and confess to her crimes. They told Wang that her parents, with whom they had spoken at length, were worried sick. "How can you be such an unfilial and selfish daughter? You are making your parents suffer so much!"

Each night, after her interrogations were over, Wang lay wide awake thinking through all of the agents' accusations, trying to figure out what it was she might have done wrong. After a week, Wang's face suddenly went white and her cellmates told the guard that she needed to see a doctor. She was given a physical exam and some mysterious pills, and then interrogated for several hours. The next morning, guards shackled her ankles and took her to a public security hospital, where a doctor placed her on an IV.

By night, she was shackled to her bed. By day, the interrogations continued, with security agents bellowing at her to sign a confession. She refused. She was distraught and on the verge of collapse. A doctor finally examined her and told the agents that they could no longer interrogate her in this way. On March 20, Wang's lawyer released a statement that she was suffering from heart problems due to long daily interrogations. "Though her situation is in control and she is out of danger, it is no longer appropriate to detain Wang Man," he said, according to Human Rights in China.

The third feminist to be jailed, Zheng Churan of Guangzhou, also suffered lasting health effects from her thirty-seven days in detention. Zheng used the slang term *pujie*—spread out on the street—to describe her state of mind while incarcerated. "In Guangzhou, we say a person is walking on the street and she isn't careful, then suddenly she's lying in the middle of the street in a horrible situation," she explains. "I felt panicked, like I was going crazy."

She did not feel as "tough" as Li Maizi, who resisted the threats and humiliation of the agents by constantly taunting them. She worried deeply about her parents, and the security agents exploited Zheng's loving devotion: "You will be charged with spying! Your parents will be charged with spying, too, and they'll be under surveillance for the rest of their lives. We're sending the police to go visit your parents now."

What exactly were the police doing to her parents? Zheng had no way to know and being unable to see the facial features of her captors without her confiscated glasses made the threats even more frightening. Only later would she learn that the security agents attempting to harass her parents at home in Guangzhou were largely kept at bay because of her boyfriend and his network of supporters in the labor rights community, who checked on Zheng's parents often to make sure they were all right.

Then the agents told her that her activist sister, Wu Rongrong, was very ill from chronic hepatitis B. From then on, Zheng cried uncontrollably throughout her daily interrogation sessions— so much that some of her older cellmates took pity on her and cared for her like a daughter. Before long, her hair began to fall out in clumps from the stress. She could not sleep and was often woken up in the middle of the night to work shifts around the detention center. Although the twenty-five-year-old had always been healthy, her knees became stiff and made cracking sounds whenever she moved. Her heart beat fast from constant anxiety.

Zheng feared that she would go blind, since her eyesight was so poor she had to squint all the time. She was overcome with self-doubt and guilt that her activist sisters had been arrested—after all, it had been her idea to hand out stickers against sexual harassment. If only she had kept her suggestion to herself, everyone could have avoided this pain and abuse, she thought.

Just as bad as the medical neglect and threats against family was the fear that their incarceration could be indefinite. Wei Tingting initially thought she would be released after a few days, so she detached herself emotionally and tried to observe her experience as an anthropologist would, treating her detention as a form of field-work. Once she realized that her detention would last longer than a few days, the interrogations pushed her into a state of anxiety and extreme disorientation, since she was virtually blind without her glasses and had no idea what was happening outside her cell. Soon she developed a habit of freezing at the sound of clanking handcuffs at the metal door, even when she was mid-conversation with a fellow inmate. "If I heard them at my door, I knew I was about to be taken away for interrogation. If it wasn't my turn, the guard would keep on walking, and I'd let out a sigh of relief," she said.

The last and most combative of the Feminist Five, Li Maizi, barely said anything during her first week of interrogations. She just smiled sarcastically at the agents who attacked her for being *lala*—a lesbian—and called her a whore. "You can yell at me all you want for being a dirty woman, a prostitute, a lesbian, it doesn't hurt me in the slightest," she said.

They accused Li of being "unfilial." "Your parents are so poor and you are a bad and ungrateful daughter," they yelled at her, before threatening her parents directly. Security agents ordered Li's father to write a letter to his incarcerated daughter, admonishing her for her bad behavior and urging her to give up her feminist activism. But when they showed it to Li, she instantly knew from the contorted, flamboyant language—urging her to "thoroughly rehabilitate herself and become a new person," for instance—that he had been dictated set phrases to write.

At one point the agents took her into a special interrogation room equipped with an intense spotlight which they shone into her eyes at close range, making it impossible for her to keep her eyes open and causing tears to stream down her face. With the spotlight forcing her eyes closed, the agents accused her of being a spy for "foreign forces."

"What? I work on gender equality—now you're calling me a spy?" Li said.

"You're a spy subverting state power!" the agents said.

Li was initially unfazed when the security agents told her she would be sentenced to five years; she calculated that she would still be young after being released and could spend her time in jail studying Chinese criminal law. But when they began threatening eight to ten years, she could no longer stay calm. Detention was alternately stressful and monotonous.

"Sometimes I felt so uncomfortable being locked in that cell all day that I'd crave being taken out for an interrogation. It was just so boring being cooped up in detention the whole time, sitting there with nothing to do. But each time I was called for interrogation, my heart would pound with nervousness," she says. She developed coping strategies to ease her mind. "I repeated these three things every day: 'Perseverance, bravery, endurance.' I said this in the morning, each time I was taken out for interrogation, and before sleeping at night," she said. "I relied on this mantra to get by."

~

Thankfully, the Feminist Five had a wave of global solidarity on their side. Wu Rongrong's lawyer issued a statement saying that she needed urgent medical attention. Her husband released medical records documenting her twelve days of hospitalization in February, while a Beijing doctor independently examined her medical records and warned that without her daily medication, Wu might suffer liver failure. Sixteen supporters delivered a letter to the detention center pushing for medical treatment for Wu Rongrong and they were arrested and held for a day. But this pressure seemed to work. The security guards, finally accepting that she was really sick, transferred Wu to a public security hospital for medical treatment. Even at the hospital, however, Wu was forced to shackle one of her ankles to the hospital bed from 6 p.m. to 6 a.m. When she went to the toilet at night, she had to drag her hospital bed by her shackled ankle to the toilet, then drag the bed back again when she was finished.

Meanwhile, the sustained global outcry over the women's detention continued, with supporters around the world joining in #FreeTheFive campaigns and protesting in the streets to denounce the Chinese government's persecution of feminist activists. In early April, the Feminist Five had seemed headed for criminal prosecution: their original charge of "picking quarrels and provoking trouble" was changed to the more serious crime of "gathering crowds to disrupt order in public places," which carries a sentence of up to five years in jail, or even longer in some circumstances. Although the Chinese government has often seemed impervious to external pressure about human rights abuses, it has also responded at times by freeing or exiling individual dissidents. We will never know the exact reasoning behind the Chinese authorities' decision to release the Feminist Five, but perhaps President Xi Jinping's blatant hypocrisy in jailing young feminists while preparing to host the United Nations' Beijing 20 summit in New York was too damaging to China's image.

After prosecutors failed to press charges against the women within the maximum thirty-seven days specified by Chinese criminal law, their lawyers demanded they be released. On the evening of April 13, Beijing authorities made the sudden announcement that all five feminists would be released immediately on bail "pending further investigation." They were labeled "criminal suspects" under investigation for "gathering crowds to disrupt order," and banned from traveling for one year without permission from the government.

In spite of their official release, however, the harassment continued—and it began almost immediately.

On the night of Wu Rongrong's release in Beijing, several agents took her to the airport and warned her to keep her mouth shut while passing through the security check.

"If someone talks to you at the airport, just ignore them and let us do the talking," an agent instructed her. When the plane landed in Hangzhou, they drove her straight to the police station and one agent began filming her with a video camera as another asked her questions.

"Wu Rongrong, did we treat you well in detention? Did you take your medicine on schedule?"

Surrounded by security agents and speaking to the video camera, Wu was afraid that they would not let her go home if she said anything bad about her captors, so she mumbled, "Yes, I was treated decently."

As the camera filmed Wu pledging to obey the authorities from now on, she became increasingly depressed.

She wanted to scream out in fury: "*You all locked me up for no reason for 37 days! You made me sleep on the floor! You deprived me of my medication and I could have died!*"

Yet she silenced herself and told the agents what they wanted to hear.

"Wu Rongrong, will you be doing any more performance art in the future?" they asked.

"I will only do good things for society from now on," replied Wu robotically, feeling more and more nauseated as the camera rolled.

When Wu's husband came to the station to pick her up, the agents made him sign a pledge that he would not permit his wife to do anything "harmful" to society. "If your wife does something like this again, we're going to come after you!" one of the agents warned her husband. Wu felt even worse at this outburst directed at her husband, as though she were not there. Why were the agents threatening him for something that she herself had done?

While Wu seethed inwardly, her husband was relieved that their family could finally be reunited. Wu's son had turned four years old while she was in detention and he was overjoyed to see his mom again. Wu broke down crying regularly, but her child was too young to detect how traumatized she was.

Since the Feminist Five had become so famous and details of Wu's life had become public, many supporters had heard about her son's fourth birthday. They deluged him with cards wishing him a happy birthday and wishing his mother well.

"Mama, why are so many people I don't know sending me birthday cards?" he asked her.

"Because your Mama is a good person and many people like me, so they like you too and want to celebrate your birthday," Wu told him. This pleased her child immensely.

But the worst was yet to come.

Less than two weeks after Wu Rongrong's release, state security agents from Beijing came to Hangzhou to interrogate her again, warning her not to tell the Hangzhou security agents they had visited. (They are supposed to inform Hangzhou's Public Security Bureau when they interrogate a citizen beyond their own jurisdiction.) The agents took Wu to a private hotel room. As soon as they entered, she was seized with fear: the blackout curtains were drawn, the room was very dimly lit, and several long tables had been arranged to mimic the Beijing detention center's interrogation cell. Then her interrogation began. The agents asked her about Lu Jun, the founder of the nongovernmental organization Yirenping, trying to get Wu to paint Lu Jun as the mastermind of her "subversive" feminist actions—just as the Haidian detention center agents had done. Wu refused.

They yelled and cursed at her, becoming so ferocious that they no longer seemed human. They seemed to transform into barking animals, standing very close to her, barking at her for hours. Then they made her kowtow three times—a traditional gesture of loyalty. She had never been as terrified in detention as she was in the Hangzhou hotel room. She began to cry. "If you keep crying, we won't let you leave," they warned.

Eight hours later, they let her go. Wu walked alone into the night, abandoned and disoriented. She felt like a wandering ghost, with no idea where she was. Headlights shone on her as she staggered alongside the road, and she felt an overwhelming urge to allow a car to plow her down. At that moment, her phone rang. It was her husband. She could do nothing but cry into her phone.

Wu Rongrong had not publicly released details of her mistreatment in detention because she had been afraid to create further trouble for herself and her family. But that night, after being locked in a state of shock for hours, she could no longer suppress her urge to scream at her captors. Her silence was suffocating her. She felt that she would drop dead if she didn't speak out and tell the world the truth about what had happened. She called her friend Zhu Xixi, a graduate student at Zhejiang University, and asked her to spread the news that she had been viciously interrogated. "My spirit is on the verge of collapse. If you don't hear from me tomorrow, it means that I am dead," read Wu's statement. Zhu sent it to rights lawyers and the feminist community, who passed it on through social media. "Either I become a person who is terrified to death of everything, or I choose resistance to regain my freedom," Wu later explained.

Another of the Feminist Five, Zheng Churan, was also severely traumatized when security agents flew her back to Guangzhou upon her release from Beijing. Zheng remained in deep shock for several weeks, afraid of being left alone and barely able to recognize that she was no longer incarcerated. Anytime she heard a knocking sound, her heart started racing. She was terrified of being arrested again and was haunted by dark, hazy images of her interrogators at the detention center. Her condition was made worse by the fact that state security agents continued to invite her for a "meal" or "tea" to "chat" and call her on the phone to question her. Though they no longer threatened or formally interrogated her, they kept her in a constant state of heightened anxiety. She feared that any friend who showed support for her would be snatched away by security agents.

Zheng believes that she was suffering from a kind of Stockholm syndrome, where she tried to cater to the requests of security agents by acting out a dutiful role. "They were trying to turn me into an obedient subject of the state and, in many ways, this was even more monstrous than anything they did to me in detention," she said. Psychotherapy arranged by friends in Hong Kong helped with her post-traumatic stress disorder. Slowly, she began to imagine vengeance against each of the men who had tormented and humiliated her. She later joked about her revenge fantasies, but it was clear that by allowing herself to tap into and express feelings of profound anger at the injustice done to her, she was able to heal from the trauma. By the end of summer she had married her boyfriend and felt ready to work again, although she promised her parents not to work for a women's rights NGO until the government dropped her criminal charges.

Toward the end of 2015, she had planned a trip to Beijing, but a security agent went to her mother-in-law's home to ask about Zheng, under the pretext that he was conducting a routine checkup for population planning. Zheng was furious and called the main security agent in charge of monitoring her. "If you want something, come talk to me directly, don't harass my mother-in-law!" Zheng told him indignantly. But the visit had served its purpose: to remind Zheng's extended family that the authorities were watching her closely, that she remained a criminal suspect, and that anyone related to her was vulnerable to harassment as well.

When Wang Man was released around midnight on April 13, agents from the detention center in Beijing drove her to her parents' home in the neighboring city of Tianjin, arriving at around two or three in the morning. A few hours later, just as Wang thought that her ordeal was finally over, new agents from Tianjin showed up and brought her to a private room in a café with no windows—designed to look like an interrogation room at the detention center in Beijing. Then the interrogations began again. "I'm ill and I have a heart condition," she begged. "Please let me rest!" Eventually, the agents let her go, worried she might have a heart attack, but not before threatening further interrogations. "I'm still going to come after you," one of them said menacingly.

This has not happened—Wang believes that they were surprised by the publicity and backed off. But the Tianjin agents still called Wang's mother repeatedly, warning her not to answer any media questions about her daughter. Back in her Beijing apartment, the police scared away Wang's roommate and instructed her landlord to evict her because of her "criminal record," so she had no choice but to move back home with her parents in Tianjin.

For Wang Man, the most painful part of her experience was being abandoned by many of her friends. Those within her closest circle, whom she mostly knew from development work and not the feminist community, did not consider themselves feminists and thought her actions were too radical. Although they said that the government was wrong to detain her, they also believed that she bore some responsibility. "Some of the friends I used to trust a lot—especially my teachers—just weren't able to understand what I had gone through and didn't want to be connected to me anymore," says Wang. "I completely understand the pressure they were under, but still, this was very painful and difficult for me to accept."

She had lost her job, her apartment, her regular circle of friends, and her independent life in Beijing and was still receiving regular phone calls from security agents monitoring her and her mother. She kept replaying in her mind the events leading up to her detention. Maybe her activism was not an important contribution to her country's development, as she had previously thought. Maybe those who treated her work with suspicion were right, and she deserved to be blamed for everything that had happened.

This was a state of near-paralysis that felt much worse to her than being in detention, and she now wished she could return. "On the inside, everything was black and white," she said. "I knew that I was innocent and had done nothing wrong, so I just needed to survive the experience and get out." Now, in the outside world, she had to face the heartbreak and disappointment of losing the support of so many she had relied on in the past.

Wang developed chronic insomnia, and her post-traumatic stress disorder often kept her from getting out of bed. She sought help from some psychologists, who told her to "examine herself" and "take responsibility" for what she had done to bring on her arrest. Coming from medical professionals, this reaction made her doubt herself even more. But in her time of greatest need, her activist sisters came through for her. They offered her moral support, assured her that she had done nothing wrong, and confirmed the critical importance of her work. They also connected her with a good psychotherapist. One of them even traveled to

Tianjin to speak to her mother about how her daughter was not a criminal and explained that she had in fact made a huge contribution to women's rights in China.

"The sisterhood offered me a safe place where I could be myself and feel secure," she said. "That feminist solidarity rescued me." In 2016, Wang began a master's degree in social work at the University of Hong Kong. Her belief in the transformative power of feminism has only strengthened.

"Many young women in China are taught that feminism is something that's off-putting or ugly and they don't want to be associated with that label, but I think feminism can be a real lifeline in emergencies. When a woman feels like she's drowning, this lifeline can pull her out and save her," she said. "This is how I feel about feminist solidarity: it can literally save our lives."

4

Your Body Is a Battleground

On the evening of her release from detention, Li Maizi insisted on taking as many accoutrements from the center as she could, such as her personally assigned blanket and eating utensils. One prison guard inspecting her belongings asked her why she wanted to keep such unlucky reminders of her incarceration. "Little girl, you're really weird," he said.

Li said she wanted to reproduce conditions inside the detention center at a public show. "This is where the spoons would go, there is where the bowls would go, this is where the blankets would go," she remarked later. "It would be a kind of performance art, where everyone in the audience would come in the room and I'd tell you how you're supposed to sleep and eat, and how you'd be interrogated."

The guards began searching through all of Li's belongings at seven or eight that evening and did not finish until nearly midnight. She had written down all the times of her interrogations on a piece of paper, which she had hidden in the elastic of her long underwear, but the guards found and confiscated it. When the search finally ended, Li packed two bags full of everything she could carry: on her left side were her prison-assigned toiletries, a pot, a bowl, a spoon, a wash basin, and a lunch box; on her right side, her blanket and mattress pad.

When we met in 2015, Li had committed many features of the detention center to memory and spent a long time drawing out a detailed map of the center to show me. First came the police station, where the feminists were held the night of March 6. Li numbered the six interrogation rooms and drew the large room with the one-way mirror and even where the tables and benches were placed. Next came the second floor of the Haidian District Detention Center. She remembered the number of each cell: She was in cell 1105; no one she knew was in the adjacent cell, 1106. Zheng Churan was in 1107, Wei Tingting was in 1103, and Wang Man was in 1101. The women were deliberately spaced apart so that they would not be able to communicate, but because the interrogation room was outside their cells, occasionally the women saw each other briefly on the way to or from an interrogation. Wu Rongrong was placed in a separate section of the center, far from the others, in cell 1203—perhaps because she was viewed as the most senior feminist organizer.

In December 2015, several other members of the Feminist Five were undergoing treatment for post-traumatic stress disorder, but when I asked Li Maizi about it she scoffed at the idea that any kind of psychotherapy would help her. It seemed to me that her meticulous drawings of the detention center were her own way of gaining a sense of control over the painful memories. In holding the women for over a month, the Chinese state had not just been suppressing dissent. They were also asserting control over the women's bodies.

The poor diet and stress inside the detention center caused Li—already slender before her arrest—to lose around ten pounds during her incarceration. Upon her release, she learned that security agents had repeatedly harassed her parents to convince her to give up her activist work. The agents had forced them from their home and held them under house arrest at the home of one of her aunts, who lived in a very remote rural area far from Beijing. They were not allowed to go out and shop or cook for themselves and had to eat takeout meals brought to them every day by their guards.

After she left the detention center, Li was also forced to stay with her parents at her aunt's village home, where they all remained under de facto house arrest. Li's girlfriend Teresa was desperate to see her, but agents constantly surveilled the home and no one was allowed to visit. The only way Teresa could reach Li was by calling her father directly.

"Don't you know we're being monitored? Don't ever call my phone again!" said Li's father.

Two days later, Teresa was permitted to visit Li in person. She knew how much her girlfriend had suffered in detention and did not want to cause her any more pain, so she stayed silent about something that was eating away at her, but that she knew Li would find deeply disturbing. With the Feminist Five attracting so much international media attention, some of the detained women's lawyers were giving regular interviews to foreign journalists about the injustice of their arbitrary detention. But there was a problem with one of the male lawyers. "Of all the lawyers representing us, he was the most reliable and supportive," said Teresa. "Whenever I wanted to talk, he would be there to listen." She trusted him implicitly, so when the lawyer suggested that she leave Beijing for Harbin in northeastern China to stay safe, she followed his advice.

Alone in the remote, freezing city of Harbin, where she knew no one, Teresa felt extremely frightened. It was not safe for her to contact her feminist sisters because the government was monitoring her so closely, so she had no idea what her friends were experiencing. The only person with whom she consistently communicated was this lawyer. Every morning, the first thing she would do was look at her messaging app to see if he had news about her girlfriend or any of the other jailed women.

Gradually, the lawyer began to make sexually explicit comments, texting her his fantasies about Teresa's relationship with her girlfriend. When she asked him for news, he insisted that she send him sexual pictures of herself before he would give her any information. Teresa felt intensely violated, but she was isolated, powerless, and desperate, so she endured the harassment at first. She was afraid to confront the lawyer, since she relied so completely on him to make the public case for releasing the five feminists. Soon she began having nightmares about him ganging up with a state security agent to interrogate and humiliate her.

Eventually she realized that the lawyer's behavior was a serious abuse of power, so she forwarded screenshots of some of his sexually explicit messages to a close friend. "These messages from [the lawyer] are making me sick, but I don't have any energy to deal with the problem right now. Please save these for me," Teresa wrote. The screenshots were inadvertently seen by another feminist activist who had been sexually harassed by the same lawyer in the past.

The other feminist began asking around and discovered that the lawyer was a serial sexual predator, deliberately hitting on young feminists in their twenties who had just become activists and did not want to "betray the cause" by speaking out about his abusive behavior. Some of them formed a closed chat group to discuss what they should do about him. Together, they sent a message to the lawyer confronting him about his behavior. The lawyer responded by sending a private apology to the group, saying that he had not meant to hurt anyone. At the time, Teresa felt that his apology was sincere and did not want to pursue the matter.

Yet shortly after the release of the Feminist Five, one of the other harassment victims told Teresa that the lawyer had continued to sexually harass her even after his apology. Teresa wanted to meet with the lawyer to confront him, but he refused to talk to her. He briefly posted a public apology on Weibo in response, then deleted it and denied that he had done anything wrong, instead attacking the feminists for "not being able to take a joke."

Teresa spoke with the director of the Beijing rights NGO where the lawyer worked and showed him the explicit messages.

As the director looked at all the evidence of sexual harassment, he appeared sympathetic. Encouraged by his response, Teresa said that his organization should rebuke the lawyer and start anti–sexual harassment trainings for all of their employees. "When we work on sexual harassment and sexual assault in the future, we would like to see your organization play a leading role in taking on these cases," Teresa told him.

Misogyny has no political boundaries; supposedly progressive, male activists have throughout history revealed deep-rooted sexism by silencing, belittling, and even abusing the women within their own civil rights movements. The scene that unfolded next could have taken place in many other parts of the world, including the United States. In Teresa's case, the head of the rights organization said that he needed to hold a meeting with his board to discuss further action, but after the meeting, he contacted her with bad news. "You're the only one who feels that he sexually harassed you; other people disagree," the man told Teresa, saying that the lawyer would be reprimanded but remain with the organization. "We're not judges who can sentence him to death with one ruling. We need to give him another chance. You need to be patient and give him more time," he said.

Teresa felt completely dejected. Then came a mounting sense of rage at the deep injustice. "*He* needs more time! What about *me?*" she fumed. Meanwhile, she could no longer keep the upsetting news about the lawyer from Li Maizi, who was still recovering from the trauma of her detention and was furious and bitterly disappointed. The extreme irony of a man who was supposed to be defending her in a dire emergency sexually harassing her girlfriend and lying about it, while representing her and other women jailed specifically for their anti–sexual harassment advocacy, was devastating.

"This whole experience taught me just how despicable people can be," says Li. The lawyer must have known that once Li Maizi came out of the detention center, she would discover the truth, so

77

there could only be two possible explanations for his behavior, she thought. Either he was so ignorant that he did not know what sexual harassment was—even though he kept talking to the media about women's rights and gender equality—or he did not believe that Li would be released from detention. "His behavior was beyond disgusting," she says.

After a while, Teresa decided that it was time to go public, so she agreed to let a feminist sister release some of the sexually explicit screenshots on Weibo—without exposing her identity. Many people—largely men—said that it was unfair to accuse the lawyer of sexual harassment, arguing that the attention would hurt the larger, "more important" goal of fighting for human rights in China. Teresa hated having strangers comment on whether his behavior constituted "real" sexual harassment and tried not to pay attention to the misogynistic remarks, but she was grateful for the strong solidarity of her activist sisters, who helped her overcome any sense of shame.

Within the human rights and LGBTQ rights communities, male activists often showed that they did not truly see women's rights as human rights. Several of the feminist activists I interviewed complained about the sexism of men who were rights activists. They told me that male-dominated rights groups often covered up other men's sexual harassment under the guise of preserving "unity." But some feminists—including Xiao Meili, Zhu Xixi, and Zhao Sile—wrote public condemnations of the rights lawyer's misogynistic abuse.

Several months after her release from detention, Zheng Churan posted an impassioned open letter about the rights lawyer on social media: "That male lawyer, his mouth full of slogans of justice and equality, sexually harassed my sisters! I went to jail because of my opposition to sexual harassment, and I'm not going to let you get away with sexually harassing my sisters!" Just like the male security agents had, many of the male human-rights lawyers also dismissed Li Maizi, Teresa, and the others as "little girls" who could not possibly be serious activists. Some had so little gender consciousness that they mocked Li's intimate relationship with Teresa, refusing to believe that the two women were actually *lala* (lesbian) and saying that they just "hadn't found the right man yet," according to Teresa.

"Most Chinese men lack even the most basic understanding of sexual harassment, so it was really important for us to go public and push back against [the lawyer]. Otherwise he might do something even worse in the future," says Teresa.

"So many of these men fly the human rights flag and see themselves as heroic figures, but they harass and traumatize women, then continue to practice as lawyers with no dent in their reputations whatsoever," Zheng Churan confided in me.

There is no reliable way to measure the prevalence of sexual harassment in China, but some surveys are worth noting. A 2016 survey of almost 18,000 students by the nongovernmental China Family Planning Association found that more than a third of college students have experienced sexual violence or harassment, with the most commonly reported being "verbal sexual harassment," "being forced to kiss or touch private parts," and "being forced to undress or expose private parts," according to the state-backed news website *Sixth Tone*. A March 2018 survey of more than four hundred women journalists by the Guangzhou Gender and Sexuality Education Center (founded by Wei Tingting of the Feminist Five) and China Women's Film Festival found that over 80 percent had been a victim of "unwanted sexual behavior, demands, language and non-verbal or physical contact" from a manager or co-worker. And a 2013 survey found that up to 70 percent of women factory workers in Guangzhou had been sexually harassed, according to the *China Labour Bulletin*. (After the arrest of the Feminist Five, the Sunflower Women Workers' Center, which conducted the survey, was also shut down.)

Veteran women's rights scholar Feng Yuan, who has worked

for decades to combat domestic violence and gender discrimination in China, believes that "99 percent of women in China" have experienced some form of sexual harassment. But Chinese law lacks a clear definition of sexual harassment, making it virtually impossible for victims to sue successfully in court. As the heavy censorship of #MeToo in China (and the detention of the Feminist Five) demonstrates, the topic of sexual harassment is still seen as politically sensitive.

The Chinese government says that about one in four married women is beaten, although the real incidence of violence is likely far higher, according to activists. China passed its first nationwide law against domestic violence in December 2015 and implemented it in 2016. But the law is poorly enforced, with restraining orders extremely difficult to obtain, and most of the country's domestic violence shelters completely unused, according to a two-year study of the law's implementation by Feng Yuan's organization, *Wei Ping* (Equality). Moreover, the anti–domestic violence law does not mention sexual violence and marital rape is not considered a crime. It should come as little surprise, then, that experiences of sexual harassment, sexual assault and domestic violence have been formative for most of China's feminist activists.

Like many other children in China, Li Maizi was born into a family with a long history of abuse. Until she turned three, Li lived in the mountains of Yanqing District outside Beijing, doted on by her loving grandma, who was so fond of her only granddaughter that she carried Li around on her back everywhere she went, even when she worked all day in the fields. Li's grandfather would come home in the evenings and beat her grandma. He also beat his children—Li's father and uncle—and they grew up thinking that domestic violence was normal. So Li's father beat her mother as well.

Li moved with her parents to another village closer to Beijing when she was three, but when she turned seven, her parents sent her back to the mountains to live with her uncle and go to school. Since her family did not own land and was only renting in Shunyi district, their household registration (*hukou*) was still in Yanqing and the government rules stipulated that she must attend school there. But Li's uncle was violent and often beat her, although he never beat his own daughter, who was four years younger. Once he burned Li's homework book in the furnace that heated their bed in the wintertime (a *kang*, common in the countryside).

"My uncle beat me because I had my own ideas and I disobeyed him," says Li. "He wanted me to do chores but I said no, why should I work for you?" She told her parents, but they made light of it and did nothing to intervene. Li felt abandoned and lonely, was treated as an outsider, and had no friends, while her school was so poor that one teacher had to teach all six grades.

But even after Li's family was able to buy a house of their own and she had moved back in with her parents in the fourth grade, her troubles continued. Despite her young age, Li knew that she was attracted to girls rather than boys, so other kids thought that she was "different" and routinely bullied her. "If anyone ever hits you, you have to hit back," her father advised.

One day when she was harvesting peanuts in the fields, a boy in the village who often bullied her finally pushed Li to her limit and she punched him. Then his nose started bleeding. "His whole family was standing around us watching, but I just didn't care," she said. "I was so angry." When the boy's older brother saw what had happened, he came over and hit Li. Then Li's father beat the older brother. "This all happened in a public place, with everybody watching, and I was watching too," says Li. "I didn't know whether to be sorry for the brother or happy because I felt avenged." After that incident, Li never hesitated to fight back whenever anyone bullied her—girl or boy—even when the boys fighting her were physically much bigger and stronger. "When there's no one you can turn to for help, you can't be a coward," she says. "Never give in. Never submit."

Meanwhile, Li's own father began beating her as well as her mother. He was six feet tall and very strong, but by this point Li was not afraid of him. One evening in junior high school, she was lingering at the home of a girl she liked and noticed that it was almost dinnertime. Her father got very angry if she was late for dinner. "After all, I was a girl," quips Li. She got on her bike and rode frantically back home, covering nearly five miles in fifteen minutes. As she walked in the door, her father started yelling at her and she immediately raised up both her clenched fists, stared him straight in the eye, and stood her ground. Her father kicked her and she went flying from the dining area all the way into the next room. "I cried, but I refused to submit," she says.

When Li was in high school, about seventeen years old, she got into an argument with her father at dinner and left the table to go to her bedroom. "You fucking bitch!" he yelled, continuing to curse her. She yelled back at him. Her father went into the kitchen, then charged into her bedroom with a large chopping knife, holding it right over her head. Li's mother and grandfather—both very short—stood on either side of the large man, trying to keep him away from Li. "Just leave now! Hurry!" pleaded her mother.

Li did not feel any fear, but was so shocked her own father would behave this way that she froze. "Go ahead, just chop me!" she said defiantly. Then Li noticed her mother's panicked expression, as though she were about to collapse. Li had never seen her mother look so frightened before, so she fled.

She rode her bike to the home of the girl she liked and sat outside in the dark, too embarrassed to knock on the door. Eventually the girl's father noticed someone outside and came out. "Who's there?" he asked. "Uncle!" Li responded, but he could not see who she was and went back inside again.

No one would ever rescue her, she thought. She rode to a public park next to the local primary school, determined to sleep on the grass all night. It was mid-autumn and the night air was very cold. After a while, Li could not stand the cold any longer and rode to her aunt's house to spend the rest of the night there.

The next morning, Li went to school and saw her mother outside, looking for her.

"I saw her worried face and I felt guilty for making her suffer so much," she says. "My Pa could die for all I cared, but I couldn't let Ma suffer any more." She returned home, and from that moment on, her father never beat her again. "He was anxious because I was their only child and if I left home, I might never come back again," she says. "That was the first time he felt the situation had gotten out of control, so he just stopped." Li's father also stopped beating his wife, although he continued to use psychological forms of abuse when he was angry, such as locking the door and not letting her in.

It was when she went to Chang'an University in Xi'an, one of China's ancient capitals, that her life was transformed. She befriended other queer students, came out as a lesbian, and became an activist in an LGBTQ rights group. She also discovered feminism and began advocating for feminist perspectives within the LGBTQ community. During her final year as an undergraduate in 2012, Li took part in many feminist actions (she and fellow activists at the time deliberately eschewed the term *protest*). In 2012, police reported her to Chang'an University for disciplinary measures after they detained her for organizing volunteers to occupy a men's public bathroom in downtown Beijing. She was already known as a troublemaker for being the only student in her class who refused to join the Communist Party. The vice president of the university summoned Li for a formal warning in his office. Would she take a work-study position on campus for 120 renminbi a month (around US$20) if she would agree to drop her feminist activism? Li refused, retorting, "How's this instead? I'll give you 250 renminbi and you give me back my freedom." By the time she graduated, later in 2012, she realized that it was her calling to become a lesbian feminist activist, fighting for women's rights and equality in China.

When I first met her in 2013, Li had begun working full-time in Beijing for the NGO Yirenping. As we ate at a small dumpling restaurant in a narrow Beijing *hutong* (neighborhood alley) outside her cramped office, she made bawdy jokes, remarking on the large number of sexually nonnormative women involved in China's feminist movement. They "go in straight and come out bent," she laughed, explaining that feminism freed women's minds and made them see the possibility for alternative lifestyle choices. She complained about how tiring it was to speak to straight men because China has too much "straight man cancer" (*zhinan ai*, roughly "straight male chauvinism" or "toxic masculinity"), then laughed wholeheartedly.

Nevertheless, it was during her detention in 2015 that she became more forgiving of her father. Her lawyer met with her father when she was detained and told him that security agents were interrogating her late at night, not letting her sleep, and generally mistreating her. Her father was enraged when he heard this and threatened to get a gun to avenge his daughter if she continued to be abused. "I was really moved by that," says Li. "He's very hot-tempered—that's just the way he is."

For an iconoclast who often makes fun of the Chinese tradition of filial piety, Li is remarkably forgiving of her father. While she crusaded against domestic violence and sexual harassment in her public life, in her private life Li believed that her father genuinely loved her. He was violent toward her and her mother because he was raised as a male chauvinist, she reasoned. At times she felt that his violent combativeness had helped prepare her for her own battles with state security agents during her detention.

She had encountered an even greater threat than her own father —the political violence of the patriarchal, authoritarian state— and felt that this was the more dangerous enemy she needed to fight. Given Li's unique history of persecution on multiple fronts, I could understand her deeply contradictory emotions about someone who had once come close to actually killing her. "Many people ask me why I became a feminist activist, but for me, I've always been resisting. Resistance is my daily life," says Li. "If I don't resist, then who am I?"

Many of the feminist activists I interviewed recounted experiences of abuse growing up, which later fueled an intensely personal commitment to the emerging feminist movement. Bai Fei was one such woman. When she was in junior high school in Shanghai, around thirteen or fourteen years old, her classmates constantly gossiped about boys, but she was not at all interested. She was attracted to girls but did not dare tell anyone, so she kept a diary about how she was in love with a female class leader. Someone discovered her diary and she became the target of routine, violent abuse from her classmates. "Whatever you can imagine, they did to me—using sharp objects to stab me all over my body, spitting in my face, holding me down and forcing me to drink urine," Bai says. She is very petite—less than five feet tall as an adult—and the fact that she was so much smaller than her classmates made her even more vulnerable to abuse.

The first time she went home with bloody scratches all over her face, her mother asked, "What did you do? Did you cause a fight?" Bai replied that her classmates had bullied her, but her father turned on her with contempt. "This only happened because you're such a coward," he told her. "It's your own fault—don't go blaming other people!"

The reaction of her parents hurt her deeply. Bai was an only child with no friends and after that exchange, she did not dare tell anyone when she was assaulted at school, until many years later. Although she had visible injuries, no teacher ever intervened to ask if she was all right, so the abuse continued through the rest of her time at high school. "I lived those years in sheer terror," she says. "I was too terrified to even look at my face in the mirror."

Shortly after she told her parents about the abuse, her father started spending most of his time with his girlfriend and rarely came home. Bai's mother—who only had a primary-school education and had a job as a sanitation worker in an apartment compound—was too unhappy about being abandoned by her husband to pay any attention to her daughter. Bai became deeply depressed and frequently thought about suicide. Whenever she drew a picture, she would draw it all black. She once tried to kill herself by slashing her wrists but survived the attempt.

Somehow, Bai graduated from high school and started life anew as a student at East China Normal University in Shanghai, majoring in sociology. She found a decent psychologist who told her, "homosexuality is not a disease." She came out as lesbian and joined an online group about HIV/AIDS, the Aizhixing Institute, run by prominent AIDS activist Wan Yanhai (who left China for the United States in 2010 because of pressure from the government). Once Bai became more active in the HIV/AIDS advocacy community, she was introduced to Wu Rongrong, who had also worked for Aizhixing.

Bai offered Wu Rongrong a place to stay for the night when Wu was pregnant and passing through Shanghai in 2011, around the time that Bai graduated from university. As they chatted that evening, Bai was so touched by Wu's generous spirit that she confided in her about the violent bullying she had endured at school. Wu listened to Bai's story intently with a kind of loving compassion that Bai had never encountered before in her life and she felt overwhelmed with gratitude. "Why don't you join our feminist movement?" Wu asked Bai when she had finished telling her personal story.

"What do you mean by *feminism*?" asked Bai.

"Come join us and you'll find out," Wu replied.

"So I just joined without even knowing anything about it at first, and then later discovered that it had so much meaning, it was truly life-changing," Bai told me later.

Wu Rongrong invited Bai to take part in a feminist training session in Hangzhou, where Bai met other activists, such as Lü Pin and Li Maizi. These training sessions often incorporated consciousness-raising, in which each woman in the group could tell her personal story of encountering sexism, abuse, or general injustice and others would listen.

Inspired and energized by her new feminist sisters, Bai threw herself into activist campaigns on issues such as sexual assault and domestic violence. In one widely reported domestic violence case, a woman named Li Yan, from a rural county in Sichuan Province, was sentenced to death for killing her husband in 2010 after suffering prolonged abuse. The husband had habitually hit her head against the wall, stubbed out cigarettes on her face and legs, sexually abused her and even cut off her finger. One night, he hit her with an air rifle and threatened to kill her—until she took it from him, used it to bash him to death, and then dismembered his body. Li Yan's lawyers said that she was at her wits' end after trying many times to seek help from the police and local Women's Federation officials, and repeatedly being told to return to her marriage and try to "bear it."

Bai Fei joined her feminist sisters to protest Li Yan's death sentence and the absence of a law against domestic violence. They wrapped themselves in white bandages and lay down in front of a court displaying a sign saying, "I Do Not Want to Be the Next Li Yan"—actions that were repeated by feminists in several different cities. She helped solicit hundreds of signatures for a petition demanding leniency for Li Yan and traveled to Beijing to deliver the petition to the Supreme People's Court. In April 2015, in a victory for the feminist activists and lawyers who had worked hard to generate a public outcry about her case, a Sichuan court ruled that Li Yan had indeed been the victim of domestic violence and suspended her death sentence. For Bai Fei, the campaign to support Li Yan and other feminist actions were a crucial part of her own healing.

"Through this feminist community, I started to understand that the mistreatment I had experienced my whole life was not my fault," she says. "I finally discovered my own worth and realized that I can be proud of myself."

When I met Bai Fei in Shanghai six months after the release of the Feminist Five, she had just posed for "Painful Words," a photo essay on homophobic abuse by Liang Yingfei in *Caixin* magazine. Bai Fei posed half-naked for her stunning black-and-white portrait, hugging her curled-up legs on a chair, with the malicious names she had been called by her classmates and her father—pervert, abnormal, "it's your own fault"—written all over her body.

Days after the Feminist Five were detained, a police officer made a phone call to Bai Fei at the company where she worked as a secretary. Her boss stood next to her and listened as the police questioned her.

"Were you planning to take part in any activities?" the police officer asked.

"What activities? I don't know about anything," she responded.

Bai had, in fact, exchanged texts with some other feminists over WeChat about going to Hangzhou for the International Women's Day event. But she denied everything and the police did not question her further—they did not need to, since her boss now knew that she was a "troublemaker." As soon as Bai hung up, her boss questioned her more about her feminist activism and fired her immediately.

"My boss thought I was a dangerous person and that the feminist movement was dangerous," says Bai.

She had gotten into trouble with the police once before, in September 2014, when she had expressed support on Weibo for Hong Kong's pro-democracy Umbrella Movement for universal suffrage (the former British colony was handed back to Chinese government rule in 1997 and has experienced a rollback of many of its freedoms). The Shanghai police came to her apartment and deleted everything on her computer and cellphone, warned her not to express support for the Hong Kong protesters, and made her sign a pledge to be a loyal and patriotic Chinese citizen.

Bai was still unemployed and looking for another job as a secretary or administrative assistant when we met in November 2015, but she said her gender-neutral appearance—very short hair, no makeup, wearing a vest and trousers—made it difficult for her. "Most people hiring for these kinds of jobs want a feminine-looking woman who knows how to put on makeup or has long hair and wears dresses," said Bai. "There's very serious gender discrimination and I haven't gotten any job offers."

Fortunately, Bai's mother had finally accepted her daughter's sexual orientation, seven years after Bai came out as a lesbian. She even invited Bai's girlfriend to come live with them in Shanghai. Her mother had the large bedroom, while Bai and her girlfriend shared the small room.

"When my girlfriend isn't working, the three of us sit and eat together, and things are quite pleasant," says Bai. "My girlfriend is very good at saying things that make my mother happy."

Despite her years of vicious, homophobic bullying at school, Bai Fei considers herself "fortunate." "Bullying is so common in Chinese schools. I was just one of many, many others who suffer this kind of abuse, but most people can't find a way out," she says. "I feel incredibly lucky to have met Wu Rongrong and other feminist sisters, so I was able to walk the road to today."

I was awed by Bai Fei's ability to feel gratitude during such a dark time. As I transcribed my interviews, listening and relistening to the women's recorded voices, something about their traumatic stories triggered long-buried memories of my own brutal sexual assault as a fifteen-year-old girl. Much of my previous research on urban women in China has attempted to illuminate how "the personal is political"—especially regarding choices and limitations around marriage. Yet, in the ultimate irony, I was incapable of seeing the damaging effects of my own childhood trauma. While

I hadn't forgotten the abuse, I had locked it away, too ashamed to admit it to anyone—other than my husband, many years later. But my interviews with Chinese feminists began to dislodge the memory. A therapist helped me to see how the experience in my early teen years had shattered my sense of self-worth.

I am the daughter of a Chinese immigrant mother who grew up in Vietnam. Her family was riven by the US war there—some fled as refugees to the United States; some to Hong Kong; some died at sea; and some, like my mother, immigrated to the United States before the war. My father was white and born in the US. Both of my parents were China scholars. They moved us from the United States to Australia when I was six and brought my brother and me with them on frequent trips to China, starting in the early 1970s.

It happened in my hometown, Canberra, Australia, when I was the last remaining girl at a party. I was fifteen and tired of playing the dutiful Chinese daughter and straight-A student. I had snuck out of my bedroom window after my parents fell asleep. A man I knew from my neighborhood waited outside to drive me to the party, telling me that the seventeen-year-old guy I had a crush on would be there. By one in the morning, my friends had left, but I stayed behind, sipping a strong alcoholic drink. I did not care for it—it tasted like petroleum—but I wanted to be rebellious. At one point I stood up to say that I wanted to go home, but my crush refilled my glass and insisted that I drink it. So I did—I wanted him to like me. Then my head began to spin and I completely lost control over my body.

The next thing I remember was being in the bathroom with two older guys as the man who had given me a ride that night watched from the side. One stripped off my clothes as I tried to fight him off me, but the second guy—my crush—also took off all his clothes. The two of them grabbed my breasts and forced themselves against me while one shoved his fingers into my genitals. I cried and yelled out, "Stop!" but my ride stood by without intervening. Terrified, drunk, and nauseated, I finally threw up, and my attackers were disgusted enough to back off me. I sank to the floor and lay naked in my own vomit. The man gave me a towel to wipe off the vomit, helped me get dressed, and then drove me home. "We're bad, but we're not that bad," he said as he dropped me off. I took that to mean that I should consider myself lucky because the abuse could have been far worse. I knew little of this man, except that he was working odd jobs around our neighborhood and was likely in his mid-twenties, but in a Stockholm syndrome way, I felt grateful to him for "rescuing" me from my attackers. Now I can see that I was just a body to him, to be delivered to his friends for their amusement.

I did not dare tell my parents—I was afraid they would discover I was not a "good girl." I confided in one or two of my girlfriends, but we were children and completely unaware of our rights. I worried that others would blame me for what had happened. Like so many girls, I was constantly subjected to street harassment from men who thought nothing of yelling obscene comments about my body parts. I assumed that sexual harassment was a normal part of being a girl that I had no choice but to accept. When I saw any of my attackers in the neighborhood, I was so ashamed that I pretended everything was normal. I did not dare speak about it to anyone else again. It took me more than three decades—and dozens of interviews with Chinese feminists about their own experiences—to break my silence.

I recall one conversation with Li Maizi in 2016, when we spoke about how so many women in China are sexually assaulted, yet very few come out publicly about their experience. "In China, rape culture is so strong that almost no one dares to admit they've been sexually assaulted because they're terrified of being blamed for it," she said.

Perhaps the most prominent example is the actor Bai Ling, who was in an army performance troupe in Tibet from age fourteen to seventeen. She told the Associated Press in 2011 that she—along with other girls in the troupe—was regularly given alcohol and sexually assaulted by several People's Liberation Army generals. One of the rapes resulted in a pregnancy, which she ended with an abortion. Bai Ling had moved to the United States and was forty-four years old when she spoke publicly for the first time about her sexual abuse. "Because of the Chinese culture of obedience, you don't ask questions," she said. "You follow and obey."

With the global #MeToo campaign of 2017, some well-known women in Hong Kong began speaking out about their experiences. In November 2017, a former Miss Hong Kong, Louisa Mak, revealed that she was sexually assaulted as a teenager while on a delegation visiting China. Hong Kong hurdling champion Vera Lui Lai-yiu spoke of being sexually assaulted by her coach when she was only thirteen. Journalist Sophia Huang Xueqin in Guangzhou came out about a senior colleague who had sexually assaulted her in a hotel room while on a business trip. Huang began her own sexual harassment survey in November 2017 of female journalists in China, which she later combined with that of the Guangzhou Gender and Sexuality Education Center. The vast majority of women said they had not told management about being sexually harassed for fear of destroying their careers.

In January 2018, a graduate of Beihang University, Luo Xixi, posted a detailed personal essay online about being sexually assaulted by her professor, Chen Xiaowu. More than a decade earlier, Luo said, her professor had lured her off campus and tried to have sex with her. Chen denied the charge but Beihang University announced that he had "seriously violated" their code of conduct and fired him after several other former students came forward to accuse him of sexual harassment. Although Luo lives in the United States, her essay went viral and inspired thousands of other students and alumni across China to sign Me Too petitions in a rare show of collective action against sexual harassment. But these petitions for the most part did not involve women publicly identifying themselves as survivors of sexual harassment.

As in virtually every other country, there is a societal ideal of the "perfect rape victim" in China. A woman who is sexually assaulted is blamed for "asking for it" if she dresses the wrong way, says the wrong thing, uses the wrong tone of voice, looks at someone the wrong way, visits the wrong place, goes out at the wrong time, drinks too much, or does not have a chaperone. "You have to be extremely strong emotionally, plus have the institutional support of an NGO to speak out about sexual assault, otherwise you will be drowned to death in humiliating attacks," says Li Maizi. She adds that it will likely be many years before women in China can have a truly open, public discussion of the deep trauma of sexual assault and harassment.

Li often says that "our bodies are our battleground" (drawing inspiration from Barbara Kruger's 1989 black-and-white photographic silkscreen of a woman's face, *Your Body is a Battleground*) in her campaigns against gender-based violence. Li's prolonged abuse while growing up demonstrates how this saying is literally true for her—just as it is for so many other women in China and globally. She and other members of the Feminist Five were jailed because they were organizing an event to highlight the severe problem of sexual abuse in China by handing out stickers about sexual harassment for people to put on their bodies.

While working on this book, I looked up Australian law regarding sexual offenses against "children and young people." I was stunned to discover that in my jurisdiction, the Australian Capital Territory, the sentence for sexual assault against children between the ages of fourteen and sixteen was ten years in jail. As an objective observer, that sentence seemed appropriate. But what surprised me more was that I had been the victim of a serious, indictable crime and had lived most of my life in fear of speaking about it. If I had been taught about consent in my sex education classes, perhaps I might have recognized that I had the right to report my assault as a crime. Instead, I recall that in one of our sex-education sessions, the counselors told us (girls only, of course) about the importance of pleasing your partner even if you did not always feel like having sex.

Had I trusted an adult enough to confide in them, perhaps I might have prevented my attackers from assaulting other girls, which in all likelihood they did. Humiliated into silence and unable to imagine that I deserved support, I had unwittingly allowed the cycle of sexual violence to continue. Today, I am so far away in time and distance from the place where the crime occurred that I have no desire to file charges. But I can still recall the full names of two of my attackers, and their three faces are seared into my brain.

Globally, according to the United Nations, up to seven out of ten women experience physical and/or sexual violence in their lifetime. In the United States, 90 percent of adult rape victims are female; girls aged sixteen to nineteen are four times more likely than the general population to be victims of rape, attempted rape, or sexual assault. Only an estimated 23 percent of rape or sexual assault cases were reported to the police in 2016, according to the US Department of Justice. A 2017 ABC News/Washington Post poll found that around 33 million women in the United States (roughly one-fifth of the female population) had experienced sexual harassment at work, but fewer than half had reported it to a supervisor. The US Equal Opportunity Commission found that 75 percent of sexual harassment victims experienced retaliation when they spoke up about it.

When retaliation is so common for women who report sexual harassment in the United States, which has an independent judiciary and a functioning legal system, one can only imagine how much greater the obstacles are for women attempting to report sexual violence in an opaque, authoritarian state like China, where there is effectively no rule of law. A woman who reports sexual abuse can easily find that the retaliation involves even more violence, especially since perpetrators are very rarely held accountable. (I wrote about some horrifying forms of retaliation against women who filed reports of domestic violence in my book *Leftover Women*.)

The Chinese government does not release reliable statistics on sexual harassment or assault, but a 2013 UN multi-country study on men and violence found that around one-half of men in its China survey had used physical or sexual violence against an intimate partner. Feminist activist Xiao Meili was shocked by the results of the UN survey when it came out in 2013 and she began looking into doing a long-distance feminist walk to raise awareness about the epidemic of sexual abuse in China.

Five years earlier, when Xiao first entered the Communication University of China in Beijing in 2008, she was a very different young woman, heavily influenced by the sexist, heteronormative standards of Chinese society. "In high school, we were never allowed to wear makeup. Then, when we started university, all of a sudden becoming a 'pretty woman' became a very important responsibility," says Xiao. "I tried hard, but it was just impossible for me to live up to all these ridiculous standards placed on women." Xiao had two boyfriends in university and felt uncomfortable about the inequality in her romantic relationships: the man's needs were constantly seen as more important than her own.

"To be honest, I even believed in the 'virgin complex' [*chunü qingjie*] for years, and so did my boyfriends," says Xiao. The "virgin complex" is a throwback to the Confucian "chastity cult" (see Chapter 7) of China's imperial era, which held that women were basically defined by their sexual purity. According to the modern version of the chastity cult—which is hardly unique to China—a sexually untouched woman is a priceless gift to be presented to her husband; when an unmarried woman has sex with a man for the first time, she effectively becomes his property and is expected to marry him eventually. Premarital sex has become much more frequent and socially acceptable over the past few decades, following China's economic reforms of the 1980s and

90s. A survey conducted in 2016 by China's chief family-planning agency found that over 70 percent of university students "agree with sex before marriage." Yet nearly a quarter of students surveyed also said "there should be no sex before marriage under any circumstances," and only 15 percent of female university students surveyed reported actually having sexual intercourse, compared with 28 percent of male students.

Young, urban Chinese are often presented in the media as having racy, unrestrained sex lives, but most of the country still has deeply conservative views about sex. China has an appalling lack of rights-based sex education, resulting in the strong policing of women's sexual behavior, widespread ignorance about sex, the vast majority of parents avoiding talking about sex with their children (often because they themselves are ill-informed), increases in HIV infection due to low rates of condom use, and high abortion rates.

Many sex-education textbooks propagate misogynistic and sexist double standards, despite growing pushback on social media. For example, the Jiangxi Province education department published a sex-education textbook for middle-school students that called girls "degenerates" if they had sex before marriage. *Senior Middle-School Student Scientific Sex Education*—originally published in 2004—contained lines like "Premarital sex does great harm to a girl's body and mind, and a girl who sacrifices her body for love won't make a boy love her more" and "The boy who 'conquers' her will see her as 'degenerate' and love her less," according to a report by Fan Yiying of *Sixth Tone*. In 2016, a teacher posted excerpts from the book on Weibo, which generated so much outrage that the publisher issued an apology and promised to withdraw the textbook.

Xiao Meili had received no sex education at all throughout her schooling and had been inundated with sexist messages that made her feel bad about herself. Even though she first encountered the term *feminism* in university, it meant little to her. Then, in her third year of college, she went to Taiwan to study at Shih Hsin University as an exchange student. There she befriended many feminist teachers and queer students. Unlike the People's Republic of China, Taiwan has one of the most progressive attitudes toward gender in East Asia, with comparatively robust support for women's rights and LGBTQ rights. In a historic May 2017 decision, Taiwan's top court issued a ruling that put the island on a path to legalize same-sex marriage for the first time in Asia.

"Like a nearsighted person with new glasses, I began to see clearly," writes Xiao. She started to identify as bisexual and threw herself into feminist activism when she returned to mainland China. As an intern at the Beijing office of *Feminist Voices* in 2011, she met another young woman passionately interested in feminism—Li Maizi of the Feminist Five—and they became lovers. On Valentine's Day 2012, they marched with Wei Tingting in the "Bloody Brides" street campaign against domestic violence. Xiao Meili was also with Li Maizi when they tried to hold an Occupy Men's Toilets campaign in Beijing in 2012 after pulling it off successfully in Guangzhou, but Beijing police interrupted the protest and questioned Li extensively because she was listed as the organizer. When they both graduated in 2012, Li began her full-time NGO job focusing on women's rights while Xiao volunteered for different feminist campaigns.

In 2013, Xiao noticed that many men had gone on long-distance walks across China, but almost no women. She started thinking about doing a feminist trek and mentioned her idea to several people, some of whom asked her, "Aren't you worried that you might get raped?" She, too, worried that a single woman walking alone long-distance might be vulnerable to rape or abduction by human traffickers. Xiao discussed her concerns with her mentor, Lü Pin of *Feminist Voices*. Lü Pin thought that connecting a long-distance feminist walk with the theme of sexual abuse would make for a powerful advocacy campaign to reclaim public space for women, stop blaming victims, and punish sexual assaulters.

"At first, I didn't think I could do it, but Lü Pin was so encouraging. She told me, 'Do it! Do it, and I'll come along with you!' Once she said that, I knew it was really possible," says Xiao. In September 2013, Xiao—then twenty-four years old—set off on her more than 1,200-mile (2,000-kilometer) walk from Beijing to Guangzhou. She called it "Beautiful Feminist Walk: Fight Sexual Abuse, Women Demand Freedom." The title of her campaign played on the name she had created for herself, Meili—a pseudonym meaning "beautiful." Lü Pin walked with her for the first several weeks, then rejoined her in 2014 as she approached Guangzhou. Xiao stayed at cheap hostels or sometimes people's houses and was often joined by other supporters for a day or several days. Along the way, she gathered signatures for a petition protesting sexual abuse of children in schools, wrote letters asking local officials to investigate abuse cases, and posted photos, drawings, videos and vignettes on Weibo.

Altogether, around sixty supporters walked alongside Xiao for different parts of her half-year journey, including feminist scholar and filmmaker Ai Xiaoming; Lijia Zhang, author of *Lotus*, a novel about sex workers in China; and the feminist, sex-worker rights activist Ye Haiyan. Ye, also known as "Hooligan Sparrow," had launched a high-profile social-media protest in 2013 against a school principal in Hainan Province who had raped six underage girls. Ye's photos of herself standing outside the school holding a sign saying, "Principal, get a room with me—leave the school kids alone," had gone viral on social media. Even the celebrity artist Ai Weiwei joined in, posting a photo of himself on Weibo with "Principal, get a room with me" scrawled across his large exposed belly.

When I first interviewed Xiao Meili in May 2016, she had not yet faced police harassment for her feminist activism, and she speculated that it might be because she did not work formally for an NGO. Instead, she ran a business on Taobao (China's version of eBay, founded by billionaire Jack Ma), where she sold her own feminist designs. Many of her designs have become extremely popular among young feminists, such as T-shirts with slogans like, "Feminism: Miracle medicine against straight man cancer and misogyny!"

During our conversation, Xiao's phone rang and she stopped to take an order for several of her products. She apologized for the interruption: "I have to keep my Taobao business going because it's my main source of income." Like most Chinese feminists, Xiao did not make any money from her activism, but considered the products she designed useful in attracting more people to the cause.

Lately, Xiao had also brought her mother on board to help with her business, since her mother had been unable to find work for many years after she was laid off from her job at a groundwater exploration company. "My Ma had nothing to do all day, so she bugged me to get married all the time. I told her many times that I'm not marrying and now she is pushing me to have a baby instead," said Xiao.

After the detention of the Feminist Five, Xiao went into hiding for a while and then moved to Guangzhou, where the political environment seemed less repressive than in Beijing. She and other feminists started a crowdfunding campaign in early 2016 for an anti–sexual harassment ad to be placed at a Guangzhou subway station, which they hoped would be displayed several months later.

More than 1,200 people within China donated small amounts to the campaign, raising more than 40,000 renminbi (around US$6,000 in 2016). Although that amount seems small by American standards, activists said that the most important purpose of their crowdfunding was to build a strong base of supporters willing to publicly identify themselves as committed to building a feminist movement—an extremely risky position to take in the current political climate.

Theoretically, it should have been very simple to rent advertising space in a subway station, but sure enough, the Guangzhou government officials in charge of subway advertising rejected the ad, complaining that the design would "cause residents to panic." The original design showed a small hand with red-polished fingernails grabbing a much larger gray hand by the wrist, with "Stop! Stop! Stop!" in speech bubbles, next to the slogan "Temptation is no excuse. Stop the groping hands." After that design was rejected, the feminists submitted several others, but authorities threw up one objection after another. A full year later, the ad was still deemed "unacceptable" for public display. Yet even as authorities harassed and stymied prominent feminists, local governments sometimes responded to the activists' demands, for example, by displaying new anti–sexual harassment ads on subways in cities like Shenzhen and Beijing.

"We have to constantly change our strategies in response to the authorities. Before the arrest of the Feminist Five, we were always 'playing table tennis on the edge' [da ca bian qiu]," Xiao says, referring to the tactic of getting close to but just barely avoiding the most politically sensitive topics. "We used to do a lot of feminist street campaigns and we're not allowed to do those anymore, so now we're very active on social media."

Shortly after my first interview with Xiao in 2016, the Guangzhou police pressured her landlord to evict her; her girlfriend, feminist activist Zhang Leilei, who had tried to file a lawsuit against Weibo for banning feminist accounts; and their third roommate, Gao Xiao, who had filed a gender-discrimination lawsuit against a Guangzhou restaurant for telling her that they only hired male cooks.

In a common tactic to harass perceived troublemakers, police pressured their landlord to give them just three days' notice before they had to move. After moving, Xiao and Zhang lived in their new apartment for just five months when their new landlord texted her, saying that the police had just called with the news that they were "lesbians who were up to no good." The landlord became anxious and asked Xiao invasive questions about her relationship with her girlfriend. Then the Guangzhou police came to her home at nine the next morning.

Xiao secretly took photos of the two uniformed policemen as they stood at her door, saying that they were "checking for fire safety." They demanded that she show her identity card and give them her fingerprints. Then they said the first two sets of fingerprints were not sufficiently clear, so she had to do them a third time. (She later regretted allowing them to take her fingerprints at all.) The police said they would be checking her apartment every month from now on. In an account she wrote and posted for her friends on WeChat (which was promptly deleted), Xiao described their exchange after the police had taken her fingerprints:

He [the police officer] suddenly said, "You still haven't written down your work address."

I wrote out my work address, then he asked for my roommate's work address.

I said, "I don't know, she's sleeping now and just a second ago you forgot to have me fill this out anyway, so let's just leave it."

He suddenly flew into a rage and yelled at me: "Listen up, I'm taking you to the police station!"

Xiao illustrated her text with a menacing photo of the young police officer, showing the man's bulging eyes and flared nostrils, mouth contorted in anger (taken by her hidden camera). Seeing that he was out of control, she tried to close the door and ask him to come back another time, but he forced it open. Xiao now felt she had to comply, so she went to get her roommate to come and write down her work address. Xiao continued her account:

"All right, see? Everything's good when you cooperate," said the police officer.

"You were the one who got aggressive first," I said.

"It was correct of me to get aggressive. If I wasn't aggressive, you would never have cooperated!" he said.

"I only shut the door because you were so aggressive," I said.

He got angry again and yelled, "You still dare shut the door? Believe me, I'm taking you to the police station!"

After more discussion, the police finally left without arresting her. Xiao filed complaints against them and they left her alone for several months.

She did not realize it at the time, but the police were collecting fingerprints as part of the Chinese government's new effort to build a vast database of DNA and biometric information from people targeted for increased surveillance. Human Rights Watch warns that the Chinese government's big-data policing platforms are much more sophisticated and invasive than previously believed. By 2017, the Chinese Ministry of Public Security had already collected DNA and other biometric data from more than 40 million people, including activists, migrant workers, and Uyghur Muslims: "It is frightening that Chinese authorities are collecting and centralizing ever more information about hundreds of millions of ordinary people, identifying persons who deviate from what they determine to be 'normal thought,' and then surveilling them."

In addition to gathering biometric data on Xiao Meili, the police were no doubt hoping that their visit—plus scaring the landlord with homophobic smears about the women—would be enough to intimidate them into silence.

But in May 2017, Xiao's girlfriend, Zhang Leilei, twenty-four at the time, started a new anti–sexual harassment campaign on Weibo with the hashtags #WalkAgainstSexualHarassment and #IAmABillboard. She dyed her hair bright pink to attract the attention of young people and posted daily photos of herself as a "living anti–sexual harassment ad," walking around Guangzhou wearing on her torso the final design rejected by transport authorities: an innocuous-looking cartoon of a small cat reaching up to stop a big pink pig's arm on a subway, saying "Stop!" in a speech bubble. It carried the same slogan as before: "Temptation is no excuse. Stop the groping hands."

Zhang offered to mail posters to the first hundred people who responded. "Action! Let your city be the first to have an anti-sexual harassment ad!" she announced on Weibo. This time, her campaign spread quickly across China. Within two days, enthusiastic women (and some men) in twenty-three different cities in China —including Beijing, Shanghai, Shenyang, and Xi'an—had volunteered to carry the sign around in public. They posted photos of themselves on Weibo: carrying the sign on the subway, posing with the sign next to their city's landmarks, designing questionnaires on sexual harassment to hand out to strangers on the street, and asking passersby to sign petitions urging transport authorities to post ads against sexual harassment.

This wave of response within just two days demonstrates feminism's unusual appeal to young Chinese women, who are fed up with being sexually harassed whenever they take public transportation. Despite the harsh government crackdown, the tightly knit group of feminist activists was able to influence public opinion and mobilize women in different parts of the country—truly extraordinary in a security state like China. "No matter how much they try to shrink our space, nothing can stop feminists from sprouting up everywhere. At any moment, we have the power to burst forth in all our magnificence," Zhang wrote in a personal essay on WeChat, which was promptly deleted by government censors.

Two weeks after the action, the police showed up at Zhang Leilei and Xiao Meili's apartment yet again. They ordered Zhang to stop her campaign or leave Guangzhou and pressured their landlord to evict the women for a third time. "This activity of yours is having too big an impact and you must end it," the police warned. "We're hosting the Fortune Global Forum here in December, so you need to move to Foshan [a neighboring city] for the next few months ...

Don't you realize that what you're doing is exactly why the Feminist Five were arrested?"

Note that the Guangzhou police tried to force Zhang to leave town seven months before the global forum even started. It is unusual even by Chinese security standards for authorities to kick a political activist out of their home for more than seven months under the pretext of maintaining security for an upcoming international meeting. Generally, the authorities make people considered politically sensitive go on a short mandatory "vacation" of several days or, at most, several weeks around politically sensitive times such as the anniversary of the Tiananmen massacre on June 4th.

Zhang agreed to stop carrying her sign everywhere she went but refused to leave Guangzhou. She also told the police that she could not stop people from continuing their own campaigns in other cities. "I'm not the only one who has been sexually harassed, and I'm not the only one calling attention to this problem," she posted on Weibo. "I hope other young women who have had troubles like me can be supported rather than ridiculed … I hope to say that what happened to you is not your fault. Sexual harassment is a social problem that must be solved," she wrote in her (deleted) essay. "I hope that more of you will tell your own stories, instead of burying your wounds deep inside your heart."

Xiao Meili and Zhang Leilei are not backing down. In her account of the police confrontations, Xiao wrote out some of the lessons she had learned—truths that also apply to countries other than China: "Whether it's violence by public authorities or domestic violence, the patterns are the same. The more you accommodate, the more you get harassed. If you don't resist, the cycle of violence will worsen. So fight for your rights, never compromise."

~

Back in 2013, Li Maizi told me that she did not expect to see any substantive progress in Chinese women's rights for about thirty more years. I was stunned. Why weren't she and other feminist activists taking bolder action? Surely there were more serious rights violations to tackle than insufficient public toilets for women, I thought at the time. I mentally contrasted the Chinese feminists' efforts to avoid antagonizing the government with the more deliberately confrontational antics of Pussy Riot, Russia's feminist punk rockers, who were imprisoned for performing songs that blasphemed Russian president Vladimir Putin:

> Virgin Mary, Mother of God, banish Putin!
> Banish Putin, Banish Putin!
> The head of the KGB, their chief saint
> Leads protesters to prison under escort.

Only after the Feminist Five were jailed did I realize that I had vastly underestimated Li and other young feminist activists in China. Their language may not have been as in-your-face defamatory, but their sheer existence as independent women's rights activists was just as subversive. Moreover, the feminists were tapping into a groundswell of dissatisfaction among hundreds of thousands of educated urban women who were just beginning to wake up to the rampant sexism in Chinese society.

"We want to challenge and deconstruct power, to build an equal society ... All of our actions are launched by [relatively unknown] individuals to avoid being labeled 'politically sensitive,'" Li said before her arrest in 2015.

Today, Li Maizi has become one of the most visible members of China's feminist movement. *Foreign Policy* named her one of its "Leading Global Thinkers" in 2015 and one of the "US–China 50" (people powering the US-China relationship) in 2017. The BBC named her one of its "100 Women of 2015." The Feminist Five were also named on *Ms.* magazine's list of "Ten Most Inspiring

Feminists of 2015," while the BBC named another Feminist Five activist, Zheng Churan, on its list of "100 Women of 2016." But the goal was always to keep attracting new recruits and building a broad-based, sustainable feminist movement across China, without a single identifiable leader.

5

Jingwei Fills the Sea

When I visited Hangzhou in November 2015—roughly half a year after the Feminist Five were released—two feminist activists in their twenties invited me to tour the city's most scenic landmark, West Lake, in the middle of a rainstorm. We paid an old man to row us across the lake in a small boat covered with an awning to keep us semi-dry. As the rain fell, Gina (a pseudonym)—who worked closely with Wu Rongrong—and Zhu Xixi, a feminist PhD student at Zhejiang University, told me how state security agents had summoned them for questioning several times since the detention of the Feminist Five. Gina's landlord had just threatened to evict her after coming under pressure from the police, while Zhu Xixi was warned that she might be expelled from her university.

After talking and rowing for a while, Gina and Zhu pointed to one of the fog-shrouded, gray stone bridges curving over the lake and said that the tomb of China's most famous feminist revolutionary, Qiu Jin, was near there. A native of Zhejiang Province, Qiu Jin was beheaded in 1907 in the city of Shaoxing, about thirty-seven miles from Hangzhou, for plotting to overthrow the Qing empire.

Zhu explained that she and her feminist sisters used to sing Qiu

Jin's protest song, "Demand Women's Rights." "But the words were too archaic and hard to remember," said Zhu. When the film *Les Miserables* came out, a team of feminists adapted one of the songs, "Do You Hear the People Sing?" and rewrote the lyrics into "A Song for All Women," which is much easier to memorize. "Will you join me / In the long fight for our rights?" goes the new song. It has become the feminist movement's anthem of solidarity.

"Hey, let's take a picture here!" Zhu suggested, so I took out my phone and we snapped some photos from our boat as Gina and Zhu smiled, holding up two fingers to flash the V-for-victory sign. That moment with young feminist activists in a rainstorm on Hangzhou's West Lake, near Qiu Jin's tomb, seemed pregnant with history.

One hundred and ten years earlier, at the tumultuous turn of the twentieth century, the cross-dressing feminist icon, Qiu Jin, was writing songs, lyrical poems, and essays aimed at emancipating Chinese women and urging them to join the Nationalist (Guomindang) revolution. In 1905, she joined the revolutionary league of the future president of the Republic of China, Sun Yat-sen (Sun Zhongshan). She also began writing one of her most important—yet unfinished—works, *Stones of the Jingwei Bird*, a song combined with traditional oral narrative in a form known as the *tanci*, which alternated between prose and sung poetry.

Qiu Jin left her husband and two children behind in China to study and give political speeches to Chinese students in Tokyo, where she wrote much of *Stones of the Jingwei Bird*. As one version of the Chinese legend of Jingwei has it, the youngest daughter of Fiery Emperor Yandi was named Nüwa, meaning "Little Girl." Nüwa longed to see the sun rise over the ocean, so she rowed in a boat out to the East Sea at dawn. As she was rowing, the cruel East Sea whipped up a heavy storm that capsized her boat and drowned her.

At the moment of her death, Nüwa transformed into a magnificent bird with a white beak and large red claws, screaming out "*jingwei, jingwei!*" in anger and pain. Jingwei, the soul of Nüwa named after the sound of her anguished screams, sought revenge by picking up stones in her claws from the mountain where she used to live, flying back and dropping them into the sea each day to fill it up. The East Sea mocked Jingwei and told her to abandon her pitiful effort. "You silly little bird, how could you ever dream of filling me up with those stupid stones?" But she vowed never to give up. Jingwei would persist every day for thousands of years—no matter how long it took—until she succeeded in filling the sea.

Qiu Jin used the myth of Jingwei as a metaphor for the struggle of Chinese women fighting for their freedom and their country. "With all my heart, I beseech and beg my [two hundred] million female compatriots to assume their responsibility as citizens. Arise! Arise! Chinese women, arise!" she wrote. "Chinese women will throw off their shackles and stand up with passion; they will all become heroines. They will ascend the stage of the new world, where the heavens have mandated that they reconsolidate the nation."

Qiu Jin herself was beheaded at the age of thirty-one, before she could finish writing *Stones of the Jingwei Bird*. Her life and work have interesting parallels with the resistance of young feminists in China today, who are so often ridiculed as inconsequential "little girls." The legend of Jingwei gave rise to the Chinese aphorism *jingwei tian hai*, "Jingwei fills the sea," meaning perseverance in carrying out an enormous task against seemingly impossible odds.

In March 2018, the *New York Times*'s Amy Qin wrote a belated obituary of Qiu Jin, 111 years after her death, part of a global series to recognize women who were not given a *New York Times* obituary when they died in the past. "More than a century after her death, many Chinese still visit her tomb beside West Lake in Hangzhou to pay their respects to the woman now embedded in the national consciousness as a bold feminist heroine," writes Qin.

Qiu Jin and other progressive intellectuals, such as Sun Yat-sen, Liang Qichao, and He-Yin Zhen (also known as He Zhen), formed part of a revolutionary movement at the turn of the twentieth century, much of which was organized in exile from Japan, Hong Kong, and the United States: "By late 1911, this revolutionary movement succeeded in toppling the Qing dynasty and replacing China's age-old dynastic system with a republican form of government." Feminism was a critical part of this "revolutionary ferment," according to Lydia H. Liu, Rebecca E. Karl and Dorothy Ko's volume, *The Birth of Chinese Feminism*.

Some of China's intellectual cross-fertilization and social-movement organizing today happens outside the country (during study abroad or visiting fellowships at universities), just as it did more than a century ago. It even happens in some of the same places: the United States and Hong Kong—though progressive Taiwan is the destination of choice for today's Chinese feminists rather than Japan. The most committed feminist activists today frequently share ideas with activists in other fields, such as rights lawyers, labor rights activists, and of course, LGBTQ rights activists.

In the last recorded chapter of *Stones of the Jingwei Bird*, Qiu Jin describes a group of young women fleeing unhappy arranged marriages by selling their dowries (which Qiu Jin also did when she fled China). Together, the women board a ship bound for Japan, holding hands and looking back at their distant homeland:

> How great these girls' ambitions must have been to break through such barriers! They had gone a thousand *li* [one *li* is around half a kilometer] from home, and now they were traveling ten thousand *li* as fast as the wind. Everyone on board looked at them and thought, "The new learning will surely thrive. One day these girls will act as the bells of freedom and save the motherland."

The emancipation of women was a central goal not just for turn-of-the-century reformers and revolutionaries who overthrew the Qing empire in 1911, but also for China's Communist revolution, which culminated in the founding of the People's Republic of China in 1949. The profound irony of Chinese authorities persecuting women's rights activists today is that the very origins of China's Communist Party in the early twentieth century lay in the revolutionary dream of women's liberation, with the publicly celebrated principle that women and men are equal. Feminism played a key but often forgotten role in China's revolutionary history.

China experienced massive political, military, and economic turmoil in the nineteenth and twentieth centuries, including the Opium Wars of 1839–42 and 1856–60, as the British Empire forced China to open up to trade through unequal treaties; the Taiping Rebellion of 1850–64, led by a man who believed himself to be the son of God and brother of Jesus Christ; the First Sino-Japanese War of 1894–95, in which Japan destroyed the Chinese navy; and the Boxer Rebellion of 1900, when foreign powers including the United States stormed and looted Beijing in response to anti-missionary rebels attacking foreign legions.

The Euro-American and Japanese invasions created pressures on China's economy that hurt women in particular, since female labor—particularly spinning and weaving—was critical to the household economy. As tariffs imposed by the British in favor of urban industries hurt China's rural economy, women were forced to work harder for fewer returns.

China's "feminist project was implicated in a problematic nationalist scheme from the start," argue historians Dorothy Ko and Wang Zheng. After its humiliating defeat by its supposedly weaker neighbor, Japan, Chinese reformers considered Japan to be both an enemy and a model for China. "Although 'women's rights' were supposedly rooted in the notion that men and women enjoyed 'natural rights,' the goal for women's rights in the eyes of its male Chinese advocates was to strengthen the nation."

Historian Mizuyo Sudo writes that the concept of "women's rights"—*nüquan* in Chinese and *joken* in Japanese—emerged when Chinese reformers adopted Euro-American terms of "people's rights" or "civil rights" (*minquan*) (often translated through Japanese texts) as a means of modernizing Qing Dynasty institutions.

Male reformers in turn-of-the-century China, such as Jin Tianhe, Liang Qichao and many others, called for better education for women and women's liberation from traditional, "weak" roles in order to ensure the nation's survival and build up its ability to stand up to foreign powers, rather than out of a genuine concern for the lives of Chinese women. The male Jin Tianhe's 1903 essay "The Women's Bell" was initially considered China's first feminist manifesto. "My two hundred million sister compatriots, however, are still kept as ignorant as before, in chains and fetters, obsessed with dreams in winter and wallowing in melancholy in spring, knowing nothing of the ideas of equality between men and women or ideas of women's participation in politics that are held by free people in civilized nations," he wrote.

Literary critic Lydia H. Liu points out the strangely racial opening of Jin's essay, in which the male reformer compares his "pathetic existence" with that of a white man in Europe or America:

> I dream of a young, white European man. On this day, at this hour, with a rolled cigarette in his mouth, walking stick in hand, his wife and children by him, he strolls with his head held up high and arms swinging by his sides through the promenades of London, Paris, Washington. Such happiness and ease!

"The desire to emulate an upper-class white European man in his marital bliss reflects the painful situation of Chinese *men* and their psychic struggles in relation to white European men. But what does this have to do with Chinese women and, more important, with feminism?" asks Liu.

Feminist writer and anarchist He-Yin Zhen was one of the first women to read Jin Tianhe's essay, according to Liu. In an act of rebellion against patriarchal naming practices, she added her mother's surname Yin to her father's surname He to adopt the rare, hyphenated name of He-Yin. After moving to Tokyo in 1907, He-Yin Zhen and her husband, Liu Shipei, launched the radical journal *Tianyi* (Natural Justice), which published her brilliantly prescient essays about gendered oppression. Historians wrongly attributed many of He-Yin Zhen's essays to her husband during the brief run of their journal. In 1907–08, she wrote a scathing essay in response to China's male reformers, "On the Question of Women's Liberation":

> Chinese men worship power and authority. They believe that Europeans, Americans, and the Japanese are civilized nations of the modern world who all grant their women some degree of freedom. By transplanting this system into the lives of their wives and daughters, by prohibiting the practice of footbinding, and by enrolling them in schools to receive basic education, these men think that they will be applauded by the whole world for having joined the ranks of civilized nations … I am inclined to think that these men have acted purely out of a selfish desire to claim women as private property.

He-Yin Zhen wrote a series of radical anarchist essays calling for the abolition of private property and the establishment of communally owned property to achieve economic equality between women and men. She advocated for the elimination of categories of gender distinction, which she argued formed the basis of patriarchal power in Confucian thought: "If sons and daughters are treated equally, raised and educated in the same manner, then the responsibilities assumed by men and women will surely become equal. When that happens, the nouns 'men' and 'women' would no longer be necessary." Shortly before the overthrow of the Qing Dynasty in 1911, He-Yin Zhen and Liu Shipei fell out with other nationalist revolutionaries; there is no reliable information about the end of He-Yin Zhen's life.

~

On May 4, 1919, thousands of university students in Beijing—female and male—gathered in Tiananmen Square to protest the Chinese government's weakness in standing up to foreign powers. They were angry that the Versailles Treaty, drawn up at the end of World War I, transferred Germany's rights to Shandong Province to Japan instead of returning them to China, and called for a boycott of Japanese goods. Anti-imperialist protests spread to other Chinese cities and fed into the much broader New Culture Movement (1915–24), which attacked traditional Chinese culture, called for democracy and science, and advocated equal rights for women.

Many new women's journals and women's rights organizations emerged from this movement, and literary critic Rey Chow argues that the construct "woman" became idealized as a metaphor for the weak Chinese nation: "If feminine self-sacrifice was the major support of traditional Chinese culture, it is not surprising that, during a period of massive social transformations, the collapse of tradition would find its most *moving* representations in the figures of those who are traditionally the most oppressed, figures that become 'stand-ins' for China's traumatized *self-consciousness*."

Just as China's young feminist activists today are mostly university-educated, so too were the "new women" of the May Fourth era, as represented in women's journals. "The feminist 'new women' had to be imagined as belonging to the nascent urban middle class for them to function as a signpost of modernity," write Ko and Wang, pointing out that virtually all of the May Fourth intellectuals were urban and middle class.

In 1918, Henrik Ibsen's play *A Doll's House*, about a woman named Nora who leaves her unhappy life with her husband and two children, was translated into Chinese and became extremely popular as the embodiment of the May Fourth era's "new woman." Nora became not just a role model for Chinese women trying to escape marriage, but also a way for young men to discuss the future of their republic and "a metaphor for their own liberation—Nora's slamming door," writes historian Susan Glosser.

114

The celebrated author Lu Xun gave a speech at Beijing Women's Normal College in 1923 called "What Happens after Nora Leaves Home?" He argued that the only possibilities for Nora after she left her family would be to become a prostitute or return to her husband, illustrating the necessity of radically transforming the moribund traditions of Chinese society. "Thus the crucial thing for Nora is money or—to give it a more high-sounding name—economic resources. Of course, money cannot buy freedom, but freedom can be sold for money," said Lu Xun. "First, there must be a fair sharing out between men and women in the family; second, men and women must have equal rights in society."

In November 1919, the young Mao Zedong began writing essays about the suicide of a young woman, Zhao Wuzhen or "Miss Zhao," who had slit her own throat as she was being taken to her future husband's home for an arranged marriage. The young woman's death "is a result of a corrupt marriage system, a dark social system, a will that cannot be independent, and love that cannot be free," wrote Mao in the *Dagong Bao* newspaper. He argued that social norms must be completely overhauled in order to find lasting solutions to the problems of marriage and female free will. "Construing the everyday relationship of women to society as an inherently violent one—Mao characterizes it as a relationship of daily rape—Mao concluded that women such as Miss Zhao (thus, most women in China) could not develop individuality in life, but could only assert free will in death by suicide," writes historian Rebecca Karl.

While the young Mao wrote, the Communist International (Comintern), sponsored by the Soviet Union, began actively planning a new Communist Party in China. The combination of domestic Chinese interests and Soviet involvement led to the sprouting of small Communist groups across China, according to Karl. In July 1921, the separate Communist groups around the country joined together to form a national organization at a secret meeting in Shanghai. Mao—future founder of the People's Republic of China—was one of the delegates.

The first woman to emerge as a leader within the Chinese Communist network was twenty-three-year-old Wang Huiwu, a May Fourth feminist activist who organized locations for the secret meetings in 1921. Wang Huiwu used her community of Shanghai women's activists to secure a space at a girls' school in the French Concession of Shanghai where the Communists could meet. When police officers raided the first meeting, she found a houseboat on South Lake in Zhejiang Province, close to Hangzhou, where delegates could pose as tourists to avoid police surveillance, according to historian Christina Gilmartin.

Wang Huiwu had written essays condemning China's arranged-marriage system as a form of lifelong imprisonment for women. Her most prominent essay, "The Chinese Woman Question: Liberation from a Trap," was published in 1919 in the journal *Shaonian Zhongguo* (Young China), whose advisors included Mao and other future prominent Communists:

> Men feared that women would work hard and be successful, acquire savings and break down the economic restrictions, whereupon the trap [of arranged marriage] would be jeopardized. So household jobs like "sewing" and "cooking" were entrusted to women with the result that women no longer had the opportunity of achieving victory ... Because of their jealous natures, men built "interior and exterior defenses" to sever women's social relations that have continued up to the present. Women were inextricably caught in this trap and never have been able to extract themselves.

Wang Huiwu and other first-generation Communist women wanted to break free of patriarchal constraints such as arranged marriage and "were attracted to the party because it provided a supportive environment in a largely hostile society," writes Gilmartin. "Indeed, to these women who were concerned with challenging traditional gender relationships and providing alternative role models, the party appeared more as a subculture than as a political institution."

After the formation of the Chinese Communist Party in 1921, the first decision of its newly appointed Central Committee was to put Wang Huiwu and another radical woman, Gao Junman, in charge of launching a Communist women's program by reorganizing the independent women's group, Shanghai Federation of Women's Circles. Wang Huiwu gained permission to sponsor two major projects: the publication of a new journal, *Funü Sheng* (Women's Voices) and a school, the Shanghai Pingmin Girls' School.

Women's Voices published its first issue in December 1921 with two women editors, Wang Huiwu and Wang Jianhong. Its authors were primarily women, and it was aimed at women readers from the May Fourth period who had gained political "consciousness," according to Gilmartin: "They portrayed women as 'the first workers' in human history, who had served as family slaves up until the present. Because most women were without property, they could in many ways be considered members of the 'propertyless class' (*wuchan jieji*), a term that served for the word 'proletariat' in Chinese." The Shanghai Pingmin Girls' School opened in early 1922, with the high-ranking Communist Li Da (Wang Huiwu's husband) as its principal, although Wang Huiwu actually did all the work of designing the curriculum, hiring teachers, running day-to-day operations, and recruiting students who could become women cadres in the Communist Party.

Yet even during the earliest revolutionary years, when male Communist Party founders such as Li Da and Chen Duxiu embraced feminist rhetoric, Wang Huiwu was never admitted as a formal member. When Li Da fell out of favor with other Communists and failed to be reelected to the Central Committee in 1922, other male Party leaders could not accept the idea of a woman holding a more important position than her husband. *Women's Voices* abruptly ceased publication and the Pingmin Girls' School permanently closed at the end of 1922.

117

Nevertheless, the Communist Party's effort to mobilize women to join the revolution received a jolt on May 30, 1925, when British police fired on a large crowd of demonstrators in Shanghai protesting the murder of a Chinese worker at a Japanese-owned textile mill. They killed around a dozen students and workers, including a female student. The killings infuriated and galvanized Chinese workers, business owners, and students into a revolutionary fervor across the country, which Communist organizers such as Xiang Jingyu (the new head of the women's program) used to recruit female student activists and labor leaders. By September 1925, the Communists had a thousand women recruits, ten times the number before the May Thirtieth Incident.

With each year, International Women's Day celebrations in major Chinese cities became increasingly radical. In 1926, in Guangzhou alone, more than ten thousand people gathered for International Women's Day, calling for an end to arranged marriage, freedom to divorce, gender equality in wages, and the elimination of concubines, child brides, and girl bondservants. But when the Communists and the Nationalists split and began a civil war in 1927, feminist programs lost their political backing.

Meanwhile, the Sixth Congress of the Chinese Communist Party in 1928, held in Moscow, passed a "Resolution on the Women's Movement" which explicitly denounced the "bourgeois feminist" women's program of the previous eight years and said it had "been a mistake to allow the establishment of independent women's associations," writes Gilmartin. "It thus facilitated a clear departure from the feminist program and the subsequent adoption of an orthodox Communist position on the primacy of economic class oppression over gender exploitation." Once Communist Party leaders decided to shift from the standard Marxist model of mobilizing the urban working class to a peasant-based revolution in the countryside, they were even less inclined to embrace feminist policies, in order to avoid antagonizing the heavily patriarchal male peasants.

~

The consequences of the Party's deliberate renunciation of feminism have reverberated through many decades, all the way to the present day. Although the Communist Party continued to endorse gender equality, Party officials shunned the term "feminism," or *nüquan zhuyi*, and shifted their focus to the elimination of private ownership and the class system. "Feminists who refused to identify with the Party's goal but focused on gender equality were called 'bourgeois narrow feminists,' a strategy copied from European socialists," write Ko and Wang. Instead, the Party adopted the terms "equality between men and women" (*nannü pingdeng*) and "women's liberation" (*funü jiefang*).

The same year that the Chinese Communist Party formally renounced "bourgeois feminism," the woman writer Ding Ling—who was writing about the experiences of urban, educated women like herself—rose to fame with *The Diary of Miss Sophia*, published in 1928. It shocked critics with its bold representation of women's sexuality and subjectivity, depicting Sophia as a woman with a strong sexual appetite who objectified a man with her lust, then had to bury her frustration in a society that forbade women from expressing their sexuality:

> I raised my eyes. I looked at his soft, red, moist, deeply inset lips, and let out my breath slightly. How could I admit to anyone that I gazed at those provocative lips like a small hungry child eyeing sweets? I know very well that in this society I'm forbidden to take what I need to gratify my desires and frustrations, even when it clearly wouldn't hurt anybody.

The Diary of Miss Sophia radically subverted the traditional male point of view, as literary critic Lydia H. Liu explains: "It is the narrator's female gaze that turns the man into a sex object, reversing male discourse about desire. Not only does the narrator objectify the man's 'lips' as if they were pieces of candy, but she ignores the phallus and feminizes male sexuality by associating it with lips (labia)."

119

Later, *The Diary of Miss Sophia* was criticized for being too "bourgeois" and divorced from more important political concerns. Mao had laid out the "correct" vision for the role of art and love in revolution at his 1942 "Talks at the Yan'an Forum on Literature and Art":

> Now as for love, in a class society there can only be class love: but these comrades are seeking a love transcending classes, love in the abstract and also freedom in the abstract ... This shows they have been very deeply influenced by the bourgeoisie. They should thoroughly rid themselves of this influence and modestly study Marxism-Leninism.

Mao's speech on the importance of ideological purity and art in service to the Communist revolution affirmed the Socialist Realist style of art developed in the Soviet Union, as well as the sexless clothing style of women from the 1940s through the end of the 1970s, when China began opening up its economy after Mao's death.

Liu argues that the "liberated" images of women presented through Socialist Realism and the bare faces and colorless uniforms—designed to further the goal of equality—"end up denying difference to women." "The category of women, like that of class, has long been exploited by the hegemonic discourse of the state of China," she writes. "In the emancipatory discourse of the state, which always subsumes woman under the nationalist agenda, women's liberation means little more than equal opportunity to participate in public labor."

Ding Ling joined the Communist Party in 1932 after her husband, the author Hu Yepin, was murdered by the Nationalists. She was then kidnapped by the Nationalists and kept under house arrest for several years until she escaped to Yan'an, which became the Communists' base after the Red Army completed its legendary Long March to escape Nationalist forces. As a prominent Communist Party member, Ding Ling renounced writing about sexuality and romantic love and embraced the Socialist Realist form of literature for the revolutionary masses.

Even so, for International Women's Day in 1942, Ding Ling vehemently criticized the Communist Party's gender politics in a damning essay about the Party's treatment of "women comrades." "When will it no longer be necessary to attach special weight to the word 'woman' and raise it specially?" she began. She discussed the pressure on women comrades to marry, as single women were the target of "slanderous gossip": "So they can't afford to be choosy, anyone will do: whether he rides horses or wears straw sandals, whether he's an artist or a supervisor."

Ding Ling pointed out the Party's double standards, with its expectation that women have children, only to deride the same women for "political backwardness" and insufficient devotion to the revolution. "I myself am a woman, and I therefore understand the failings of women better than others. But I also have a deeper understanding of what they suffer," she wrote. "Women are incapable of transcending the age they live in, of being perfect, or of being hard as steel." She called on men in the Communist Party to consider the suffering and "social context" of their female counterparts: "It would be better if there were less empty theorizing and more talk about real problems, so that theory and practice are not divorced, and if each Communist Party member were more responsible for his own moral conduct."

Party officials accused Ding Ling of having "narrow feminist" feelings and holding "a nonrevolutionary view of the relationship between women's liberation and class struggle," according to Rebecca Karl. In retaliation for her criticism of the Party, Ding Ling was fired from her position as editor of a literary journal and ordered to re-educate herself. She later recovered politically, only to be sent for re-education among the masses during the anti-rightist campaign in 1957 for speaking out about women's "double burden": "Women were celebrated in their public role as 'iron women,' for their heroic contributions to production.

Meanwhile, they were forced to silently struggle with household chores."

Even as the Communist Party subjected its own women cadres to sexist double standards, it used the rhetoric of gender equality to mobilize masses of women into joining the revolutionary cause. In 1949, the Communists won their war against the Nationalist forces and founded the People's Republic of China (PRC), with gender equality enshrined in its new constitution. Historian Gail Hershatter describes these deeply transformative early Communist Party policies, aimed at bringing hundreds of millions of women out of the home and into paid labor in the public sphere: "During that first decade ... ambitious state initiatives sought to reconfigure landholding, marriage, the organization of work, the very under-standing of one's self, one's community, and one's past."

A cornerstone of the Communist revolution, the Marriage Law of 1950, abolished arranged marriages, the purchase of child brides, polygamy and prostitution. It also granted women more financial independence and life-changing new freedoms, such as the right to divorce abusive husbands and remarry (although Party officials later backed away from strictly enforcing the law because of strong resistance from elders). "This was an ambitious attempt to alter daily social practice and to raise the status of women, par-ticularly in rural areas, where 'feudal' ideas had been less often challenged than in the cities of pre-1949 China," writes Hershatter. In addition, the new Party-state sponsored literacy classes for rural women, most of whom did not know how to read. As one rural Party cadre told Hershatter, "Why did we start with literacy? At that time, families would only let a woman go out of the house if she was going to learn how to read. When women enjoyed more contact with the outside world by attending literacy classes, their thinking became more liberated little by little."

The Communist Party established a state agency, the All-China Women's Federation, to "protect women's rights and interests." Yet the term *feminism* had become so taboo that the members of the Women's Federation had to hide any real efforts to promote a women's rights agenda through what Wang Zheng calls "a politics of concealment." At the same time, by the early 1950s the national Women's Federation had employed tens of thousands of officials to set up local branches from large urban settings down to the most remote villages. The Shanghai Women's Federation mobilized more than 300,000 women—of whom 250,000 were housewives—to turn out for a mass rally on International Women's Day in 1951 to protest the US "imperialist" rearming of Japan, writes Wang.

Although the rally's theme was anti-imperialism, an internal report commented on its participants' "feelings of empowerment." As Wang notes, "Participants in the parade all felt that women have power and status now. Even men said, now women are a big deal." The revolutionary roots of March 8, International Women's Day, in China's own history make it all the more hypocritical—and indicative of the current government's paranoia about social stability—that Communist Party security agents in 2015 would jail young feminists for planning an event to commemorate that day. The Party is no doubt haunted by its own historical success in mobilizing millions of women to join the revolution.

In the mid-1950s, Mao Zedong launched his rural collectivization drive, a radical move to abolish industry and private property formerly owned by the wealthy. In 1958 he unleashed the Great Leap Forward, a catastrophic drive to have China catch up with the United States and Britain in steel and grain production. The policy called for setting up large-scale people's communes by diverting millions of farmers from agriculture to work in factories, while at the same time exponentially increasing the procurement of grain from the countryside. Local officials trying to please their Party bosses engaged in mass falsification of data, reporting their "extraordinary successes" in production. Ultimately, the Great Leap Forward caused food shortages so severe that tens of millions of people died in the worst famine of the twentieth century.

The phenomenon of the "iron woman" was born during the Great Leap Forward to draw on women's labor power—traditionally in agriculture—to boost industrial production in male-dominated fields. "Women competed with one another and with men for high productivity,'" writes Karl. "This was the fulfillment of Mao's desire for and commitment to female 'liberation through labor.'" In 1952 women had accounted for fewer than 12 percent of workers in Chinese state-owned enterprises, but during the Great Leap Forward, women were assigned en masse to work in state-run enterprises, writes sociologist Jiang Yongping. By the end of the 1970s, the labor-force participation rate for urban women in China had reached more than 90 percent as the state established the largest female workforce in the world. "Since they did not need to seek permission from their fathers or husbands, this signaled the emancipation of urban women from the control of male heads of households. In addition, people came to accept women's employment as a normal part of the social economy," argues Jiang.

Yet the 1950s and 1960s were a time of great suffering for women, as anthropologist Guo Yuhua documented in a study of women's memories of the collectivization period in a northern Chinese village. Women were required to perform all domestic chores—often letting babies and young children go hungry, sitting in their excrement during the day in the absence of help—while they went out into the fields to work alongside the men. As Guo Yuhua writes, "being liberated [by the Party] was not true liberation."

There is a great deal of controversy over whether women's gains during the early Communist era were real or merely rhetorical. One of Mao Zedong's most famous sayings is his declaration that "women hold up half the sky." Heroic propaganda images of women produced by the Communist state after 1949 showed muscular, red-cheeked women welders and bulldozer drivers working for the glory of the new nation. Just as the rhetoric of women's emancipation by male reformers at the turn of the century and during the May Fourth era was more about modernizing and strengthening China than about improving real women's lives, so too the "liberation" of women in the Communist era was in many ways largely symbolic. The Communist Party touted women's liberation to demonstrate the success of its proletarian revolution, but the voices of women are missing from official Party history, according to Guo Yuhua.

Following several decades of Communist Party–mandated equal employment for women and men in the planned economy after Mao Zedong's death in 1976, the government under the new leadership of Deng Xiaoping introduced sweeping economic reforms. Although life had undeniably been harsh and cruel for everyone during the Mao era, gender inequality skyrocketed as China's postsocialist market reforms took hold.

In 1978, China's State Council codified rules from the 1950s mandating that women in labor-intensive fields must retire at age fifty, while ordinary male workers could retire at sixty. The rationale behind differential retirement ages, derived from the Soviet Union, was to require women to retire at young ages so they could manage domestic chores while their grown daughters worked full-time. (White-collar women who are public servants must generally retire at fifty-five, while white-collar men may often work until sixty-five.) Although the government recently announced that it would slowly raise the mandated retirement age, the five-to-ten-year gender gap remains basically in place today.

Urban women's labor participation dropped precipitously from its high at the end of the 1970s when China began dismantling the planned economy. The massive state-owned enterprises that had provided workers with an "iron rice bowl" of guaranteed life employment began firing tens of millions of workers. Women at state-owned companies were the first to be fired—or told to retire at forty-five—and the last to be rehired later, according to Liu Jieyu. State enterprises also closed childcare centers, hurting the younger women workers who remained employed, since women were—and continue to be—primary caregivers for children and the elderly.

In the late 1980s and 1990s, a "Women Return to the Home" (*nüren hui jia*) movement gained popularity as unemployment increased, along with calls on women to give up their jobs for men. As free-market reforms deepened, gender discrimination in hiring became rampant; this persists today, with many job ads blatantly stating that they are only seeking to hire men. Or, if the jobs are open to women, they often specify that the women must be married with children, or be of a certain age, height or weight, or look a certain way. (Gender discrimination in hiring is one issue Chinese feminists frequently take on.)

After the Tiananmen massacre of 1989 crushed a massive uprising of pro-democracy protesters and the Soviet Union collapsed, it became even more politically urgent for the government to accelerate market-oriented economic reforms to prop up the Communist Party's legitimacy. The resulting "economic miracle" of double-digit GDP growth rates in effect co-opted most Chinese citizens, who ceased to demand political reforms as long as their living standards were rising.

In 1995, China hosted the UN World Conference on Women, and the Chinese government agreed to allow the formation of some women's rights NGOs in exchange for the privilege of being host country, according to veteran women's rights advocate Feng Yuan. "But behind the rhetoric of openness, there were always tight constraints on our activities," says Feng, who began her career as a journalist, then joined with other women journalists to set up the NGO Media Monitor for Women Network in 1996.

Until the 1995 UN women's conference—made famous by Hillary Rodham Clinton's speech proclaiming that "women's rights are human rights"—most women in China did not know what *domestic violence* meant. In 2000, Feng cofounded the Anti-Domestic Violence Network, a nongovernmental organization that played a major role in pushing through China's 2016 law against domestic violence. That group has now closed down; Feng Yuan cofounded another women's rights NGO, *Wei Ping* (Equality) in 2014.

The nongovernmental, women's rights organizations in the mid-1990s through early-2000s were closely affiliated with the All-China Women's Federation and never completely independent from the government. As Feng Yuan says, there was a big difference between the Communist Party's "movement of women" (*yundong funü*)—the top-down mobilization of women in service to the nation—and a bottom-up "women's movement" (*funü yundong*). Still, veteran activists working in women's NGOs paved the way for the emergence of independent feminist activists today. In 2003, filmmaker and women's studies professor Ai Xiaoming directed her students in the first Chinese-language performance of Eve Ensler's *The Vagina Monologues* at Sun Yatsen University in Guangzhou, inspiring a new group of young feminists.

Meanwhile, gender inequality continued to deepen in tandem with China's accelerating economic reforms. China's gender income gap has widened significantly since the 1990s. In 1990, the average annual salary of an urban woman was 77.5 percent that of a man, but by 2010, urban women's average income had fallen to just over 67 percent that of men, according to official data from China's National Bureau of Statistics. Rural women were even worse off, making only 56 percent of men's annual income on average in 2010.

Women's labor-force participation in China has also dropped precipitously since the onset of market reforms. In 1990, 73 percent of Chinese women fifteen and older were in the workforce, but by 2017, that figure had plummeted to just 61 percent, according to the World Bank. By contrast, 76 percent of men fifteen and older were in the labor force in 2017. Many different forms of persistent gender discrimination have caused China to place in the bottom third of all countries evaluated for their gender disparities. The

World Economic Forum's Global Gender Gap Index ranked China 100 out of 144 countries in its 2017 report.

I discovered, through my PhD research at Tsinghua University in Beijing, that an even more important indicator of women's declining economic status relative to men was China's astonishing gender gap in property wealth, which had emerged following the privatization of the housing market in the late 1990s. Under the planned economy of the early Communist era, the government allocated public housing through work units and rent was negligible. After the State Council ended government distribution of housing and launched a market-based system of homeownership, China's real-estate boom took off. Urban home prices skyrocketed from the mid-2000s on, a trend that continues despite frequent warnings of a real-estate bubble.

As I detail in *Leftover Women*, Chinese women have largely missed out on what is arguably the biggest accumulation of residential real-estate wealth in history, worth around 3.3 times China's GDP, or around US$43 trillion, at the end of 2017. The dynamics are extremely complicated but, in short, I argue that many women lost out on China's explosion of housing wealth because the urban homes that were appreciating exponentially in value tended to be registered solely in the man's name. Chinese parents tended to buy homes for sons, not daughters. Women often transferred all their assets to their husband or boyfriend to finance the purchase of a home registered in the man's name alone. To make matters worse, in 2011, the Supreme People's Court issued a new interpretation of the Marriage Law stating that, unless legally contested, marital property essentially belongs to the person who owns the home and whose name is on the property deed. In China that person is usually a man (at least up until the latest available data in 2012).

I was extremely troubled to find out, through extensive personal and online interviews I conducted from late 2010 through early 2013, how many intelligent, university-educated women were willing to cede ownership of their expensive new homes to their boyfriends or husbands, even when the women had contributed their life savings to the property purchase. I discovered that many young women truly believed the sexist messages coming from the state media and their own parents telling them that they would never find a husband unless they were prepared to make major financial and emotional compromises. Time and time again, I was demoralized by the low awareness of sexism among urban women in their twenties and early thirties, revealing how deeply patriarchal norms were still embedded in society.

When *Leftover Women* was published in mainland China in 2016 (with some censored passages, which I posted on my personal website), I wrote a special prologue for Chinese women, in the hope that more would recognize the importance of fighting for their economic independence. Here is an excerpt from my prologue to the Lujiang 2016 edition, translated by Li Xueshun:

> To those Chinese women who are single and considering marriage, I have two pieces of advice:
>
> 1) If you decide you must marry and buy a home, make sure that you register your name on the property deed. Do not forfeit ownership of the most valuable asset you will ever have in your life.
>
> 2) Do not marry just for the sake of marrying. There are many paths to happiness in life and you may find the greatest self-fulfillment if you remain single, surrounded by like-minded friends who support you in your aspirations.

I received thousands of personal messages and tagged posts on Weibo from women describing how they were pushing back against intense marriage pressure, but very few messages from women who were buying their own homes. I have not seen much evidence that China's severe gender gap in property ownership has fundamentally changed since 2013. But even if all the women in China could suddenly afford their own apartments now, they have already missed out on the greatest wealth-accumulation period, from the late 1990s through the late 2000s.

Leftover Women also examines the resurgence of traditional gender norms, in particular China's crass propaganda campaign, launched in 2007, to stigmatize urban professional women in their late twenties who are single. I argue that the term "leftover women," or *sheng nü*, was a deliberate propaganda campaign to shame educated, "high-quality" (*gao suzhi*) women into getting married, which would theoretically promote social stability (in part by absorbing some of the excess men caused by China's sex-ratio imbalance). I pointed out that the media campaign targeting these women appeared shortly after China's cabinet made an important policy announcement in 2007 to "address unprecedented population pressures."

The State Council "Decision on Fully Enhancing the Population and Family Planning Program and Comprehensively Addressing Population Issues" said that the "low quality of the general population" made it hard for China to "meet the requirements of fierce competition for national strength." It also declared that "upgrading population quality [*suzhi*]" was a key goal. I argue that the Chinese government's marriage campaign would serve its eugenics purpose of "upgrading population quality," because "high-quality" educated women could produce "high-quality" babies for the good of the nation.

Against this alarming backdrop of the resurgence of gender inequality driven by breakneck economic development, China's new feminist movement was born. Today, for the first time since before the 1949 revolution, young women's rights activists independent of the Communist Party eagerly embrace the term *nüquan zhuyi* (feminism). These feminist activists focus on transforming the personal lives of real, flesh-and-blood women in all their complexity, so they can join together and pressure the government to change its unjust, sexist policies.

When I first met with Hangzhou feminists near the tomb of the revolutionary Qiu Jin in 2015, Wu Rongrong of the Feminist Five was still recovering from post-traumatic stress disorder brought on by her mistreatment in detention. Gina, her young deputy, had spent almost two months traveling more than 1,200 miles by bus, fleeing the security agents deployed in a multiprovince crackdown on feminist activists. Over many hours during that rain-soaked afternoon, she recounted her ordeal as a fugitive.

On March 6, 2015, Gina was eating lunch at the Weizhiming Women's Rights Center with half a dozen colleagues and volunteers when she received a call from the Hangzhou Public Security Bureau saying they wanted to meet with her.

"I don't believe you. How do I know who you are? We get a lot of crank calls," Gina replied.

"We know your boss, Wu Rongrong."

"Then call Wu Rongrong directly. Please don't call our office," said Gina.

Gina had begun working for the women's center less than a year earlier, when she graduated from university in Henan Province in the summer of 2014. Only twenty-four years old, Gina had never been questioned by the police before and did not know what to do. She felt like getting some fresh air to collect her thoughts, so she went downstairs.

Gina noticed the building guard talking in the foyer with several men who mentioned her office number, and she realized they must be state security agents. She called up to her office and told everyone there to leave right away. Then she called the Public Security Bureau, offering to meet them at a public mall close to the police station.

Two men and a woman from Hangzhou state security waited for her at the meeting place and said they needed to have a "proper chat" at the police station. Gina suggested talking at a fast-food restaurant, in public, but they said it was not a suitable place. "The police station is here to protect the people's safety," said one of the agents.

This worried Gina and made her even more determined not to go to the station. She kept on walking and proposing different public places to chat, until the agents relented and booked a private room at a restaurant. By the time they arrived, the private room had six or seven agents—all but one of them men—already seated around a table. The new agents did not identify themselves, but Gina could tell by their accents that they must have flown down from Beijing.

"Who organized this sexual harassment activity? The timing is very bad. Don't you know the National People's Congress [China's parliament] is meeting?"

Gina said she did not know who had organized the activity and that she had just seen it on the internet. She brought along samples of the anti–sexual harassment stickers they were planning to hand out and tried to explain the problem of gender inequality in China, but none of the agents wanted to listen. "Cancel your activity now."

After several hours of questioning, the agents let her go. By this time, it was late at night and Gina had heard that some of her feminist sisters, including Li Maizi and Zheng Churan, had been arrested in different cities, so she began packing up the stickers at the women's center. Then she climbed into her bunk bed in the adjacent room of the two-room office (which doubled as her residence) and slept fitfully.

Early the next morning, March 7, Gina took the box of stickers over to Zhu Xixi's dorm room at Zhejiang University. Wu Rongrong arrived at the Hangzhou airport at around two in the afternoon and texted that she was back. Gina called Wu repeatedly but her phone did not pick up. She deduced that Wu must have been detained by state security.

Gina called the Hangzhou security agent who usually monitored Wu Rongrong (Gina had saved his phone number), and he confirmed that state security agents from Beijing had come to Hangzhou to arrest Wu. Gina waited at Zhu Xixi's dorm room and fretted with several other feminists about what they should do now, when the agent called again: "We must meet with you immediately." Gina called the women's center and told everyone to leave and shut down their cellphones. Then Zhu Xixi also received a call from a Hangzhou security agent demanding to meet with her on campus.

"You need to go into hiding too," Gina told Zhu. They all left the dormitory, had dinner one last time together, then scattered.

Gina and one friend stuck together. They decided they could not leave Hangzhou by train because they would have to show their identity cards to buy tickets, making it easy for security agents to track them down. Instead, they spent that night at the home of a stranger, arranged by their feminist "rescue team." Early the next morning, they boarded a public bus bound for a distant suburb.

They could not stay at any hotels because they would be required to register their identity cards, so they arrived at the next town late at night and slept at a twenty-four-hour McDonald's, then got on another bus the next morning. If they headed through several provinces, they believed that it would be much more difficult for security agents to track them down.

First they headed west through Jiangxi Province to the city of Wuhan in Hubei Province, central China, about 450 miles from Hangzhou. They stayed with a friend of a friend in Wuhan for about a week, then traveled 540 miles north by bus (staying at KFC or McDonald's at night) to Jinan, the capital of Shandong Province, where a "training of trainers" course had been planned long in advance.

Gina had arranged to meet with another feminist attending the training session in Jinan, since she had thought that they would be safe so far from Hangzhou. But when she and her friend headed toward the meeting place, Gina was stunned to see police and plainclothes agents obviously patrolling and filming the area. Gina and her friend scrambled to turn back before anyone noticed them. Once they were out of view, Gina texted the third woman to warn her about the security patrols. "Don't go back to the hotel! The police are there, let's meet somewhere else," Gina texted.

One of their supporters found a room for them at an obscure hostel in Jinan where they would not have to show any identification. That night the three women stayed together. The next morning, the third activist fled separately, while Gina and her travel companion boarded the first bus out of Jinan. This time they headed far south, to Jiangxi Province almost 800 miles away, where a feminist colleague had set up a safe house for them for several weeks.

Gina had cut herself off from her social media networks and felt extremely anxious not knowing what was happening or what lay in her own future. After a while, she used an internet phone service to call her parents in the mountains of rural Henan. Gina had barely told her parents anything about her feminist activism and dreaded their questions. When she was growing up, Gina's parents had let her younger brother run around the mountains by himself because he was a boy, but they would not let her do the same and made her do housework instead.

"You're a girl, you can't just do what the boys do," her mother had said when Gina complained. Gina's father also beat her mother when he was angry, and her mother silently accepted the violence. From her childhood on, Gina could not tolerate these stifling traditions, and she told me that she felt she had become a true feminist long before she even heard the term. Gina studied very hard and, in the end, she was the one who went on to get a university degree while her brother never finished junior high school.

To her relief, Gina's mother answered the phone. "Ma, there's been a problem with my company, Weizhiming," she said.

Her mother was worried and wanted to know if she could help. "There's nothing you can do, Ma, try not to worry too much," she said. Gina told her mother not to say anything to the security agents if they came by, and to tell her friend—a designated intermediary—if the agents did anything to them.

The next time she called to check on her parents while in hiding, her father answered. "You come home this instant!" he yelled at her. "No, I can't," she replied, but her father would not stop yelling, so she hung up.

Gina returned to Hangzhou after the Feminist Five were released from detention. With Wu Rongrong still recuperating, Gina felt a heavy responsibility to take charge of feminist organizing in Hangzhou. Wu and her partners had decided to announce the closure of the Weizhiming Women's Center because of a new law restricting foreign-funded NGOs, requiring them to find government sponsors and register with the police. Informally, however, their group was hearing from more young women than ever before, all expressing keen interest. "The detention of the Feminist Five was awful, but on the other hand, so many more people started paying attention to our cause and volunteering," said Gina.

Virtually all of the student volunteers for feminist activities in the past had been undergraduate or graduate students, but for the first time, Gina started getting messages from high-school students wanting to help organize campaigns. In response to the surge of new interest, Gina—a little too hastily—organized a public discussion on gender inequality and advertised it on WeChat. But the police, who closely monitored her communications, told her to cancel the event.

"I had thought that the political environment would improve, but now I feel so hopeless," said Gina, becoming agitated as she talked to me during our long taxi ride through Hangzhou's rainy streets, returning from our visit to West Lake:

Lately with the feminist movement, I just can't see the way forward. So much of what we do doesn't get any media attention, so nobody knows about it. Then I start asking myself, is it worth it to do something so risky when no one will ever report it? I mean, since Wu Rongrong was released, I've had to take on so many responsibilities. I have to train new recruits just

135

graduating from university, but I'm only barely out of university myself. Sometimes I feel like I just can't handle everything.

It began to pour outside and the rain beat down noisily on the roof of our car. The driver turned up the speed of his windshield wipers, sweeping rhythmic torrents of water back and forth. Gina paused to look out at the rain, then started sobbing. This determined young woman was clearly traumatized by her run-ins with state security, yet she remained deeply committed to building a feminist movement that could endure.

I asked what those outside China could do to help.

She said she didn't know. "When I was in hiding, I cried myself to sleep almost every night. I heard about a woman who was taken into a detention center for some little thing and no one was allowed to visit her, and then all of a sudden she died there. Sometimes you wonder, what does it take to behave like a real human being in this terrible environment—when you're not even treated like a human being yourself?"

As our taxi approached its destination—another meeting with feminist activists—Gina quickly wiped away her tears.

"We must keep training new recruits so that if we get taken away, there will always be more people behind us to take our place," she said.

6

Feminists, Lawyers and Workers

As young people in China increasingly embrace the basic ideal of gender equality, feminism is beginning to influence other, traditionally male-dominated, social movements. Some male labor rights activists are starting to recognize that there can be no economic justice without gender justice. In recent years, sexual violence and gender discrimination have been at the center of important lawsuits. The ability of Chinese feminist activists to connect the grievances of different marginalized groups—potentially combining them to create a mighty, intersectional force of opposition—is another reason that the Communist Party sees feminism as a threat.

Wang Yu, the rights lawyer who defended Li Maizi of the Feminist Five, is a feminist crusader in her own right. She has taken on the most politically sensitive legal cases, the ones no other lawyers dared touch—representing members of the banned spiritual group Falun Gong; Professor Ilham Tohti, a moderate Uyghur academic who was jailed for life on the charge of separatism; feminist activists; and the parents of primary-school girls sexually abused by their principal. Journalists have written extensively about Wang Yu as a human rights lawyer, but much of the writing divorces her human rights activism from her *women's* rights activism, which is of critical importance. Her legal advocacy for women's and girls' rights is a powerful example of what can be accomplished when the field of human rights law adopts a gender perspective and shows the inextricable connection of gender justice to other forms of social justice.

Around four in the morning on July 9, 2015, a group of security agents drilled out the lock on Wang Yu's door, shoved her onto her bed, handcuffed her and put a black hood over her head. They dragged her out to a van waiting outside her home and drove her to an unknown location. Eventually, she arrived at a detention center cell with ten beds, but she was the only inmate, guarded by very young women (Wang guessed that they were around twenty years old). One young woman told Wang they were going to do a "routine inspection," with surveillance cameras mounted on the walls:

> I was told to take off all my clothes, stand in the middle of the room for inspection, and to turn my body three times. I objected to this insulting order. But these young girls didn't care.
>
> They rushed forward, pushed me against the floor, and stripped me. I was crying, and pleading with them at the same time. Why would they insult me like this? Why didn't they have any compassion? Why were they so violent to a small woman like me?

Wang Yu was the first Chinese rights lawyer to be taken away in what would become a sweeping round of detentions, disappearances and interrogations of around three hundred rights lawyers and legal assistants—called the "709 crackdown" after July 9, the date the detentions began.

The authorities subjected Wang Yu to brutal treatment and interrogations for many months before announcing her formal arrest in January 2016 on suspicion of "subverting state power," a charge that could result in life imprisonment. Her husband, Bao Longjun, who had worked with her as a trainee lawyer, was charged with a slightly lesser crime of "inciting subversion of state power." Security agents also traveled across the Chinese border in October 2015 to Myanmar to kidnap and repatriate Wang's sixteen-year-old son, Bao Zhuoxuan, who was attempting to escape to the United States. They placed him under house arrest and made him live with his grandmother in Inner Mongolia, under police surveillance. By crossing to another country and kidnapping a child under the age of eighteen to punish him for what his mother did, Chinese authorities violated Article 2 of the UN Convention on the Rights of the Child, which prohibits any form of punishment of children for the actions of their parents.

Authorities released Wang from detention in August 2016 after she was shown on state-owned media giving a videotaped "confession." In the tape, she renounced the legal profession and blamed "foreign forces" for using her to smear the Chinese government. The American Bar Association had chosen to honor her with its inaugural International Human Rights Award in July 2016, but in her "confession" Wang promised to reject any awards from foreign organizations, saying, "I am Chinese and I only accept the Chinese government's leadership."

Only a year later did the truth begin to come out. In July 2017, Wang Yu made a statement to Yaxue Cao of *China Change*, thanking her supporters. "These last two years of hardship have given me a deep appreciation of our citizens, human rights lawyers and international friends … It is you who made us realize that we are not alone," she said. "Of course, the road before us is very long, and walking it will be a test of our courage and self-confidence. I will carry on as I did in the past, my friends—please have faith!"

Wang Yu was part of a new wave of women's rights lawyers who were seized with feminist zeal as they volunteered for cases about sexual abuse, domestic violence, and gender discrimination —cases that did not directly challenge the legitimacy of the Communist Party but came to be treated as politically sensitive. The Chinese government succeeded in silencing Wang—at least for the moment—but before her arrest, she helped set in motion a nascent feminist trend in Chinese rights law.

Liu Wei, feminist lawyer and former executive director of Yirenping's office in Zhengzhou, describes how Wang Yu and several other women lawyers decided on this path. In April 2013, Liu and Wang attended a conference of rights lawyers in Wuhan. The women lawyers there proposed a network for rights lawyers across China, to form connections so they could support each other. Liu said the male lawyers were largely opposed to the idea and called it too "risky," so it was not taken up. "Personally, I think a lot of China's male lawyers have very strong personalities and do a lot of talking, so they didn't see a need for this kind of network," she says.

After dinner the first night of their conference, the lawyers broke up into small groups. Unusually, Wang Yu and Liu Wei formed a group with more women than men. By the end of the evening, their discussion had sparked an epiphany in Liu.

"I realized for the first time that it's my life mission to fight for the rights of women and girls," says Liu. Wang, Liu, and some of the other women decided to cofound a network on their own, one just for female lawyers working on women's and girls' rights. They called it the Public Interest Collaborative Network for Women Lawyers in China.

Over the following few weeks, they wrote a mission statement and posted it online to recruit other women lawyers around China who wanted to give free legal representation to sexual abuse victims, domestic violence victims, and others. They also planned to provide support to women's rights lawyers and allow them to team up more easily with lawyers in different regions, with the hope of making it less dangerous when working on politically sensitive cases. By the end of May, the women lawyers' network had grown to several dozen members and began holding meetings and training sessions in different cities and regions, including Beijing, Guangdong, Henan, and Sichuan.

Just after the network formed, in May 2013, news broke about a school principal and government official who had raped six girls ages eleven to fourteen, after taking them to a hotel room in the city of Wanning in Hainan Province. Wang Yu went down with a group, including the prominent women's rights activist Ye Haiyan (Hooligan Sparrow), to offer legal help to the victims' families and draw media attention to the epidemic of sexual abuse of girls in schools. At the same time, other volunteers from the network began collaborating closely in several sexual assault cases.

Liu and a team of lawyers took up a case involving a village school for children through the third grade in Tongbai County, Henan Province, where a male teacher had over many years sexually assaulted around twenty young girls, most between seven and nine years old. Liu's team of lawyers offered free legal representation to the families of the victims. "Once we accepted the case, we won the trust of the villagers," says Liu. "Soon, other families of girls in surrounding villages who had been sexually assaulted by the teacher came to tell us about their abuse."

The teacher had abused so many girls over the years that Liu's team needed around fifteen lawyers working together to persuade families to come forward and testify. The teacher's oldest victim had already married and had a child. Despite the offer of free legal services, almost none of the families were willing to testify at first—partly because of the legal hurdles, but also because of a sense of humiliation. "Most people think rape is a family shame that needs to be hidden," says Liu. In 2013, Chinese criminal law still classified child rape as "having sex with underage prostitutes," victim-shaming language that discouraged many families from coming forward.

The victims who did agree to speak out had horrifying testimonies. Even though the court only considered the cases of girls abused within the past two years, it found the teacher guilty of raping two young girls, aged just seven and eight, in his own home. It also found him guilty of sexually assaulting sixteen young

141

girls during class in front of other classmates, often by groping their genitals. He had threatened to hurt them even more if the girls told their parents about the abuse.

Chinese law generally only recognizes evidence of physical injury as valid and eligible for compensation, according to Liu. It is extraordinarily difficult to win damages for the emotional pain and suffering caused by sexual violence. "Some of the girls had a broken hymen, and their parents would buy some cheap ointment from the pharmacy to rub on their wound," says Liu. "But all the girls were deeply traumatized and in desperate need of psychotherapy." Her team argued to the judge that the victims' worst injuries were emotional and they required compensation for psychological counseling. The judge told Liu, "In China, we don't have this kind of legal provision, but if you can find evidence that they have been harmed, I will admit it."

Liu believes the judge was convinced that her team would never be able to provide evidence of harm, but they found a psychological counseling center in Zhengzhou that was willing to help the victims and brought some psychologists from Zhengzhou to evaluate the abused girls. In the end, they testified that each girl had suffered long-lasting trauma and needed to pay for years of psychotherapy.

Since there were no visible, physical injuries in the case, Liu's team arranged an out-of-court settlement of 1.3 million renminbi (around US$206,000), to be divided among the families that had taken part in the lawsuit. This is believed to be the highest amount of damages ever received in litigation related to sexual assault of a child in China. Yet even this important victory failed to address the deep shame felt by some family members. In 2016, Liu found out from a colleague that a parent of two young girls who had been raped by the teacher had committed suicide by jumping off a building.

The increasing publicity surrounding severe child sexual assault added fuel to the activist momentum started by other pioneering women's rights lawyers such as Guo Jianmei, the founder of Zhongze Women's Legal Counseling Center (which was forced to shut down in 2016). In 2015, the National People's Congress abolished the law classifying child-rape victims as "prostitutes," categorized sex with children as rape, allowed boys and men to be included as victims of sexual assault, and increased the maximum penalties for perpetrators of child rape. But laws on sexual assault and rape are still extremely flawed. And because China lacks an independent judiciary, even when the laws appear to be thorough, women's rights lawyers say they are extremely hard to enforce. The Henan and Hainan cases were just two among countless other cases, but the Chinese government does not release reliable data on sexual assault.

The sexual violence prevention center Girls' Protection Foundation said that from 2013 to 2015, the media reported at least 968 incidents of sexual assault against children under age fourteen involving more than 1,790 victims, the vast majority of whom were girls. In 2016, there were at least 433 cases of sexual assault of children reported in the media, with over 778 victims, 92 percent of whom were girls, according to the foundation. Needless to say, these numbers are absurdly low for a country of almost 1.4 billion and a mere fraction of the actual incidence of sexual assault, according to women's rights lawyers.

By comparison, in the United States, the Associated Press in May 2017 found 17,000 official reports of sexual assault of students in high schools, middle schools, and even elementary schools between the fall of 2011 and spring of 2015. Even this report, the most complete accounting yet of sexual assault in US schools, said that "it does not fully capture the problem because such attacks are greatly under-reported, some states don't track them and those that do vary widely in how they classify and catalog sexual violence."

In November 2017, Chinese authorities announced an investigation into conditions at childcare centers across the country, following a public uproar over accusations of sexual abuse at a prestigious Beijing kindergarten run by RYB Education, a company listed on the New York Stock Exchange (RYB stands for red, yellow, blue). Xinhua News wrote that the children were "reportedly sexually molested, pierced by needles, and given unidentified pills." Angry middle-class relatives of children had gathered outside the kindergarten, several kilometers from the Communist Party leadership compound, while tens of thousands of people on Weibo demanded answers from the government—but public discussion was quickly squelched. RYB Education fired the head of the school and police arrested one teacher, while government authorities issued a censorship directive to all news agencies in China that said, "Don't report or comment on Red Yellow Blue [RYB] New World Kindergarten in Beijing's Chaoyang district," according to *China Digital Times*.

By contrast, when Liu Wei's legal team settled their case in Henan in October 2013, many Chinese reporters wrote about it and interviewed Liu about the epidemic of sexual assault in Chinese schools. This was not the first time that Liu had taken on a case involving sexual abuse of girls, and until then the government had sometimes viewed her work as helpful in identifying corruption among local officials. But the 2013 case attracted so much media attention that a government official in Zhengzhou visited Liu and warned her not to take on big sexual abuse cases anymore. "We can tolerate what you've done so far, but if you take this any further, you will be viewed as opposing the Communist Party and opposing society," said the official. He warned her not to do any more interviews and to stay away from foreign reporters in particular, who he said were just using her "as their tool."

Liu had always been very careful not to speak too much about her work and rarely gave interviews, but she was enraged by this explicit threat and vowed to resist. Not only was she determined to continue speaking out, she felt that it was her *calling* to do so. "The government doesn't care if your work isn't attracting much attention," says Liu. "But once you start talking to the media and you take on big cases that draw a lot of public attention—when different groups in society collectively stand together and speak out about a problem—then you are seen as a threat."

Liu threw herself with even more zeal into her women lawyers' network and resigned from Yirenping. She and other cofounders recruited new lawyers and formed small groups specializing in sexual abuse, reproductive justice, employment discrimination, domestic violence, and legal reform. They decided not to register as an official organization to protect their members, but within a year of its formation, the group had attracted around 150 women lawyers across China.

Around this time, feminist attorney Huang Yizhi filed a gender discrimination lawsuit in Beijing on behalf of a twenty-three-year-old woman using the pseudonym Cao Ju. She had been rejected from a job as administrative assistant at a private tutoring firm, Juren Academy, because recruiters said that the firm was only looking to hire men. In December 2013, Cao was awarded 30,000 renminbi (around US$4,500), a landmark settlement in what is believed to be the first case of its kind in China's history.

Feminist activists in other cities wanted to seize on the momentum of the legal victory. In 2014, the Hangzhou feminist activist calling herself "Gina"—twenty-three at the time—applied for a job with the New Oriental Cooking School, which had advertised explicitly for a male administrative assistant. When Gina called school recruiters to ask why they only hired men, they told her outright that the male director needed a man to carry his suitcases on business trips. This was all the evidence Gina needed for her lawyer to file a gender-discrimination lawsuit, and in November 2014, the West Lake District Court in Hangzhou ruled that the cooking school had violated the applicant's equal employment rights. This was a major Chinese court ruling related to gender discrimination in employment, setting another legal precedent. Yet the court awarded a paltry 2,000 renminbi (just over US$300) in damages to the plaintiff, for "mental distress."

State media outlets such as the *Global Times* reported on the ruling as a victory for women's rights, but Gina worried about the small sum. "Since the compensation was so little, most female university graduates will think it's not worth it to file a gender-discrimination lawsuit," she says. She filed an appeal for more compensation and a formal apology from the cooking school, but when the Feminist Five were arrested in March 2015, she had to leave Hangzhou to go into hiding for almost two months (see Chapter 5). By the time Gina returned to Hangzhou, the short statute of limitations on her court appeal had already expired.

Meanwhile, after the high-profile Henan case, police and state security agents began to monitor feminist lawyer Liu Wei much more aggressively. They drove regularly around her apartment in Zhengzhou and she was afraid that they might threaten her five-year-old son or her husband. On the weekends, she insisted on taking them to the suburbs to "go sightseeing," thinking that they would be safer in a crowded, public place away from their apartment.

In May 2014, Liu's former colleague, Yirenping lawyer Chang Boyang, was arrested. Chang was representing clients who had attended a memorial meeting in advance of the twenty-fifth anniversary of the Tiananmen massacre in Beijing, though he himself did not take part in the meeting. Afterwards, police raided the Zhengzhou Yirenping office and froze its bank accounts. (The Beijing Yirenping office stayed open because it had a different business registration.) Liu and other key members of the women lawyers' network decided they should meet in Hong Kong in July to discuss how to adapt to the worsening political environment. Hong Kong provided a safer environment in which to discuss their work, and July happened to be in the middle of school holidays. Liu had been feeling guilty about not spending enough time with her son, so she brought him along for what she thought would be a vacation when her meetings were over.

Shortly after her plane landed in Hong Kong, Liu received a text from the police informing her that she was a criminal suspect and wanted for interrogation in the case of Yirenping's "illegal business operation." She went completely numb. She had been anxious for months about the security agents tailing her in Zhengzhou, but she never imagined that she would be formally named as a criminal suspect. Some of the women lawyers meeting in Hong Kong saw how bad her emotional state was and recommended a psychotherapist to help her as she planned her next move. They advised her to stay out of mainland China if at all possible.

Liu only had a seven-day visa, but the psychotherapist wrote a letter to the Hong Kong government requesting an extension on medical grounds, which she received. She had applied for a fellowship with the Global Network for Public Interest Law (PILnet) in New York and contacted them to see if she could start a year earlier. They quickly said yes and rushed the immigration paperwork so that she could begin the following month and travel directly from Hong Kong. As Liu passed through immigration controls in Hong Kong and New York, she was terrified that Chinese police would suddenly show up and arrest her, but on August 8 (eight is considered a very lucky number in China) Liu and her child arrived safely in New York. *Am I really here in America?* Liu thought.

For the first few months after their arrival, Liu woke up disoriented. She brought her son with her to afternoon and evening law classes, then spent her nights frantically communicating with members of her women lawyers' network in China. I met Liu Wei for the first time at a New York café in April 2016, when I was a visiting professor at Columbia University and she was a visiting scholar at New York University's US-Asia Law Institute. She brought her son—then eight years old—and he kept tugging at her shirt: "Mama, look what I drew!" Each time, Liu stopped speaking to smile at him and say, "Yes, look at that!" Then she would resume talking intently about women's rights and the crackdown on rights lawyers in China.

As Liu recalled the life-altering sequence of events in July 2014, her eyes welled with tears of gratitude over the good fortune that her child happened to be with her in Hong Kong when she was summoned by the police. "I don't know what state I would be in if he weren't with me now," she says. Later, when Liu watched Wang Yu's videotaped "confession" purporting to renounce the legal profession in August 2016, she completely understood. She said that anyone else with a child would have done the same thing: Wang had obviously "confessed" for the sake of her teenage son.

After receiving a master's degree (LLM) in international law and justice at Fordham University in 2017, Liu Wei was more convinced than ever that feminist consciousness should be a critical component of human rights law in China, and that only a lawyers' network led by women with a feminist perspective could push effectively for the reforms needed to better protect women's legal rights. Some members believed that the network should accept male lawyers who supported women's rights, but Liu disagreed, given men's generally low awareness about sexism and misogyny. "I think it's best not to include men," she said.

Dozens of women lawyers dropped out of the network following the arrests of Wang Yu and other rights lawyers in 2015, while the remaining members continued to meet and strategize. Feminist activists collaborated with some of them in their training sessions, using encrypted forms of communication and never discussing their plans on phone calls or WeChat, which were heavily monitored. (Another group for lawyers also formed, which was open to male members.)

"The government went after Wang Yu first because she was the most courageous and outspoken of all of China's rights lawyers," says Liu. She believed that the government crackdown on rights lawyers would be able to slow but not stop an underlying, inexorable trend: the growing interconnectedness of different social justice movements.

In 2016 and 2017, the wives of detained male human-rights lawyers built a small but powerful movement of their own. They demonstrated in acts of performance art inspired by feminist activists, dressing theatrically with bright red slogans written on their clothes, carrying red buckets outside jails and courts, and demanding access to their jailed husbands, according to the *New York Times*.

"You see a clear trend of rights lawyers linking up with nongovernmental organizations on some big cases, attracting ordinary citizens who support us from the sidelines," says Liu. "This is what the Communist Party fears the most—that all these different social forces coming together will be unstoppable."

Separate from the movement of women's rights lawyers is another potentially unstoppable force: strikes and worker protests rose to record levels of over 2700 in 2015 and around 2650 in 2016— almost double the number of incidents in 2014 (when 1379 strikes were publicly reported), according to the *China Labor Bulletin*. The *Bulletin* notes that these public reports of strikes are just "the tip of the iceberg." Independent trade unions are banned in China and the only officially permitted union, the All-China Federation of Trade Unions, exists largely to control workers. (Similarly, the primary purpose of the All-China Women's Federation is to control women, even though its stated mission is to "represent and uphold women's rights and interests.")

The growing intensity of workers' collective action is vividly portrayed in the 2017 documentary film *We, the Workers* by Huang Wenhai and Zeng Jinyan. Worker unrest has soared because of multiple factors, such as rising expectations among a younger generation of workers, increased communication and networking among workers through social media, and growing automation or relocation of factories to other countries with cheaper labor.

"Workers today know their rights and are not afraid of the authorities," said Han Dongfang, the veteran labor organizer who founded the *China Labour Bulletin*. Today's workers are much more defiant than the older generation of workers in the 1990s and early 2000s, who silently put up with major rights violations, months of unpaid wages, and brutally long shifts in exchange for factory jobs.

During the Tiananmen pro-democracy uprising of 1989, Han was a twenty-six-year-old railway worker in Beijing who quickly emerged as the charismatic leader of an independent union. After the Tiananmen massacre of June 4th, the Chinese government placed Han on its list of most-wanted labor leaders and he was jailed without trial for almost two years. When he developed drug-resistant tuberculosis, Han was permitted to receive medical treatment in the United States, where he had most of one lung removed. In 1994 he moved to Hong Kong and established the *China Labour Bulletin*. I first met Han in 1997 when I was working as a journalist for Radio Free Asia, which had just begun Mandarin-language broadcasts out of Hong Kong (and later added Cantonese broadcasts). Soon afterward, Han started a regular call-in radio show for Radio Free Asia, *Labour Bulletin* (*Laogong Tongxun*), talking with workers in China about their daily struggles and labor disputes. Han has continued his radio show ever since and the *China Labour Bulletin* has formed partnerships with many labor rights activists and lawyers.

Of all the exiled Chinese rights activists I have met from the Tiananmen protest generation, Han is one of the few who have remained closely engaged with ordinary Chinese citizens, perhaps because of his focus on what he calls "pragmatic, real-life" concerns rather than the more abstract goal of transforming a dictatorship into a democracy. Han was impressed by young Chinese feminist activists' solidarity with striking workers in Guangdong Province and their tackling the ubiquitous, entrenched problem of gender discrimination by employers. Women are more likely than men to be employed in China's low-paid manufacturing and services jobs, so women workers have been on the front lines of China's growing labor unrest.

"Since foreign-invested companies in particular hire more women workers, of course, many women are taking part in protests about labor conditions," he told me in September 2016, when I met with him in Hong Kong. "But so far it's still mostly men who are doing the collective bargaining with management." Han wanted to bring gender perspectives into labor dispute resolution to improve working conditions for all people, not just men. Several years ago, *China Labour Bulletin* began recruiting factory women for its skills-training programs in Guangdong, to help them take leadership roles in collective bargaining with management.

"If we can have three women leading the collective bargaining, we think that's even more important than having three hundred women participating in a strike but not having a seat at the negotiating table," said Han. "Of course, the three hundred women workers protesting are very important, but if you have women trained in the specific skills to lead collective bargaining with management, they can motivate even more women workers to come out and have their needs represented."

When most of the labor-capital negotiations are led by men, women's rights are all too often discarded in favor of a narrow focus on wages or pensions alone. Yet women are extremely vulnerable to gender-based forms of discrimination in the workplace, such as the denial of reproductive health-care coverage and maternity leave, sexual assault and sexual harassment in the workplace, and unfair dismissal due to pregnancy.

In a typical case from June 2017, a pregnant woman in the western city of Xi'an took her former employer, Xi'an Giant Biogene, to arbitration for unfair dismissal after she told her supervisor she was pregnant. The supervisor held seven meetings with her to push her to leave her administrative job for a more physically demanding production job with less pay, then threatened to fire her when she refused to comply, according to *China Labour Bulletin*. And in December 2017, three women who were fired after getting pregnant filed a joint pregnancy-discrimination lawsuit against China Railway Logistics Group in Beijing, in what is believed to be China's first collective case of its kind. A Beijing court ordered the company to pay one woman 10,000 renminbi (one month's pay); the two other women's cases were still in progress as this book went to press.

Although women are becoming more aware of the need to stand up for their rights as workers, "there is still a big gap between general rights awareness and mastering the skills needed to lead negotiations with management," says Han. He sees one of the important roles of the *China Labour Bulletin* as helping aggrieved workers turn a major labor dispute into collective bargaining, encouraging women to come forward and do the bargaining, training them in negotiating skills, and educating male labor organizers to accept women as their equals.

"We say to everyone, well, 80 percent of your factory workers are women, but 90 percent of your collective bargaining leaders are men, so don't you think it would be easier to mobilize your workers if you had more women leaders?" Han says. "And they admit, 'Yes, more women representatives could help us in our bargaining efforts.'" His group told worker leaders to seek out and recruit women workers who were active and interested in representing all the workers in negotiations. "Slowly, slowly, more women workers start taking the lead in collective bargaining," he says.

China Labour Bulletin held regular collective bargaining training sessions for fifty to eighty worker representatives at a time, with Han personally leading training sessions in Hong Kong from 2012 to 2014. It also supported a labor rights group in Guangdong Province, the Panyu Workers' Center. One of Panyu's employees was a charismatic woman, Zhu Xiaomei, who had been fired in 2014 from her job at the Hitachi Metals factory in Guangzhou for organizing workers and campaigning for a trade union. She sued and won a major out-of-court settlement from Hitachi of 230,000 renminbi (around US$36,500).

Zhu worked as an organizer for Panyu on many labor disputes involving thousands of workers, including a strike by hundreds of sanitation workers at Guangzhou's University Town in August

2014. The employer, Guangdian Property Management, had told workers that they had to move with the company away from their homes or lose their jobs. Workers were demanding fair severance pay and a promise that the company taking over the new cleaning contract for University Town would hire them all.

In one video of the collective action, Zhu spoke before a group of striking workers—mostly women—who were fanning themselves in the heat. "At first you might be a little afraid and think it's better to let other representatives go and talk. But once you go yourself, as some of you already did today, you will discover that the management can't actually do anything to you, isn't that right? Are you afraid?" asked Zhu.

"No!" they shouted.

"That's what I'm talking about!" Zhu responded enthusiastically. "Don't think that going in and talking to them [management] is something very scary! We are always scaring ourselves, but actually, there's nothing to fear. We keep telling you, don't worry, go and talk to them, but you say, 'No, no, no, I'm not good enough.' Those of you who watched the negotiations today should have a sense of what it's like, and I hope you can go out and tell the people around you about it. In these collective labor disputes, we are all victims, but we can all benefit too, right?"

After weeks of strikes and negotiations, Guangdian Property Management agreed to pay the workers 3,000 renminbi (around US$450) for each year of service, social security, and housing benefits; they also received contracts with the new company taking over the cleaning contract, according to the *China Labour Bulletin*. But in December 2015, police arrested at least eighteen labor organizers in Guangdong Province. In September 2016, a Guangzhou court sentenced three of the arrested activists to suspended jail terms on the charge of "gathering a crowd to disturb public order." The organizers included Zhu Xiaomei, who was nursing a baby at the time of her arrest. Two men were given suspended jail terms: Zeng Feiyang, director of the Panyu Workers' Center, and

Tang Jian. Another man, Meng Han, was released in April 2017 after spending twenty-one months in jail.

Han Dongfang says the government fears that Chinese workers might become as organized as the Polish Solidarity (Solidarność) independent trade union. Solidarity was formed in 1980 and was suppressed by Poland's Communist government, but then went on to defeat the Polish Communist Party in partly free elections in 1989. Its triumph was a historic milestone in the collapse of communism in Eastern Europe and the Soviet Union.

In a *China Labour Bulletin* essay for International Labor Day 2017, Han calls on international brands to take responsibility for working conditions at Chinese factories in their supply chains:

> Since 1989, the Chinese government has repeatedly sentenced labor movement leaders fighting for freedom of association; the court rulings were tools for political intimidation. But in the 2016 sentencing of four staff members of the Panyu Workers' Service Center, the Chinese government has for the first time issued a retaliatory ruling on behalf of a business against those who were assisting workers to engage management in a successful case of collective bargaining …
>
> To put it bluntly, these global brands took the lion's share of profits, but what have they left for China? For Chinese workers, nothing but poverty; for China's labor relations, nothing but endless disputes; for Chinese society at large, nothing but police repression of workers and labor NGOs. It is time for global brands to acknowledge their role in these serious violations.

In May 2017, Chinese authorities detained another three labor activists who were investigating working conditions at shoe factories in southern and eastern China owned by Huajian International, which made shoes for the brand of Ivanka Trump, daughter of (and advisor to) US president Donald Trump. The three labor activists were held at a detention center in Ganzhou, Jiangxi Province, until the end of June, then released on bail pending a trial. Several workers from the Ganzhou factory reported long hours stretching past midnight, low pay, and verbal abuse. One worker said that an angry manager had hit him in the head with the sharp end of a high-heeled shoe, causing his head to bleed, according to the Associated Press. Ivanka Trump and her company repeatedly declined to comment.

Despite the extremely repressive environment, labor protests and strikes continue, with women workers increasingly on the front lines. In March 2018, around a thousand factory workers—70 percent of whom were women—went on strike at the Simone luxury handbag plant in Guangzhou to demand back payment of their social insurance contributions. The South Korean firm Simone Accessories is one of the biggest manufacturers for global designer brands, including Michael Kors, Marc Jacobs and Coach, with locations in countries such as China, Cambodia and Vietnam. Simone Accessories began moving operations from its Guangzhou factory to cheaper locations in 2017, and the Guangzhou workers worried that they might never receive their long-overdue social insurance and housing fund benefits. The largely women workers went on strike, and after nine days of collective bargaining, reached an agreement with management over their demands.

Zheng Churan of the Feminist Five has linked her feminist activism with a deep concern for labor rights and working-class women ever since she was a student at the prestigious Sun Yat-sen University in Guangzhou. In August 2014, she went almost daily to take photographs and hand out protest stickers to the striking University Town sanitation workers. Their strike attracted a lot of media attention, but Zheng says reporters were only taking pictures of the male workers, even though 80 percent of the sanitation workers were women: "Why weren't the women workers being shown? I decided I had to take my own pictures of the women, and we also handed out stickers to the women workers to express their demands and stick them on their faces and clothes. It was all very visual." She posted an online photo essay with the title, "These Are Women with Strength and Power."

One of Zheng's photos showed a woman worker smiling at the camera, with a sticker across her forehead that said, "Guangdian Property, Stop Doing Evil." In another photo, a woman worker had her fist raised, with a sticker on her cheek that said, "Pay Me for My Labor." Another showed six uniformed women workers huddled together, laughing as they reached out their hands to do a team cheer, their faces covered with stickers saying things like, "She Gave Nine Years of Blood and Sweat/You Used Her Then Threw Her Away." A male co-worker stood beside the women, cheering them on.

"Too many of our media outlets lack gender consciousness so they overlook and erase the women in our social movements," says Zheng. "We can't let that happen." The striking sanitation workers also won support from many students: more than nine hundred at Sun Yat-sen University signed a petition to demonstrate their solidarity with the workers.

When the Feminist Five were arrested, some of the supporters expressing solidarity with them on social media were workers who had been personally helped by Zheng. One of the most striking pictures posted on Weibo was that of a male worker with a bare upper torso, displaying large red characters written on his back: "Giant Rabbit, always proud of you! The proletariat supports you!" (Giant Rabbit is Zheng's nickname.)

Ever since her release from detention, Zheng has continued to think about strategies to build solidarity between the rapidly growing numbers of middle-class feminists and working-class women. "The outpouring of support for us has been tremendous. But in this kind of political environment, the most acceptable form of feminism revolves around consumerism and elite women," she says. "This is politically safer and won't get us arrested, but we need to come up with ways to use this trend to do something for less educated, women workers, who have very different problems."

Even though some leaders in the labor rights movement are women, like Zhu Xiaomei, thus far few have linked their collective action to an explicitly feminist cause. Any large-scale, cross-class collaboration between middle-class feminists and working-class women would likely be viewed as yet another threat to the Communist Party. The Communist revolution of 1949 succeeded because elite Communist intellectuals joined forces with tens of millions of peasants and workers. No one mobilized women workers and rural women better than the Communist Party during the 1930s and 1940s, but that kind of grassroots mobilization of the masses is virtually impossible in China's repressive environment today.

Zheng notes that it is much easier to see fast results when feminist activism is aimed at university-educated women, pointing to the proliferation of "Lean In" groups among urban professional women across China as just one example of burgeoning "neoliberal" feminism for the elite. "But if someone had the resources to really invest in feminist consciousness-raising among factory women, the results would be incredible," she says.

Still, Zheng is heartened by the hundreds of thousands of young women who are already pushing back against sexism and misogyny and starting to change mainstream Chinese society. Young Chinese women are particularly concerned about rampant gender discrimination in employment, because it directly affects their own lives. "We can see a process of awakening in these women on social media. Anything related to gender discrimination in employment attracts a huge number of angry comments. At first, the women don't recognize that sexism is a problem, or maybe they know it's a problem but they think there's nothing they can do to change it," says Zheng. "Then they see activists like us doing something interesting to highlight the problem and they realize it's actually okay to express their opinions in public and call out sexism when they see it."

In spite of the recent surge of interest in feminism and gender inequality among urban women, Zheng and other feminist activists are cut off from funding within China and banned from many events because they are still officially "criminal suspects." Chinese professors have told Zheng outright that they would love to invite her to campus but their university would not give permission for her to speak. Most women's studies departments cannot invite feminist activists who are not approved by the government-sanctioned All-China Women's Federation, because of increased scrutiny of "hostile foreign influences" on Chinese campuses. Even some international organizations self-censor and do not invite independent, feminist activists to speak at their events, for fear of offending the Chinese government.

Zheng continues to receive warnings from security agents, although she was allowed to visit the United States in December 2017. One week after the BBC named her on its list of 100 "inspirational and influential women of 2016," Zheng received a call from a security agent asking why she had appeared on the BBC's list. "Our leaders found out about this list and they're very unhappy," said the agent. "How did they decide on the list? Did they give you any money? Do they want you to travel there?" Zheng told him she didn't know anything about the BBC, but that she was probably listed because of her new business plan to "help women get ahead in the workplace." That answer seemed to satisfy the agent and he did not insist on meeting her in person. "If something like 'Lean In' becomes politically sensitive, then there really *will* be a revolution in China," she jokes.

Zheng adds that the Guangzhou security agents monitoring her after her release were not the same ones who arrested and interrogated her in 2015. "I don't know what happened to those guys—they just disappeared. Maybe they're all dead!" Zheng laughs uproariously at the thought. "I'm so bad!" she says, still laughing, obviously deriving some stress relief from her revenge fantasies. "Everyone feels a lot of pressure now and no one feels safe, but we all get together often to eat, drink, and have some laughs," she says. "It's important to keep having fun together, because no matter how dark things get, we feminists are staying put. We cannot be extinguished."

China's Patriarchal Authoritarianism

L
u Jun, co-founder of the NGO Yirenping, showed up to our first meeting at a café in midtown Manhattan in 2016 wearing a black T-shirt with "This is what a feminist looks like" emblazoned on the front in Chinese characters. The T-shirt—designed by feminist activist Xiao Meili and inspired by the famous retort of the American women's rights icon Gloria Steinem, "This is what forty looks like"—has become practically a uniform for China's feminist movement. He has lived in self-imposed exile in the United States for several years and has been called "one of China's most wanted social activists."

In 2006, Lu Jun founded Yirenping in Beijing, then opened another branch in 2009 with his colleagues Chang Boyang and Yang Zhanqing in Zhengzhou, Henan Province. At first, they focused on discrimination against people with hepatitis B (including Lu Jun himself), who were banned from working in a wide range of jobs. They also took up consumer rights and HIV/AIDS, since Henan had been ravaged by an HIV/AIDS epidemic that was spread by an illegal blood trade and covered up by the local government. Virtually no Chinese foundations dared give money to NGOs working on citizen rights, so a large portion of Yirenping's funding came from the US-based National

Endowment for Democracy, which receives annual support from the US Congress.

Yirenping in Beijing expanded its work to include women's rights after feminist Wu Rongrong joined the organization as a new college graduate in 2007. In May 2009, Wu Rongrong led Yirenping's first major women's rights campaign, highlighting the case of Deng Yujiao, a twenty-one-year-old woman who had killed a Chinese official in self-defense while he was sexually assaulting her (see Chapter 1). Then in late July, two officials came with a police officer to search the Beijing office of Yirenping for unspecified "illegal" documents. "We refused to let them search our office because one of the officials' identity cards had expired, so we told them their search was illegal," said Lu Jun. He also received word that the rights lawyer Xu Zhiyong (with whom he had worked on a 2008 case about tainted baby formula that sickened tens of thousands of babies) had just been arrested.

Lu Jun and his colleagues refused to be intimidated. "We just sat there, arguing with them the whole time and I even called the police department to report their illegal search," he says. At 6 p.m., the officials left without doing a search, although they took away several dozen anti-discrimination newsletters, saying they would "study" them. Later, the police officer came back and asked Lu to apologize to the government officials, but Lu Jun refused.

The government initially denied Lu Jun permission to go abroad for a European Union human rights conference, but in December 2009, he was allowed to leave for several months to visit the University of Hong Kong and Yale Law School. By the time Lu Jun returned to China to start Yirenping's disability rights program in 2010, the police didn't bother him much anymore, except for a "chat" over tea or a meal every few months. Yirenping was largely left alone to pursue its programs until May 2014, when Chang Boyang was arrested for representing clients who held a vigil for the twenty-fifth anniversary of the Tiananmen massacre.

Although local authorities closed down the Yirenping office in Zhengzhou, the Beijing office was allowed to stay open.

Now central government officials suddenly realized that there was an influential rights organization that they had not considered to be "dangerous" before—but Lu Jun was already in the United States, beginning his fellowship as a visiting scholar at the US-Asia Law Institute of NYU School of Law. "The central government started paying close attention to all NGOs in China that received foreign funding and of course Yirenping, because of our foreign funding, became an important target in the crackdown on NGOs," says Lu Jun. "They started looking through all of our programs, but it was hard for them to find any political problems." Women's rights stood out as potentially posing the greatest danger to the government. It involved provocative street activism, and it had been successful in organizing women—and some like-minded men—in different cities across China. So the authorities "decided to use women's rights as their entry point," says Lu Jun.

After authorities arrested the Feminist Five in March 2015, security agents raided the Beijing office of Yirenping, took away all the computers and files, and detained one of the center's employees. At a Chinese Foreign Ministry briefing on March 25, foreign correspondents asked about the detained feminist activists. "No one has the right to ask China to release relevant persons, so we hope that relevant people will stop interfering in China's judicial sovereignty in such a manner," said the government spokesperson.

Lu Jun points out that authorities had only begun paying attention to feminist activists in 2012, because they had mobilized so many supporters. "The feminist movement has made huge leaps compared to just a few years ago. It actually looks like a real social movement now ... I think all the people in China are like scattered sand and if you can organize the sands, you will be stronger than the forces that are scattered," he says. "Right now, feminist voices can be heard because they are well organized. But if they can't organize, their voices will fade."

Lu Jun has no doubt that Xi Jinping, China's paramount ruler since November 2012, is opposed to feminism and women's rights in general: "China's feminists today have a new enemy: Xi Jinping," he says. "And this enemy is very powerful."

China's legislature formally ended presidential term limits in March 2018, granting vast new powers to President Xi and setting him up to be China's strongman ruler for life. The Communist Party has ruled China for almost seventy years—nearly as long as Communist rule in the Soviet Union. After the Tiananmen massacre of 1989, many journalists and academics predicted the Party's demise, but it has defied these predictions and further strengthened its hold on power.

Most analysts of China's authoritarianism regard gender as a marginal issue, but I believe that the subordination of women is a fundamental element of the Communist Party's dictatorship and its "stability maintenance" system (*weiwen*). I argue that Xi Jinping, like other strongman rulers around the world, sees *patriarchal* authoritarianism as critical for the survival of the Communist Party. Even before the ascent of Xi, sexism and misogyny had long underpinned China's authoritarian control of its population. (Other reasons for the Party's longevity include its ability to adapt to social change and to deliver rapid economic growth while cracking down ruthlessly on political dissent.)

Today, for the first time since the founding of the People's Republic in 1949, organized feminist activists independent of the Communist Party have tapped into broad discontent among Chinese women and developed a level of influence over public opinion that is highly unusual for any social movement in China. Growing numbers of women—particularly educated urban women—are recoiling from the state's relentless efforts to coerce them into heterosexual marriage and child rearing. It is no wonder, then, that China's all-male rulers feel threatened by young feminist activists, who are calling for an individualistic emancipation of women that has nothing to do with nation building.

The Chinese government's backlash against feminism is a form of state-level, fragile masculinity, terrified at the prospect of emancipated women rising up to challenge the Communist Party's political legitimacy. The threat from feminist activists was perceived to be so dire that in May 2017, the *People's Daily* online—the official mouthpiece of the Party—published an announcement from the vice president of the All-China Women's Federation warning that "Western hostile forces" were using "Western feminism" and the notion of "putting feminism above all else" to attack China's Marxist views on women and the country's "basic policies on gender equality." "Some are using the banner of 'rights defense,' 'poverty alleviation' and 'charity' to directly meddle in our country's women's affairs, attempting to look for weaknesses and make a breach in the field of women's issues," Song Xiuyan warned. She went on to add that all cadres specializing in women's affairs must follow the wise guidance of Xi Jinping and guard against Western efforts to interfere with China.

Shortly after Xi became general secretary of China's Communist Party in November 2012, he gave a pivotal speech in which he explained the Soviet Union's collapse. "A few people tried to save the Soviet Union; they seized Gorbachev, but within days it was turned around again, because they didn't have the instruments to exert power. Yeltsin gave a speech standing on a tank, but the military made no response, keeping so-called 'neutrality.' Finally, Gorbachev announced the disbandment of the Soviet Communist Party in a blithe statement," he said. "A big party was gone, just like that. Proportionally, the Soviet Communist Party had more members than we do, but nobody was man enough to stand up and resist."

The independent journalist Gao Yu (jailed several times for her role in the 1989 Tiananmen protests and other criticism of the government) was quick to respond. "'Nobody was man enough!'" she wrote. "How vividly this captures Xi Jinping's anxiety over the fall of the Soviet Communist Party and the collapse of the Soviet Union!"

Xi's first major speech as Party leader signaled that—contrary to predictions that he would proceed boldly with economic and political reforms—he saw his primary role as stamping out any destabilizing forces that might provoke widespread social unrest and lead to the Party's collapse. President Xi was declaring that, unlike Gorbachev, he was "man enough" to stand up for the Communist Party; he possessed the manly qualities needed to defend China from those seeking to undermine Communist rule.

In April 2013, the Party circulated an internal memo titled "Document No. 9," warning officials to be vigilant against the infiltration of dangerous views from the West. It singled out seven "Western" concepts it called the "seven unmentionables" (*qi ge bu jiang*), including universal values, Western constitutional democracy, civil society, Western freedom of the press, and the historical errors of the Communist Party. Shortly afterward, the government began its sustained, harsh crackdown on civil society.

For the first several years of his presidency (until early 2016), Xi was quite literally called "Xi Dada"—the rough equivalent of "Big Daddy Xi"—in the state media, which built up a personality cult around him the likes of which had not been seen since the 1966–1976 Cultural Revolution, when Mao Zedong was eulogized through song, dance, propaganda posters, and news reports as China's one and only savior. This language celebrates Xi Jinping for his manliness and upholds the patriarchal family as the basic foundation of a strong and stable state.

Like Orwell's Big Brother, China's "Big Daddy" is always watching you. Propaganda images depict Xi as father of the Chinese nation, in a "family-state under heaven" (*jiaguo tianxia*). He is officially general secretary of the Communist Party, president, chairman of the Central Military Commission, chairman of the Central National Security Commission, and chairman of the newly established Central Commission for Integrated Military and

Civilian Development—to name just a few of the muscular titles Xi has amassed.

In October 2016, the Communist Party bestowed on Xi the new title of "core leader," a term previously only given to Mao Zedong, Deng Xiaoping, and Jiang Zemin. (Xi's immediate predecessor, Hu Jintao, was never described as a "core leader.") Then in October 2017, the Party elevated Xi even further—in theory, to the same status as Mao Zedong, founder of the People's Republic. At the conclusion of the Nineteenth Party Congress, Xi's ideas were enshrined in the Party Constitution under the unwieldy name "Xi Jinping Thought for the New Era of Socialism with Chinese Special Characteristics."

According to established rules limiting Party leaders to ten years in power, Xi should have named a successor and prepared to step down in 2022, but the sudden abolition of term limits in 2018 has moved the Communist Party sharply away from its norm of consensus-based leadership of the past few decades.

When Xi became president, pop and hip-hop songs emerged idolizing him not just as a father but as an ideal husband too, with titles such as "Be a Man Like Xi Dada," "Xi Dada Loves Peng Mama" (China's "first lady," Peng Liyuan), and, one of the most popular of all, "If You Want to Marry, Marry Someone Like Xi Dada." The video for the last song flaunts militaristic and macho images of Xi greeting thousands of soldiers from the People's Liberation Army in a parade down Tiananmen Square to a thrusting disco beat while a soprano belts out, "If you want to marry, marry someone like Xi Dada, a man full of heroism with an unyielding spirit."

Xi's hypermasculine personality cult became so extreme that some Party officials felt it had gone too far, and in early 2016 urged the state media to drop the term "Xi Dada." Nonetheless, Chinese state media continue to present the nation as one big, male-dominated family, which needs strong, masculine leadership in the form of Xi, the paternalistic patriarch.

Yet just how strong is the strongman Xi in reality? Behind the manly titles and macho propaganda videos, Xi's hold on power is much more fragile than it appears. China's economy has entered a protracted slowdown, just as the country is beginning to face the severe demographic crises of an aging population and a shrinking workforce. By most accounts, China's decades-long "economic miracle" of double-digit growth rates is now over. The government announced a projected GDP growth rate of around 6.5 percent in 2018, as the economy is widely expected to cool. China's labor productivity growth has also slowed significantly, while its financial system is plagued by capital flight and ever-increasing public debt caused by excessive state investment. The investment agency Moody's downgraded China's debt rating in May 2017 for the first time since November 1989, just months after the Tiananmen massacre.

Today, with the Chinese government struggling to deliver on its promise of constantly rising living standards, dissatisfaction is mounting among many sectors of the population—and the government's response has been to tighten ideological controls everywhere. As law professor Carl Minzner argues, China is reversing its progress toward greater ideological openness over the past several decades and "China's one-Party system is beginning to cannibalize itself." Since the Communist Party can no longer rely on rapid economic growth to bolster its legitimacy, Chinese propaganda under Xi's leadership has revived some sexist elements of Confucianism, in particular trying to push the notion that a traditional family (based on marriage between a man and a virtuous, obedient woman) is the foundation of a stable government.

The collection *Women and Confucian Cultures in Premodern China, Korea and Japan* illuminates how premodern rulers deliberately used Confucian discourse to prescribe models of feminine behavior that would consolidate their hold on power. "We have found the state—staffed by pragmatic officials intending to centralize power and by idealistic scholars bent on civilizing society —an unusually active agent shaping terms of gender interactions. In propagating laws as well as canonical and didactic texts, the state was instrumental in naming the category 'woman' and defining norms of womanhood," write the editors.

In one of the volume's essays, "Competing Claims on Womanly Virtue in Late Imperial China," Fangqin Du and Susan Mann write that during the Yuan Dynasty (roughly 1279 to 1368), the government explicitly promoted a neo-Confucian model of family and womanly virtue as its official ideology, which was essential to its statecraft. Yuan rulers followed an early classical text, *The Great Learning*, which taught that "regulating the family was the first step in administering the state." As part of its political strategy, the Yuan government actively promoted the norms of female chastity and wifely sacrifice. "Yuan rulers drew an explicit parallel between a wife who dedicated herself to her husband and a subject who was absolutely loyal to his ruler: 'a man dies for his country and a woman dies for her husband; this is *yi* [righteousness],'" write Du and Mann.

While filial piety (*xiao*) was considered the dominant womanly virtue in the Song Dynasty (roughly 960 to 1279), by the middle of the Qing dynasty (1644 to 1911), Confucian didactic texts focused even more on a "chastity cult" emphasizing woman's "marital fidelity and sexual purity" within the family, according to Du and Mann. The Qing Dynasty text *Biographies of Exemplary Women* (*Lienü zhuan*) said that a stable government is formed through the accretion of "harmonious" families—based on marriage between men and women:

> The daughter obeys her parents; the daughter-in-law reverently serves her parents-in-law; the wife assists her husband; the mother guides her sons and daughters; sisters and sisters-in-law fulfill their appropriate [duties.]

When every member behaves this way, a family achieves harmony; when every family is harmonious, the state is well governed.

It is striking how much recent Communist Party propaganda preaching "family values" harkens back to the Confucian discourse from the imperial era on womanly virtues.

China's official Xinhua news agency ran a long article on March 29, 2017, entitled "Ever Since the Eighteenth Party Congress, Xi Jinping Has Talked This Way about Family Values" (the Eighteenth Party Congress in 2012 named Xi China's top leader). Xinhua proceeds to explain why Xi places such great emphasis on traditional family values (*jiafeng*): "Today we publish a new article to study with you the good family values advocated by Xi Jinping, to understand the relationship between family values and national values (*guofeng*)."

Xinhua points out that the Chinese word for "family," *jia*, is also part of the compound word for "nation," *guojia*: "The family is the smallest nation, the nation is 10 million families. The 'family' [*jia*] in family values is not just the small family, but also the family in our nation [*guojia*]. Since the Eighteenth Party Congress, Xi Jinping has often stressed the importance of family values. He says 'little family' but he has in mind the 'big family' [the nation]."

The article features a photo of Xi as a filial son, strolling through a garden hand in hand with his elderly mother, with stern warnings to keep family members in line: "Every cadre must place great emphasis on family values, stay honest and clean, cultivate one's character, govern one's family well, and in addition to controlling oneself properly, set strict demands on spouses, children and close colleagues." Xinhua also restates the frequent Communist Party line that family forms "the basic cell of society" and that "a harmonious marriage is the foundation of a harmonious society."

In March 2017, just as Weibo was imposing a month-long ban on the *Feminist Voices* social media account and erasing feminist essays posted on WeChat, Xinhua ran an article (picked up by media outlets across China) entitled, "A Review of President Xi's Greetings to Women over Five Years," accompanied by photos of adoring female delegates smiling at him and applauding. "President Xi in many of his keynote speeches addressed the dialectical relationship between national development and family construction, showing the Communist Party Central Committee's great concern on women and family work," Xinhua reported. "Women play an active role in nurturing traditional family values ... Virtues are precious treasures for the promotion of family harmony, social stability and the well-being of the next generation," Xi was quoted as saying.

At no point did the Xinhua article mention the critical importance of working women to China's long-term economic growth. Rather, it focused entirely on how much Xi emphasized women's obligations within the family—in particular, taking care of children and the elderly. "Women should take responsibility for youngsters' education; boost the traditional positive virtues of the Chinese nation; and, contribute to the social ethos," Xi was quoted as saying. "He said Chinese traditions and virtues of family harmony and affection should not be forgotten, so as to ensure that the young grow up healthily and senior citizens are being taken good care of," Xinhua reported. The government's aggressive promotion of traditional gender norms predates Xi's ascendancy, but Xinhua is now sending the message that President Xi himself is giving his imprimatur to the notion that traditionally virtuous wives and mothers are key to solving China's most pressing social problems.

In March 2018, the All-China Women's Federation in Zhenjiang, Jiangsu Province, started a series of courses for "New Era Women" (for Xi Jinping's "New Era") to "raise the quality" (*tigao suzhi*) of young women by teaching them how to cross their legs, sit, kneel, apply make-up and decorate the home like proper ladies, according to "traditional culture." These government-sponsored schools are disturbingly similar to the unofficial women's "morality schools" appearing in recent years, which teach women to obey their husbands. "Don't fight back when beaten. Don't talk back when scolded. And no matter what, don't get divorced," said one teacher from the Fushun Traditional Culture School, in a leaked video posted online in November 2017.

Meanwhile, in almost seventy years of Chinese Communist history, there has never been a single woman on the Politburo's elite Standing Committee. Why? I believe that China's all-male rulers have decided that the systematic subjugation of women is essential to maintaining Communist Party survival. The already severe underrepresentation of women in elite politics actually got even worse with the appointment of new Party leaders in 2017. Today, there is only one woman on the twenty-five-member Politburo. Female representation on the Central Committee—the largest of the Communist Party's top political bodies, with 204 full members—declined from a paltry 6.4 percent on the Seventeenth Central Committee in 2007 to an even more dismal 4.9 percent today. There was not a single woman heading any of mainland China's thirty-one provincial administrations in 2017, according to the Brookings Institution. By contrast, both Hong Kong and Taiwan—which are part of "greater China"—are now led by women.

The Chinese government wants women to be reproductive tools of the state, obedient wives and mothers in the home, to help maintain political stability, have babies and rear the workforce of the future. When China began opening its economy to free market reforms in 1979, it also introduced the catastrophic "one-child policy," which grossly violated the reproductive rights of all of China's women. The egregious abuses of Chinese women throughout more than thirty-five years of the one-child policy—large-scale forced abortions, sterilizations, and compulsory birth control, including the coercive insertion of intrauterine devices (IUDs) on a mass scale—have been extensively documented by authors such as Mei Fong in her book *One Child: The Story of China's Most Radical Experiment.*

China's fertility rate was 2.8 births per woman on average in 1979, when the one-child policy was first introduced. By 2015, the fertility rate had collapsed to just 1.6 births per woman—far below the population-replacement rate of 2.1, according to the World Bank. After ignoring many years of warnings from academics and activists about a looming demographic disaster, the Chinese government suddenly announced with great fanfare at the end of 2015 that it would ease the one-child policy practiced for over three decades and officially allow married couples to give birth to two children. Yet, by most accounts, the end of the "one-child policy" has come far too late to reverse long-term demographic trends. Some heralded the change as a move toward greater reproductive freedom, but the government was only embarking on yet another grand experiment in population engineering: this time it was urging women—though only the right sort—to reproduce for China.

In addition to plummeting birthrates, China must grapple with a drastically aging population and a shrinking labor force—all of which are closely linked to China's decelerating economic growth, labor productivity growth, and fundamentally, the political legitimacy of the Communist Party.

The National Bureau of Statistics population development plan projects that one-quarter of China's population will be over sixty years old by 2030. In 2017, one-third of Shanghai's residents were already over sixty, according to Xinhua News. China's dependency ratio—showing the number of children (birth to fourteen) and older people (over sixty-five) to the working-age population (fifteen to sixty-four)—is projected to rise from 36.6 percent in 2015 to 69.7 percent in 2050, according to the CSIS China Power Project. China also has one of the world's most skewed sex-ratio imbalances, with roughly 34 million more men than women and 113 boys born for every 100 girls in 2015, according to Xinhua

News. (I analyze the Chinese government's perception of the sex-ratio imbalance as a threat to social stability in my book *Leftover Women*.)

Xinhua initially proclaimed the "two-child policy" a roaring success—"China's Two-Child Policy Results in Largest Number of Newborns since 2000," one headline boasted in March 2017. Officials had originally estimated that the two-child policy would lead to about 3 million additional births annually through 2020, adding more than 30 million people to China's labor force by 2050.

But there has been no baby boom. Figures released in January 2018 show that China's birthrate fell by 3.5 percent in 2017 compared with the previous year. The number of births in 2016 increased by just 1.3 million over 2015—less than half the projected figure and falling far short of expectations, according to government data (with total births of 17.25 million). According to official statistics, the number of children born to parents who already had one child did rise in 2017, but the number of first-child births dropped.

In response to the lower-than-expected birthrates, Wang Peian, vice-minister of the National Health and Family Planning Commission, announced in February 2017 that the government was considering "birth rewards and subsidies" to couples who already had one child to have one more. Meanwhile, Huang Xihua, a lawmaker at the 2017 National People's Congress annual meeting, proposed lowering the legal marriage age from twenty for women and twenty-two for men to eighteen for both sexes, in order to "encourage more births as the nation grows old."

The government has even offered to remove the IUDs forcibly inserted into millions of women from the 1980s through the 2000s so that they may have a second child. But Chinese women have lambasted the plan. The forced implantation of IUDs amounted to "involuntary, forced acts of mutilation," Han Haoyue wrote in a post shared thousands of times on Weibo, according to Sui-Lee Wee of the *New York Times*. "And now, to say they are offering free removal as a service to these tens of millions of women—repeatedly broadcasting this on state television as a kind of state benefit—they have no shame, second to none," wrote Han.

In May 2018, some news outlets reported that the government might eliminate birth limits, but at the time *Betraying Big Brother* went to press, there were no signs that women would be granted real control over their bodies. Whatever the demographic program, the Communist Party continues to view women as reproductive agents for its development agenda. Feminists like Lü Pin say that any new birth policy is likely to place even more pressure on women to have babies.

Shortly after the government announced that it was ending the one-child policy in 2015, Lü Pin wrote an online essay that posed some crucial questions:

> If the state is truly returning our reproductive rights, who will end up controlling these rights in practice? This is a critical issue for the well-being of women. Is it the husbands, the mothers-in-law [*gongpo* or husband's mother], parents, or is it women themselves? Is it possible that control over reproductive decisions will move from the patriarchal state to the patriarchal family? That women will go from being forced not to have children to being forced to have children?

Absent any new government initiatives to provide more and better childcare and eldercare, the two-child policy (or any future policy) is likely to add to women's burdens both in the home and the workplace. Although gender discrimination in employment is technically illegal in China, companies have little incentive to hire women and employers do not want to assume the cost of paying for women's maternity leave. With the heavily gendered division of labor in families, most unpaid family caregivers are women, so the state is transferring the heavy, public burden of childcare and social security onto women in private families. "China's model of economic development relies on the exploitation of women," says Lü Pin.

China's "two-child policy" has been accompanied by a new propaganda campaign to drive up plummeting birthrates, especially among urban, educated women, who are considered to be "high quality" (*gao suzhi*) according to the eugenics-minded population planners. When I wrote about the Chinese government's media campaign about "leftover" women, which began in 2007, I thought that the propaganda might eventually subside. Instead, the Chinese state media became even more aggressive about pushing urban, educated women in their twenties to marry and have babies following the end of the "one-child policy." After more than three decades of forcing women to have abortions, China's state media suddenly did a U-turn and started churning out slogans, articles, and images about the glories of having two children—preferably as soon as possible.

"Don't miss out on women's best years for getting pregnant!" warn some headlines in state media. Those years supposedly are between the ages of 24 and 29, according to the government; beyond that, it says, beware birth defects. One December 2015 article originally published in the *Beijing Youth Daily*, an official publication of the Communist Youth League, was illustrated with a photograph that could have come straight out of Margaret Atwood's dystopian novel *The Handmaid's Tale*, about women being forced to have sex and bear children in a country where fertility has plummeted. The photo featured the blacked-out silhouette of a woman wearing a university-graduation gown with a mortarboard on her head, holding an infant (in full color) in her arms. The article states that when female university students look for jobs before graduation, employers invariably ask them, "When do you plan to have children?" Rather than criticizing this omnipresent (and illegal) gender discrimination, the author urges female university students to hurry up and have babies because employers are "more likely" to hire women once they have gotten their childbearing out of the way: "Many female university students discover that women who check the box 'already married, already had baby' [*yihun yiyu*] stand a much higher chance of success in their job search."

The article was widely reprinted in different media outlets across China with varying headlines: in the *People's Daily* online, it was "University in Beijing has over 10 female student mothers: Bright job prospects" and " 'Already had a baby' becomes a sought-after quality in the job-hunting season—more female university students prepare for pregnancy" (sohu.com).

Other media reports showcase gorgeous "university-student mothers" who flaunt how happy they are to be having babies while still in graduate school or even college. One article on the website sohu.com in March 2017 had the headline "Female University Student's Joyful Love: Freshman Year—Live Together, Sophomore Year—Get Pregnant, Junior Year—Have Baby." The article featured a photograph of a conventionally beautiful young woman beaming beatifically in her graduation gown and mortarboard, one hand resting on her prominently pregnant belly, the other arm holding her toddler.

At the same time, the government discourages single women from having babies because it sees marriage and family as a pillar of social stability, so mass matchmaking initiatives are also intensifying. In May 2017, China's Communist Youth League made a widely publicized announcement that it would "help unmarried young people find significant others" through activities such as mass blind dates and "educate young people to establish proper values for love and marriage."

The *Global Times* reported many Weibo users complaining about state-owned companies forcing their young, single employees to take part in the blind dates at parks and stadiums and counting it as "absenteeism" if they refused to go. The article quoted an expert on population planning, Yuan Xin at Nankai University, as saying that "the high rate of single people will affect social stability." Yuan went on to say that a "high population of single males might also cause many other social problems such as sexual violence and women and child trafficking, not to mention the pension burden they will bring about when they get old." It cited statistics from *China Youth Daily* saying that China's population of "single people" had reached 200 million in 2015, a figure it called "worrying" for the government.

That same month, censors abruptly shut down China's leading lesbian app, Rela, which had around five million registered users. Weibo simultaneously deleted the lesbian social media account without offering any reason. The Rela app and its entire website disappeared just days after Taiwan's top court issued a historic ruling on May 24, 2017, in favor of legalizing same-sex marriage. Some users speculated that the app was banned because Rela had supported the mothers of LGBTQ children who wanted to take part in a popular matchmaking event at Shanghai's People's Park. Needless to say, lesbians freely loving each other adds up to fewer women willing to enter heterosexual marriage, thus harming China's population-planning goals. Although censors have cracked down on gay men's apps as well, the Chinese government in general is more tolerant of gay male activities, perhaps because there are around 33 million more men in the population than women, according to Xinhua. In addition, around 80 percent of China's gay men are already married to or will marry women, according to studies by Zhang Beichuan, a retired professor from Qingdao University Medical School.

Yet China's misogynistic, single-shaming, and often homophobic propaganda is increasingly falling on deaf ears—thanks in no small part to young feminists' influence on social-media discourse. Virtually all of China's persecuted feminist activists come from the exact demographic that the government is targeting in its pro-marriage, pro-natalist policies: university-educated, middle-class women in their twenties and early thirties.

Although Chinese feminist activist campaigns eschew the appearance of overt political opposition, their underlying message is extraordinarily radical. By mobilizing women to break free of China's patriarchal institutions of compulsory marriage and child rearing, feminists are sabotaging the government's fundamental objective of ensuring that ("high-quality," educated, Han Chinese) women remain baby breeders and docile guarantors of social stability.

One American feminist from the "second-wave" movement of the 1960s and 1970s, Shulamith Firestone, articulated a vision of society that would destroy what she argued was the primary instrument of men's tyranny over women: the biological family structure, which must be uprooted through revolution. Passages from her 1970 book *The Dialectic of Sex: The Case for Feminist Revolution* would strike terror in the heart of any Communist Party population planner, particularly since her Marxist revolutionary language and "population biology" is so familiar to them:

> So that just as to assure elimination of economic classes requires the revolt of the underclass (the proletariat) and, in a temporary dictatorship, their seizure of the means of *production*, so to assure the elimination of sexual classes requires the revolt of the underclass (women) and the seizure of control of *reproduction*: not only the full restoration to women of ownership of their own bodies, but also their (temporary) seizure of control of human fertility—the new population biology as well as all the social institutions of child-bearing and child-rearing.

Firestone's call for the overthrow of the biological family structure and "the freeing of women from the tyranny of reproduction by every means possible" was viewed as far too radical for mainstream American feminists. But in some ways, we are beginning to see in China what it might look like for women to "seize control of human fertility" en masse.

Millions of young women in China's rapidly growing middle class are beginning to experience an awakening about their rights, with profound consequences for China's future. As individuals, most may be unwilling to challenge Communist Party rule, but as a collective—through their reproductive choices—women's rejection of marriage and childbearing could imperil the government's most urgent population-planning objectives. A May 2017 survey by Zhaopin, one of China's largest job-recruitment websites, of over 40,000 working women found that just over 40 percent of working women in China without children do not want to have babies at all. Almost two-thirds of working mothers with one child do not want to have a second child. The women surveyed said their top reasons for not wanting children were "not enough time and energy," "concerns over career development," and "too expensive to raise children." More than half of all working women surveyed said their biggest concern about having children was "difficulty in returning to work after childbearing," while just under half said they were mostly concerned about "being replaced by others."

Many of these women, under extreme pressure from their families and the government to sacrifice their personal desires for the "greater good" of society, may end up having one or two babies anyway. Nevertheless, the implications of almost half of China's working women without children saying that they do not ever want to have babies are staggering when one considers the enormous size of China's rapidly expanding middle class. In 2016, the Economist Intelligence Unit estimated that the number of Chinese belonging to upper-middle-income or high-income brackets, which reached 132 million (or 10 percent of the population) in 2015, would rise to 480 million (and 35 percent of the population) by 2030.

Marriage rates are starting to fall after rising for many years. In 2016, the number of Chinese couples registering for marriage decreased for the third year in a row (falling by almost seven percent from just one year earlier), while the divorce rate continued to climb for at least eight consecutive years since 2008, according to Ministry of Civil Affairs statistics. These patterns of women rejecting marriage are long-established in other parts of East Asia, such as Japan, South Korea and Singapore, but they have only just begun to emerge in China. Although it is too early to tell if marriage rates will continue to fall, I have met a surprising number of young Chinese women in the past few years who express militant opposition to marriage because they do not want to be beholden to a man and his family.

Meanwhile, there are single women who want to have a child but are penalized for doing so. If the Chinese government merely wanted to boost birthrates overall, an obvious solution would be to lift penalties on single mothers. Taboos about single parenthood are eroding in many countries around the world, but in China, single women without a valid "reproduction permit" from the government are often denied birth certificates for their children. Without a birth certificate, the child will not be given an official household registration (*hukou*) and will have trouble gaining admission to school and access to affordable healthcare. Moreover, if women cannot produce a marriage certificate upon giving birth, they are frequently slapped with "social maintenance fees" for violating population-planning restrictions.

The fact is that the two-child policy to date applies only to married heterosexual couples, largely those in urban areas (since rural couples already routinely have two children or even more). Some women in their twenties and thirties in cities such as Beijing and Shanghai say they have no desire to get married, but they are doing it for the sole reason that they want to have a child. Allowing single women to have babies would likely cause marriage rates to fall further—a prospect that no doubt threatens the Communist Party's vision of heterosexual marriage as the basic foundation of social stability.

Chinese authorities are so loath to grant single, fertile women any freedoms that might deter them from getting married that single women are banned from using assisted reproductive technology. In response, some wealthy, single women are traveling abroad to freeze their eggs. In July 2015, one of China's most famous movie stars, Xu Jinglei—who was forty-one at the time—told a Chinese magazine that she had flown to the United States to freeze her eggs. News of Xu's revelation became a hot topic on Weibo and even the infamous male blogger Han Han, known for boasting about his womanizing and sexual conquests, came out in support of Xu's choice. "Isn't it okay to just want a child but not want to marry a man?" he asked, prompting tens of thousands of comments in response.

The eugenic undertones of China's population-planning policies are unmistakable. Even as officials urge college-educated, Han Chinese women to marry and get pregnant, they are discouraging, sometimes through coercion, ethnic minority women they regard as "low quality" (*di suzhi*)—in particular, Uyghur women in the northwest region of Xinjiang—from having more children. Han-dominated China had for decades permitted ethnic minorities living in the countryside to have three children or sometimes more. But the government is now tightening its population-planning restrictions on Uyghur women. In January 2015, a senior Communist Party official in Xinjiang Province, Hou Hanmin, said the government needed to combat "worryingly high birthrates" in southern Xinjiang, according to the *Global Times*. "This negatively affects not only the physical and mental health of children and women, but also the population quality in the region, posing risks to social stability," Hou is quoted as saying.

In November 2015, southern Xinjiang Province doubled payouts to Uyghur couples who agreed to have fewer than their allotted quota of children—to 6,000 renminbi (roughly US$950), according to the *Economist*, which quoted Xinjiang's Party chief as saying the government needed to lower fertility and introduce "a family planning policy 'equal for all ethnic groups,' as part of efforts to fight terrorism." In 2014, southern Xinjiang officials offered cash bonuses to interethnic couples with one Han Chinese partner marrying a member of an ethnic minority group, plus housing, education, and other benefits, in an apparent effort to dilute the Uyghur population.

In addition to cracking down on unapproved births in Xinjiang province, the Communist Party in April 2017 issued a list of banned Muslim baby names, such as Islam and Quran, for all newborns. It banned all Uyghur women from wearing face veils and all young men from growing beards, in the name of fighting "extremism." Xinjiang Province has for many years been the site of Muslim Uyghur uprisings against Han Chinese rule. In July 2017, authorities in Xinjiang invoked "ethnic equality" to announce that they were ending the decades-long policy of allowing Uyghurs and other ethnic minority groups to have one more child than families from the Han majority. An article in the state-run *Global Times* about the policy change quoted Wang Peian of the National Health and Family Planning Commission as saying that southern Xinjiang had serious problems with "poverty, rapid population growth and serious public health deficiency."

Among the majority Han Chinese population, the growing numbers of Chinese women resisting marriage and childbearing pose a challenge to one of the key means of the Party's security apparatus to bring trouble-making citizens into line—by threatening the troublemakers' own spouses, parents, and children and making them responsible for monitoring their relatives. For example, Lu Jun believes that state security agents subjected Wu Rongrong to more severe abuse than the other members of the Feminist Five because she had a husband and child. "It was very easy for the government to use her family members to threaten her. The others were not married and did not have children, so it was much harder for security agents to find something with which to threaten them," says Lu Jun.

When interrogating the unmarried members of the Feminist Five, security agents used the young women's parents to pressure them. The agents exploited their sense of filial duty and preyed on their guilt at being "bad daughters" who would cause their parents great suffering if they did not "confess" their crimes. This strategy was particularly effective with activists such as Zheng Churan, who had a very close relationship with her parents and felt immense guilt at the idea that her feminist activism was imposing undue burdens on them. But for activists who did not feel as bound by traditions of filial piety—such as Li Maizi, who had been abused by her father—it was easier to resist security agents' accusations that she was an "unfilial daughter." Li scoffed at the notion that she should give up her line of work just because her parents did not like it.

The more women are free agents, independent and beholden to no one, the more they can resist and disrupt the patriarchal authoritarian order. Following the release of the Feminist Five, state security agents took the four unmarried women back to their parents' houses—regardless of how many years they had been living independently—and warned the parents that they were responsible for keeping their daughters under control. When Wu Rongrong was taken back to her husband and child, Hangzhou agents specifically threatened her husband, saying that they would "come after him" if his wife engaged in any further feminist activism. *Feminist Voices* founder Lü Pin points out that the persecution of the Feminist Five demonstrates a key strategy in authoritarian "stability maintenance": to exploit the love of "troublemakers" for their family members and enlist entire families into keeping their rebellious relatives under control.

Security agents use such threats against many other activists as well. For example, feminist activist Liang Xiaowen was just twenty-two when she was targeted by a state security sting operation in Guangzhou because she organized a seminar for lawyers at the British Consulate on women's rights and population planning. Late one night in February 2015, a large group of state security agents reached out to the boss of Liang's father, who worked at a wood trading company. The agents made the boss accompany them to barge into Liang's parents' home at midnight, ordering her father to tell her that she must not go through with the event at the British Consulate.

Liang was no longer living with her parents, but she had only just graduated from college, so the agents must have figured that the most effective way to intimidate her was to put pressure on her parents. Liang's father called her after midnight to say that more than ten men—state security agents, the police, and his boss—were at his home. "There are many uncles from the police here right now and they tell me you're organizing an event at the British Consulate," Liang's father told her. "Whatever it is you're planning, you need to cancel."

Liang agreed not to go. A week later, she was "invited" to a formal dinner with security agents, Guangzhou police, her parents, and her father's boss. The state security section chief in Guangzhou presided over the dinner and said that he was formally recognizing Liang Xiaowen as his "Goddaughter." "I will be your Godfather, so if you ever have a problem, you can turn to me for help. Now we're all part of one family!" he announced. A month later, when the Feminist Five were detained, Liang went into hiding. In 2016, she began a master's degree in law at Fordham University in New York.

From the perspective of state security, university students are generally easier to discipline, because Communist Party advisors at their schools can threaten to give them demerits or expel them. For this reason, although state security initially rounded up at least ten feminists on the eve of International Women's Day 2015, the university students—such as Teresa Xu—were released within twenty-four hours and sent back to their universities for further disciplinary measures. Recall that in April 2018, Peking University also pressured the mother of college senior Yue Xin to try to stifle her daughter's #MeToo activism on campus.

In December 2016, President Xi gave a major address to university heads and Communist Party officials, urging them to tighten ideological controls on campus and transform universities into "strongholds of Party leadership." One Party discipline inspector in March 2017 singled out Shantou University in Guangdong Province—which had a vibrant women's studies program and feminist community, as well as a reputable journalism school—for a particularly harsh public warning. Chief Inspector Yang Hanjun said the Communist Party committee at Shantou University was "weak" and "untimely in implementing decisions from the central and provincial Party leadership." He urged the university to more closely monitor teachers' and students' comments in class and on social media, according to the *South China Morning Post*.

Feng Yuan, who has lectured at several universities, says that ideological controls have tightened for all gender studies programs, which had very few resources to begin with and must generally be approved by the All-China Women's Federation. She characterizes the Chinese government's stance on feminism today as "full of contradictions": the Communist Party officially endorses gender equality and wants to demonstrate to the world that it takes gender discrimination seriously. China's desire to be recognized as a major global power is why the government finally enacted its anti–domestic violence law in 2016. But two years after its passage, some of the law's most important provisions—including the issuance of restraining orders against accused perpetrators—have not been properly implemented, according to a study conducted by Feng's group, *Wei Ping* (Equality). Women who seek restraining orders are routinely told to return to their partners to preserve family "harmony" and social stability. Tightening restrictions on NGOs also make it very difficult for victims of domestic violence to seek help. "We can't just rely on slogans, saying 'women and men are equal' without enacting real policies that combat gender inequality," says Feng.

When I first interviewed Feng Yuan in 2012, she said, "There is basically no space for an independent women's movement in China." As long as the Communist Party remains in power, that statement will likely remain true. China's patriarchal security state will not tolerate a large-scale, independent women's movement. But the fact that young feminists have already succeeded in building a community that has mobilized and inspired so many women and girls is astonishing. In spite of China's deeply entrenched gender inequality and the ongoing government crackdown on feminist activism, Feng believes that growing public rights consciousness has helped to create a "richer environment" for women's rights advocacy. "So many people used to think that feminism was unnecessary because the Communist revolution established equality between women and men," she says. "But more people today see that, actually, we have a lot more work to do to improve women's rights."

Now that the government has passed an anti–domestic violence law that makes China look more like a responsible global power, I believe the Communist Party is unlikely to ever enforce the law properly, because keeping the patriarchal family structure intact— even when the woman's life is in danger—is central to political stability and Communist Party survival. By extension, violence against women is an inherent part of China's patriarchal authoritarianism. No matter how brutally oppressed a man is by the state, he can always go home or elsewhere and take his anger out on a woman with impunity. No matter how low the man is in society, the woman attached to him (whether wife or girlfriend) is even lower. As long as the government continues allowing men to abuse women—in the home, on public transportation, or in the workplace—men are more likely to accept a one-party dictatorship.

According to the Chinese government, women must marry men to preserve social stability, provide an outlet for men's violent urges, and perform unpaid labor at home. Women must breed babies to relieve the aging of the population and the shrinking of the workforce (although, as noted, in line with Han Chinese–supremacist eugenics, only educated Han Chinese women are supposed to have more babies). Education is only necessary in order for women to play their proper role as mothers, so that they can build up a highly skilled workforce for China's future. Finally, women must care for the elderly, so the government does not have to spend money on a comprehensive welfare program, and women must nurture the "harmonious family" at the heart of the authoritarian state.

As feminist activists continue to disrupt the patriarchal, authoritarian order, the government will likely find new ways to persecute them. Yet growing numbers of Chinese women now recognize that they deserve to be treated with dignity and are pushing back against gender discrimination, sexual violence and misogyny. They are seizing control of their own reproduction, threatening the population-planning goals that are central to the Chinese Communist Party's strategy for surviving beyond the Soviet Union's seven-decade run. Even if all the feminist activists in China are arrested or otherwise silenced, the forces of resistance they have unleashed will be extremely difficult to stamp out.

Conclusion

A Song for All Women

I met Li Maizi and Teresa Xu for dinner in December 2015, eight months after the release of the Feminist Five, at a hipster café in Beijing's Wangjing neighborhood. They shared a motor scooter and wore industrial-grade pollution masks to screen out the toxic night air. Li had just painted her left-hand nails bright aqua and her right-hand nails bright pink; Teresa wore deep red lipstick. In July 2015—several days after the US Supreme Court's historic ruling legalizing same-sex marriage—Li and Teresa held a wedding ceremony in Beijing to celebrate their union and to protest the ban on same-sex marriage in China. They invited around twenty friends and almost as many journalists, sang "A Song for All Women," and posed for photos kissing in the private room of a Beijing restaurant, decorated with rainbow flags. (They broke up in 2017.)

Li had planned to bring to our meeting two of the red-stained wedding dresses she, Wei Tingting, and Xiao Meili had worn in their "Bloody Brides" protest against domestic violence in 2012. "It's best if I give the wedding gowns to you because I can't leave them in the mainland," she said, knowing that I was talking to Lü Pin of *Feminist Voices* about staging an exhibition in Hong Kong on Chinese feminist activism.

"Once the exhibition is over, will you please take good care of the wedding gowns?" Li said. "Maybe we can donate them to a feminist museum."

I asked her if she really thought she would no longer be able to find any use for the wedding gowns in the mainland. Li looked uncharacteristically dejected.

"There's no space for us to demonstrate in public anymore," she said.

Had she thought about studying abroad?

"Yes, but I'm very conflicted," said Li. "If I leave, what will happen to my work in China?"

These concerns about not wanting to leave the country oppressing them have been shared by famous dissidents, such as the imprisoned Nobel Peace Prize winner Liu Xiaobo—who died of liver cancer in 2017 while still in custody—and famed Russian Nobel laureate Andrei Sakharov, who was called the "voice of conscience" for his resistance to human rights abuses in the Soviet Union. It is extraordinary that Chinese feminists in their twenties would have to confront the same gut-wrenching existential questions and be threatened with charges of "subversion" when the Chinese government itself officially supports gender equality.

I did not end up taking the dresses. But just before New Year's Day, Li Maizi posted pictures of Teresa and another young woman wearing the faux blood-stained wedding gowns on Weibo and WeChat, their faces made up to look bruised and beaten, each carrying a doll also painted with black bruises. This was meant to highlight the problem of abusive ex-husbands kidnapping children from their mothers, as divorce cases in China continue to rise. Most of the children abducted by ex-husbands are sons, who are seen as more important for passing on the family line.

Teresa and the other feminist activist posed on a public street in Beijing, holding two large signs saying, "Marriage may end / Domestic violence does not cease" and "It's a crime to kidnap a child." Li Maizi was not photographed on the scene, but she wrote captions to the photos, explaining that China's new anti–domestic violence legislation failed to protect divorced women and their children from violent ex-husbands. Li had found a way to make use of her wedding gowns after all. She was passing the torch to other activists, so the feminist movement stayed alive.

All of the Feminist Five suffered psychological and, in some cases, physical mistreatment during their detention. Yet despite their ordeals, the women became even more committed to feminist resistance. Even as they struggled with post-traumatic stress and state persecution in the months after their release, they were deeply aware of their critical importance in providing inspiration for other feminists.

Just weeks after authorities released them, Xiao Meili announced a playful competition on Weibo, calling for women to post photos of their unshaven armpits to challenge stereotypes about femininity and celebrate alternative forms of beauty. In June 2015, Xiao announced the winners of the contest. In first place was a graduate student in Hangzhou: none other than Zhu Xixi, who had herself been interrogated by state security agents about her feminist activism. Zhu's winning picture showed her arching her neck in a dancer's arabesque, blissfully smiling with her eyes closed, wearing a sleeveless dress, arms raised to lift up her long hair as she showed off her unshaven armpits. For this honor, Zhu Xixi won a hundred condoms. "I'm even prouder of my armpit hair now," Zhu told reporters.

Even before the contest ended, the photos attracted well over a million views on Weibo. The contest appeared innocuous and apolitical, but left unsaid was the fact that it functioned as an ingenious means of broadcasting images of the five feminist "criminal suspects" beyond China's strict internet censors to a larger audience on Weibo. It held up the Feminist Five as glitteringly appealing role models who loved their bodies and had an irreverent sense of humor.

The woman who tied for the second-place prize (a vibrator) was activist Li Maizi, who posed with her upper body completely nude, lips painted fire-engine red, arms stretched provocatively above her to show small tufts of hair in her armpits, with the Chinese characters for "Armpit Hair is Love / Domestic Violence is a Crime" written in black across her bare breasts.

Tied for third place was the Feminist Five's Wei Tingting. Wei's winning photograph showed her wearing nothing but a bra, smiling triumphantly as she raised her arm in a clenched power fist—the universal sign of resistance to oppression.

Even while Chinese authorities attempt to silence and restrict the movement of activists, China's feminist movement has begun to expand outside its borders, as Wu Rongrong described to me in December 2016. I met with her and Zheng Churan when they were visiting Hong Kong. It was the first time I had seen Wu since just after her release from detention and I was stunned by the marked improvement in her appearance. Her face had lost its puffiness and sallow color, and she exuded radiant energy. As we chatted over a Cantonese dinner, her five-year-old son played under the table.

Wu had resigned herself to being a constant target of state security surveillance, but she was relieved that the Hangzhou police now seemed to be treating her with more respect as they monitored her. She even developed a sense of humor about her surveillance. Just before Hangzhou's G20 summit in September 2016, she received a call from a security agent.

"Wu Rongrong, what are your plans for the G20?" he asked.

"I don't have any plans. Maybe I'll go sightseeing somewhere," Wu replied.

"That's a very good idea. Where would you like to go on vacation? We'll take you."

"Well, my son wants to see Disneyland in Shanghai."

"When would you like to go? The end of August and first week of September are ideal," he said, as though he were a travel agent carrying out a customer's request.

In Shanghai, Wu did not want the agents constantly following her and her child around Disneyland. But she knew that if she complained about their surveillance, the agents would react harshly, so she tried another tactic: flattery.

"My son is such a handful, so I really appreciate having you here to help me take care of him!" she gushed. The agents promptly ran off and left them both alone for the rest of the trip.

Meanwhile, since I was about to move from Hong Kong to New York, Zheng Churan asked if I could bring something to her close friend Liang Xiaowen, the feminist activist who had left Guangzhou to pursue a master's degree in law at Fordham University in New York. Zheng pulled out one of the hairs on her head: a symbol of how much she missed her feminist sister. "There's a saying that one strand of hair contains a person's DNA, so this hair means that I will always be together with Xiaomen [Liang's nickname], even though we are far apart," she said.

By the time I gave Zheng's friendship token to Liang Xiaowen in New York, Liang was already heavily involved with Lü Pin's new US-based group, the Chinese Feminist Collective. She and dozens of other Chinese feminists in the United States converged on Washington, DC, for the January 21, 2017, Women's March, joining several million Americans who protested Donald Trump's inauguration in the largest single-day protest in US history. They posted pictures and videos on WeChat so that their feminist sisters in China could be inspired as well.

Liang led a feminist activism workshop for Chinese women in New York, together with Li Maizi (passing through town on one of her global speaking trips) and two US-based feminists, Liu Xintong and Di Wang. Afterward, Liang, Li, and some other women headed to Trump Tower for a bilingual protest against misogyny and sexual harassment.

Liang spoke at a Chinese women's leadership conference at Barnard College in April 2017, saying that she was "raised in China's feminist movement" and that Chinese women should use their privilege of studying or working in the United States to raise awareness of the government assault on women's rights in China. "Everyone should speak out bravely about feminism in public," she exhorted her mostly female audience, urging them to organize their own Chinese feminist groups at each university campus and send information back to their friends in China.

When Weibo announced a ban on the *Feminist Voices* social media account in February 2017, ostensibly for posting an article about the global women's strike on International Women's Day, Liang, Liu Xintong, and other feminists filmed themselves protesting the ban at Times Square, bandaging their mouths and wrapping themselves with plastic to demonstrate their anger at being silenced. The 2017 ban on *Feminist Voices* lasted only one month, but on the night of March 8, 2018—International Women's Day—Weibo imposed a new ban, which appeared to be permanent when *Betraying Big Brother* went to press. This time, feminist activists inside and outside China (including New York's Central Park) donned multi-colored, carnival-like outfits and masks reminiscent of Russia's Pussy Riot, posting pictures of themselves dancing in "funeral/rebirth ceremonies," waving banners that said, "Feminism will not die!" and "Feminism is immortal!"

"As a woman, I have no country. As a woman, I want no country. As a woman, my country is the whole world," says Lü Pin, quoting Virginia Woolf. She believes that Chinese feminists—whether in China, the United States, or elsewhere—must form alliances that cross national boundaries, or the feminist movement will be unable to sustain itself through the years of uncertainty and peril that lie ahead. As Chinese authorities become increasingly belligerent about shutting down feminist social-media accounts or persecuting individual activists, she sees it as critically important to globalize the feminist movement and "fight on several battle-grounds at the same time."

In addition to the United States, Chinese feminists are building a diaspora in the United Kingdom, Hong Kong, Taiwan, Canada and elsewhere. Wu Rongrong was accepted for a master's program in law at the University of Hong Kong in the spring of 2017, but Chinese authorities at first did not permit her to travel. The Public Security Bureau of her hometown in Shanxi Province rejected her application for a travel permit to Hong Kong, saying that she was banned from leaving China for ten years because of her involvement in "illegal cases yet to be handled." When Wu went to the Shanxi police station to appeal her travel ban, an officer told her, "Don't continue to go to school. What's the point? Go home and live well."

Wu hired a lawyer and filed lawsuits against two county offices of the Shanxi Public Security Bureau, then posted constant pictures and accounts of her arguments with public security officers on Weibo. Finally, just as her classes were beginning at the University of Hong Kong in September 2017, the authorities backed down and gave her a travel permit, allowing her to enroll as a student.

Wang Man pursued an MA in social work at the University of Hong Kong, and Xiao Meili and other feminist activists were planning to apply for overseas study programs. Meanwhile, Peking University was threatening one of its students for her #MeToo activism in April 2018, but many of her classmates and students at other universities continued to resist efforts to stop them from speaking out against sexual violence.

Although the antifeminist crackdown in China had driven some feminists to study or work abroad, very few of the persecuted activists I interviewed said they wanted to give up their activism. In 2017, Bai Fei moved from Shanghai to Beijing to try to set up a feminist bookstore/library there. A popular feminist bookstore/library in Shanghai, *Nüshu Kongjian*, founded by Ying Zhu and managed by Gloria Wang, had been pressured by police surveillance to close down in 2016.

Guangzhou emerged as a feminist epicenter: Wei Tingting moved there from Beijing to work on a new NGO, the Guangzhou Gender and Sexuality Education Center. In September 2017, Wei released a documentary she directed, *Bi China*, about the lives of bisexuals in China. "Gina" moved from Hangzhou to Guangzhou in 2016 and is still deeply involved in feminist organizing.

Li Maizi, the most widely publicized member of the Feminist Five, began an MA program in the theory and practice of human rights at University of Essex in October 2017. She has traveled and given speeches internationally—often in English, which she diligently studied following her release from detention. Li was about to return to Beijing for several months when I had breakfast with her in New York in April 2017. I asked if she was ever nervous about getting arrested again, especially because of her continued, vocal criticism of the government. She said she believed the authorities would not dare arrest her while she was about to start an MA program at a British university, since the Chinese government was trying to project an image of itself as a world leader in higher education.

"Besides, there's just no point in worrying about this—and I'm not going to censor myself," said Li.

Her international speaking trips had taught Li to connect the concerns of Chinese women with those of other women around the world. "The worsening political environment in China is in line with global trends, like Russia inflaming its nationalist populists to strengthen Putin's hold on power. There's this backsliding of democracy around the world," she said. "It's the same in places like Egypt, India, and in the United States with Trump."

Now that Li had received so much publicity, she saw her future role as communicating Chinese feminism to a global audience and helping to build international feminist solidarity. "Our global feminist sisters launched many campaigns—online and offline—to help us in the past, and if we build and sustain international connections, then we can all help each other in the future," she said. "There are so many similar problems facing women all around the world."

Li warned that the Chinese government was becoming increasingly effective at using propaganda on social media to unleash extreme nationalistic, xenophobic, and Islamophobic sentiment among its young people—some of whom would do anything to defend China's reputation from perceived humiliation. Witness the coordinated hostile reaction to Yang Shuping, a Chinese woman who gave a graduation speech at the University of Maryland in May 2017 in which she praised America's clean air and democracy. "The moment I inhaled and exhaled outside the airport, I felt free. … Democracy and freedom are the fresh air that is worth fighting for," Yang told the crowd.

Yang's speech was streamed online and watched by millions of Chinese, some of whom immediately inundated her with vicious online abuse. The *People's Daily* fomented virulent nationalistic anger toward her, personally targeting her in an article with the headline, "Chinese Student at University of Maryland Slammed for Biased Commencement Speech." The article accused her of "playing up the wrong stereotypes about China" and quoted outraged Chinese observers saying things like, "… the false contents (lies) in the speech hurt the feelings of a large group of people and damage the image of a nation."

The *People's Daily* attack opened the floodgates for Weibo users to post much more sexist and abusive comments, such as, "She has an incredible ability to lick feet. Don't worry about coming back to China. Our motherland doesn't need a bitch like you." Yang called the hostile response "deeply disturbing" and posted an apology on Weibo. "I deeply apologize and sincerely hope everyone can understand, [I] have learned my lesson for the future," she wrote.

Li Maizi said that government-orchestrated rabid nationalism online often takes the form of misogynistic abuse and singles out Chinese feminists as being "anti-China" traitors. "Feminists are smeared and slandered as 'foreign forces' to try to turn the people against us," said Li. "This kind of nationalism is likely to get even worse in the future, so our situation is critical." The government has managed to make the term "feminist" so politically sensitive and objectionable that any woman who publicly declares herself to be feminist is making herself vulnerable to a torrent of vicious and sexist online trolling.

Ironically, just as the government is intensifying its crackdown on feminist activism, large corporations are beginning to recognize the commercial power of consumer feminism and tap into China's potentially massive market for brands that represent women's empowerment—in an apolitical way, of course.

In 2016, for example, an emotional ad by the Japanese cosmetics firm SK-II about "leftover" women pushing back against marriage pressure went viral in China, attracting millions of views during its first few days alone. The video, "Marriage Market Takeover," featured real women celebrating their single lifestyles as an alternative to the norm of compulsory marriage. (In full disclosure, I was a consultant for Forsman & Bodenfors, the ad agency that made the video, although I was not told that SK-II was involved.) The online comic Papi Jiang also became a pop-culture feminist in 2016, winning more than 25 million Weibo followers and millions of dollars in company endorsements for her satirical "self-media" (*zi meiti*) videos, which made fun of sexist double standards in Chinese society.

The entertainment industry is beginning to see that it can profit from the enormous demand among young Chinese women for music and films that challenge traditional gender norms. One of China's biggest pop stars is a woman, Li Yuchun (also known as Chris Lee), who cultivates an androgynous image with extremely short hair and oversized trousers, saying that she likes to "go against the traditional," according to the *Guardian*. Her 2016 album *Growing Wild* sold more copies in the first sixteen days after its release than Beyoncé's *Lemonade* during an entire year. She also signed deals with L'Oréal and Gucci and in 2017 became a brand ambassador for Diesel.

Following in Li Yuchun's footsteps, China's newest genderfluid band, Acrush—made up of five young women who present themselves like a "boy band"—attracted more than 750,000 adoring, mostly female fans on Weibo even before they unveiled their first single in April 2017. The name Acrush stands for Adonis, the Greek god, and was the result of a deliberate effort by the pop-music company Zhejiang Huati Culture Media to attract young urban women who reject the cloyingly feminine standards pushed by mainstream Chinese media, according to news reports written about the band's debut. Zhejiang Huati conducted a nationwide talent search for young women who would fit the nonconformist, genderfluid image of the band. "They just enjoy the male appearance, the carefree style, and want to sing like men," CEO Wang Tianhai told the *Guardian*, insisting that the band did not stand for anything political.

The band's hip-hop and rap-influenced debut single was even named "Activist" (*xingdong pai*) (although English translations later used "action" instead). The video features the five women in close-cropped hair, trousers, and leather jackets, one with a baseball cap on backward, dancing while grabbing their crotches. In more ways than one, the song, about smashing barriers imposed by society and the state, is clearly influenced by the language of Chinese feminist activists:

> I refuse to lead an insignificant existence any longer …
> How do I tear off these labels?
> So that I can control my own life? …
> I'm sick of enduring this weakness
> Come back as an activist! …

Lu Keran, a twenty-one-year-old band member who used to be chased out of women's bathrooms for looking like a boy, told the

Guardian, "An important message we want to convey to our fans is that it's important to be true to who you are." The five band members—whose ages range from eighteen to twenty-four—are affectionately called "handsome youths" by their female fans, who scream and shed tears of excitement at the band's public appearances.

But in a reminder of China's extremely restrictive political environment, the five women are reportedly prohibited from talking publicly about their sexual orientations. As Chinese feminist researcher Di Wang points out, although the thousands of people who took part in China's Me Too campaign demonstrate that the general public is increasingly willing to call out sexual harassment, "it has not yet provided a supportive space in which survivors are comfortable disclosing their sexual orientation, gender identity, or gender expression."

Still, China became the world's second-largest movie market in 2012 and there are signs that films about women's empowerment could make record-breaking profits there—if the Chinese government refrains from restricting them. A Bollywood film released in China in May 2017, *Dangal*, was based on the true story of two young Indian women trained by their father to be wrestling champions. One daughter, Geeta, beat up boys who bullied her as a girl, then grew up to become the first Indian woman ever to win a gold medal in wrestling at the Commonwealth Games. The film became a commercial sensation and by October had become one of China's highest-grossing films ever, earning around $200 million at the Chinese box office. The film, directed by Nitesh Tiwari, portrays the women wrestlers challenging the same kinds of gender stereotypes in India that hold women back in China, such as sexist double standards and pressure to marry young.

In June 2017, the Warner Brothers/DC superhero movie *Wonder Woman* opened in theaters around China and made more than $90 million by October, almost one-quarter of its total international box-office earnings, making China by far the movie's biggest market outside the United States. *Wonder Woman*—Hollywood's first blockbuster featuring a female superhero and directed by a woman director, Patty Jenkins—outperformed some other male-led superhero movies on their opening weekends in China, such as *Guardians of the Galaxy* and *Man of Steel*. Chinese film companies Tencent Pictures and Wanda Pictures also invested in the film, according to *China Daily*.

Zheng Churan wrote an interesting essay for *Feminist Voices* in June 2017 about her reaction to *Wonder Woman*. She critiques the film for not meeting her feminist expectations in many ways, such as overemphasizing the sexiness of the Wonder Woman character, Diana, and her romantic relationship with the male lead. But what fascinated me was the second part of her essay, which becomes a feminist manifesto. Despite having outlined what she sees as major flaws of the film, Zheng begins to identify with the demigod Diana. She weeps as Diana fights the boundless cruelty of "mankind" and experiences the same bitter disappointment when Diana's naive hopes about saving humanity from destruction are dashed. "I, too, am a fervently idealistic feminist: I want the emancipation of women, I want gender equality and I want everyone to be able to live free from oppression and cruel mistreatment," writes Zheng.

She sees parallels between Diana's struggle with self-discovery and her own experiences as a persecuted feminist activist in China, realizing with horror that society is far more barbaric than she had initially thought and questioning whether it will ever be possible to rid the world of its ugly, misogynistic violence.

These last few years, so many people keep asking me, how, precisely, will we be able to realize our idealistic goals? Communism? Capitalist, liberal democracy? A feminist utopia? Diana is a demigod, but even she was unable to avoid making many mistakes in her search for an end to the brutality of war. We [feminist activists] are mere mortals, how can any one of us be expected to provide the one and only correct strategy for our long, slow movement?

Zheng writes that every woman has her own unique path to feminist awakening, which may be very slow, with devastating failures along the way. Perhaps we achieve insight through a new gender identity or sexual orientation; perhaps we are victims of traumatic sexual violence. "Our awakening may be accompanied by deep pain, excitement, or terror, until in that flash of enlightenment, the truth bursts forth with savage power," she writes.

Since her release from detention, Zheng has been reading about women's rights movements in other countries. In southern Russia in August 2017, five women who had gathered by the Black Sea to camp and discuss feminism were detained and interrogated by police. Russian police only released the women after they agreed to sign statements saying that they had been warned not to engage in "extremist" activities. In Mexico, dozens of feminist activists have been brutally murdered in retaliation for their advocacy. In Argentina, a series of vicious femicides sparked huge protests in 2015 and reinvigorated the women's movement. In Brazil, there were even more brutal femicides than in Argentina—witness the assassination of Black, lesbian feminist councilwoman Marielle Franco in Rio de Janeiro in March 2018. And, of course, Donald Trump was elected president of the United States.

When Zheng Churan visited New York for the first time, in December 2017, I went with her and activist Liang Xiaowen to a #MeToo protest outside Trump Tower for survivors of sexual violence. We also went out to dinner with several other Chinese feminists and the Egyptian-American feminist Mona Eltahawy, author of *Headscarves and Hymens: Why the Middle East Needs a Sexual Revolution*. During Egypt's 2011 revolution, Mona had been detained, beaten and sexually assaulted by Egyptian security forces, who broke her left arm and right hand. Later, Mona wanted to "celebrate her survival" by getting tattoos on both of her arms. She showed Zheng her tattoos, including the Egyptian goddess Sekhmet—the goddess of retribution and sex, "both of which I want," said Mona. After listening to Mona's story of assault and healing, Zheng reached out and embraced her for a long time, tears streaming down her face.

"Feminists around the world all have their own battles, but whenever there's a crisis, we can stand together and support each other," Zheng said in another one of our conversations. "The forces of authoritarianism and crony capitalism are linking up around the world and getting stronger, so we feminists need to come together too, otherwise we're letting these forces split us apart."

But although Zheng often cracks jokes about the Communist Party, neither she nor any of the feminist activists I know ever calls for the overthrow of the government. "People often talk about what will happen if the Communist Party collapses, but even if the Party falls, we will still have to face these male chauvinist leaders and the patriarchy," says Zheng. "We have to preserve and sustain our strength over many years."

Some Chinese feminists—including Zheng, who believes that capitalism inherently exploits women—lament the fact that their originally radical message about fighting women's oppression is being co-opted by corporations selling an apolitical form of consumer feminism. Yet Lü Pin argues that the new corporate interest in feminism in China might, paradoxically, help keep the political movement alive. "It's not necessarily a bad thing if corporations want to capitalize on the huge market for feminism in China; they use us, but we can also use them," she says. "When the government wants to silence us, [corporate feminism] may help us to get our message out and expands the space for the discussion of women's rights." She cites a Chinese idiom: "The pond that is too clean has no fish" (*chi zhi qing ze wu yu*), which she takes to mean that a movement cannot survive if it is too ideologically pure. "No institution will ever be 100 percent feminist, and intellectuals who do nothing but criticize others can never bring about a revolution, because they are incapable of making compromises or cooperating with other people," she says. "As activists, we have to work in the real world and solve real problems."

Lü Pin describes the antifeminist crackdown as "loose on the outside, tight on the inside" (*wai song nei jin*), meaning that the authorities want to give the world the impression that they are not too repressive, but that their aim is to wipe out the feminist movement entirely. She foresees an extremely difficult battle in the years ahead, perhaps driving all feminist activists independent of the Communist Party entirely underground.

"We must out-survive our enemies," says Lü Pin.

As I finish this book in April 2018, it is impossible to predict whether China's nascent feminist movement will be able to survive. In the long run, feminism may eventually triumph and lead to a more open society. Years from now, the detention of the Feminist Five may be regarded as a critical turning point in the history of organized resistance to the patriarchal, authoritarian rule of the Communist Party.

China's male rulers see gendered oppression as crucial for the future of their dictatorship, but feminism—which demands that women control their own bodies and reproduction—is in direct conflict with the eugenic, pro-natalist, population-planning goals of the Chinese state. As China's demographic challenges become more acute and the battle for Communist Party survival more fraught in coming years, the crackdown on feminism is likely to intensify.

Indeed, the backlash against feminism might escalate not just in China, but around the world. According to the Freedom House, democracy faced its most serious crisis in decades in 2017, as the United States ceded its global leadership role to a rising China, while misogynistic autocrats bent on rolling back women's rights were emboldened in countries from Russia to Hungary and Turkey.

In this time of crisis, how should we respond to rising authoritarianism in China and around the world—including the United

States? By fighting the patriarchy. Supporting feminist activists and promoting women's rights are the most effective way to stop the growing, misogynistic assault on democratic freedoms globally.

In the video for "A Song for All Women," the song with which this book began, Zheng Churan stands barefoot on a beach in southern China, holding her sandals in her hands. The ocean waves crash beside her, leaving trails of white foam as she sings of her longing for freedom from abuse. The video moves between the five feminists in Beijing, Hangzhou, and Guangzhou, singing of women rising up against their oppression.

> We believe in a world with equality.
> This is a song of freedom and dignity.
> Will you join me
> In the long fight for our rights?
> I want to go out without fear.
> I want to be beautiful without being harassed.

Under close surveillance by the security state, the Feminist Five sing of their innocence and of a menacing male predator:

> Wake up from your sleep! Seize him.
> I am not the one who committed a crime.

Wei Tingting and Wang Man, filmed in a lush bamboo grove in Beijing, defy sexist caricatures of feminists as ugly, humorless prudes:

> I sing for myself
> Not for your judgment.

Wu Rongrong sings from a green garden in Hangzhou:

> I have brilliant dreams
> And deep desires.

The song closes with Zheng Churan sitting beside Li Maizi, the two of them smiling and celebrating their spiritual liberation:

> Faced with suspicion and ridicule
> Hardship has made me grow stronger.

An anonymous interviewer asks the women about their lives after detention, with the rousing melody playing in the background as the young activists poke fun at themselves and the security state that persecutes them.

"Now that I've lost my job, I get kind of bored sitting around at home every day," says Wei.

Li jokes about the confiscation of her passport and the loss of her job. "Drop the charges already! When am I getting my passport back?"

Zheng quips, deadpan, "After my rights organization was closed down, I changed careers. Now I have become an unsuccessful businesswoman."

The video concludes with a slow-motion montage of all five women laughing, finding joy in solidarity, refusing to submit to their oppressors. Before it fades to black, the women flex their biceps and flash the V-for-victory sign. Li looks straight into the camera and announces with unalloyed confidence: "I believe that China's feminist movement will grow stronger and stronger."

Li Maizi, Zheng Churan, Wei Tingting, Wu Rongrong, and Wang Man are shown as opponents of patriarchy, singing to women across the country, "Wake up from your sleep!" Through song, they have transformed themselves from ordinary human beings—who can be crushed by the security state's brutal intrusion into their daily lives—into avenging angels calling on all women to resist oppression. They have faced the world's most powerful authoritarian regime, yet they have persisted and, so far, prevailed. Despite the government's attempts to silence them, China's Feminist Five have become a kind of incandescent myth, soaring like the legendary bird Jingwei, determined—no matter how long it takes—to fill the sea.

Acknowledgments

To everyone who told me their stories: I hope that I have done you justice and not fallen short in trying to make some sense of this complicated moment in China's history. I am especially indebted to Lü Pin, Zheng Churan, Li Maizi, Wu Rongrong, Wei Tingting, Wang Man, Teresa Xu, Lu Jun, Xiao Meili, Zhang Leilei, Zhu Xixi, "Gina," Liu Wei, Li Yuan, Feng Yuan, Liang Xiaowen and Han Dongfang. The people I named in this book represent only a tiny part of China's feminist movement, and I hope that many more will write about the movement in years to come.

I am grateful to my conscientious editor, Audrea Lim, who recognized the importance of this book and suggested imaginative ways to improve it. I thank the team at Verso Books, in particular, my copy editor, Sarah Grey; production editor, Duncan Ranslem; publicist, Emily Janakiram; and US marketing manager, Anne Rumberger.

I was very fortunate to receive the invaluable comments of Eileen Chow, who generously critiqued the first and final drafts of my manuscript. I am also grateful to Lisa Estreich for her insightful comments on several of my chapters.

I am indebted to Dorothy Ko, who recommended me for a 2016

Mellon visiting professorship at Columbia University, where I developed ideas for this book. Thank you to the Weatherhead East Asian Institute at Columbia University for inviting me to give a talk in March 2016, "Gender and Social Control in the Era of Xi Jinping," in which I presented some of my early ideas on China's patriarchal authoritarianism.

A huge thank you to my agent, Marysia Juszczakiewicz, for believing in me. Thank you, Mona Eltahawy, for your passionate encouragement of this book and for showing me how to let go of my fears. Thank you, Rebecca Karl, for your brilliant scholarship and incredible support for my work.

Some parts of this book appear in a different form in op-eds I have written. Thank you, Karen Attiah, who edited my 2018 *Washington Post* op-ed, "Xi Jinping's authoritarian rise in China has been powered by sexism," and Stéphanie Giry, who edited my 2018 *New York Times* op-ed, "China dropped its one-child policy. So why aren't more Chinese women having babies?" Thank you, Hannah Bloch and Alex Leff, who edited my 2018 NPR op-ed, "China is attempting to muzzle #MeToo." Thank you to Kaavya Asoka and Sarah Leonard for inviting me to contribute an article, "China's Feminist Five," for the fall 2016 issue of *Dissent* magazine. Thank you, Anna Leach, for editing my 2016 *Guardian* op-ed, "How Chinese feminists can inspire women to stand up to Trump." Thank you, Nancy Naples, for inviting me to write "Feminism, Chinese" for *The Wiley Blackwell Encyclopedia of Gender and Sexuality Studies* and Jeffrey Wasserstrom, for inviting me to contribute to *Dissent* magazine in 2013.

I am indebted to Didi Kirsten Tatlow, whose excellent reporting on feminist activism in China was a great resource for me, and who introduced me to the incredible anti–domestic violence advocate Kim Lee. I am grateful to all of my professors at Tsinghua University's Department of Sociology, where I did my PhD research. I am grateful to the co-founder and editor of WAGIC.com and the Twitter account @halfthesky49, Séagh Kehoe.

So many people have helped me in various ways to persevere in my work on China, when I thought of giving up. I am especially grateful to Stephanie Kleine-Ahlbrandt, Oscar Alcantara, Ted Anthony, Alec Ash, Bao Pu, Angie Baecker, Sophie Beach, Sarabeth Berman, Bill Bishop, Laurel Bowman, Tania Branigan, Adam Brookes, Julia Broussard, Melindah Bush, Melissa Chan, Yuen Chan, Elaine Chen, Chen Yaya, Renee Chiang, Farai Chideya, Mike Chinoy, Joanna Chiu, Lenora Chu, Clifford Coonan, Heather Cross, Kath Cummins, Maura Cunningham, Deborah Davis, Rangita de Silva de Alwis, Julia Famularo, Mei Fong, Howard French, Paul French, Michelle Garnaut, Bonnie Glaser, Jeremy Goldkorn, Jorge Guajardo, Paul Haenle, Elizabeth Haenle, Jane Hayward, Gail Hershatter, Albert Ho Chun-yan, Hanson Hong Fincher, Mara Hvistendahl, Denise Hyland, Susie Jakes, Sarah Jones, Jan Kiely, Deborah Krisher-Steele, Suzanne Kuai, Kaiser Kuo, Shiamin Kwa, Elizabeth LaCouture, Indira Lakshmanan, Christina Larson, Susan Lawrence, Ching Kwan Lee, Kim Lee, Louisa Lim, Lydia H. Liu, Jonathan Man Ho-ching, Lu Miaoqing, Kristie Lu Stout, Melissa Ludtke, Elizabeth Lynch, Darcy Mackay, Rebecca Mackinnon, Evan Medeiros, Judy Melinek, Trey Menefee, Carl Minzner, T.J. Mitchell, David Moser, Tamara Nopper, Brendan O'Kane, Evan Osnos, Eileen Otis, Malin Oud, James Palmer, Pan Yue, Brenda Pitts, Vivien Pong, Oliver Radtke, Melissa Rayworth, Maguena Reimers-Fincher, Sophie Richardson, Bernice Romero, Robert Rutledge, Paola Sada, Sarah Schafer, David Schlesinger, Andrew Shaw, Peggy Shaw, June Shih, Victor Shih, Christoph Steinhardt, Dermot Tatlow, Nora Tejada, Kate Threlfall, Kirk Troy, Kellee Tsai, Anne Tumlinson, Corinne Vigniel, Gloria Wang, Alice Wong, Minky Worden, Wang Yajuan, Yan Hongjun, Charlotte Yang, Xu Xi, Zeng Jinyan, Tianqi (Kiki) Zhao and Ying Zhu.

I am grateful to the Chinese Feminist Collective. The Human Rights in China timeline on events related to the arrest of the Feminist Five was a great resource for me. Thank you to everyone who invited me to give talks or attended talks on my first book, *Leftover Women: The Resurgence of Gender Inequality in China*. Thank you to everyone who ever cited me or expressed support for my work on social media.

I thank my mother, Beverly Hong-Fincher, for being the very definition of a feminist pioneer. Thank you to my late father, John Fincher.

I thank my children, Aidan and Liam, for bringing me so much joy. I hope that you will keep trying to make the world a better place as you grow up.

Finally, I am grateful to my husband, Mike Forsythe. Thank you for your sharp editing, cheerleading, friendship and unwavering faith in me over the years.

Notes

On the night of March 8, 2018, International Women's Day, censors banned the Weibo account of *Feminist Voices* and the following day, WeChat erased *Feminist Voices*. Many of the online essays I refer to came from *Feminist Voices* and state media are constantly deleting posts, so I have only provided some of the online links in my notes. Most of my information comes from personal interviews, which I recorded, but in some cases I have supplemented these with secondary sources, for which I have provided notes. I have tried to be conscientious in my fact checking and any errors are entirely my own.

Epigraph

p. vi Qiu Jin, "Excerpts from *Stones of the Jingwei Bird*," in *Writing Women in Modern China: An Anthology of Women's Literature from the Early Twentieth Century*, edited by Amy D. Dooling and Kristina M. Torgeson (New York: Columbia University Press, 1998), 45.

Introduction

p. 1 "a cappella in Chinese." This passage appeared in a different form in Leta Hong Fincher, "How Chinese Feminists Can Inspire

Women to Stand Up to Trump," *Guardian*, November 23, 2017, theguardian.com.

p. 1 "A Song for All Women" is my translation of their song, *Nüren zhi ge*. The Youtube of their song, posted six months after the release of the Feminist Five, is titled "Do You Hear The Women Sing." Also see Conclusion: A Song for All Women.

p. 2 "Xi hosting a meeting on women's rights at the UN while persecuting feminists? Shameless." @HillaryClinton, tweet, 7:39 a.m., September 27, 2015.

p. 3 "The proletariat supports you!" Some of these posts have been translated and preserved at Wei Zhili, "Free the Women's Day Five! – Statements from Chinese workers and students," Nao's blog, March 13, 2015, libcom.org.

p. 4 "rest of his life." Parts of these passages appeared before in Leta Hong Fincher, "Xi Jinping's Authoritarian Rise in China Has Been Powered by Sexism," *Washington Post*, March 1, 2018, washingtonpost.com.

p. 5 "from taking off." Mimi Lau and Mandy Zuo, "#MeToo? Silence, Shame and the Cost of Speaking Out about Sexual Harassment in China," *South China Morning Post*, December 8, 2017, scmp. com; Merriam-Webster, "Word of the Year 2017: 'Feminism' Is Our 2017 Word of the Year," n.d., accessed February 16, 2018, merriam-webster.com.

p. 5 "wear on the streets." Qiao Long, "Chinese Feminists Forced to Leave City Ahead of Fortune Global Forum," *Radio Free Asia*, December 1, 2017, translated and edited by Luisetta Mudle, rfa.org.

p. 5 "violated regulations." Jiayun Feng, "WeChat Censors Victim of Sexual Harassment in Shanghai, Who Is Criticized for 'Overreacting,'" *SupChina*, November 30, 2017, supchina.com.

p. 6 "70,000 followers on WeChat." Jiayun Feng, "Chinese Social Media Censors Feminist Voices," *SupChina*, March 9, 2018, supchina.com.

p. 6 "in 1949." These and some other passages in the book appeared in a different form in Leta Hong Fincher, "China's Feminist Five," *Dissent*, Fall 2016, dissentmagazine.org.

p. 6 "in the 1990s, gender inequality deepened" See also Isabelle Attané, "Being a Woman in China Today: A Demography of Gender,"

China Perspectives 4 (2012): 5–16. Philip N. Cohen and Wang Feng, "Market and Gender Pay Equity: Have Chinese Reforms Narrowed the Gap?" in *Creating Wealth and Poverty in Postsocialist China*, edited by Deborah S. Davis and Wang Feng (Palo Alto: Stanford University Press, 2009).

p. 6 "worth around 3.3 times China's gross domestic product," Zhang Zhi Ming, Dilip Shahani and Keith Chan, "China's Housing Concerns," HSBC Global Research Report, June 7, 2010, p. 5. The value of China's residential real estate surpassed 3.27 times China's GDP, at RMB 109 trillion, in February 2010.

p. 6 "end of 2017." Based on 3.3 times China's GDP at the end of 2017, around RMB 273 trillion, which is equivalent to around US$43 trillion.

p. 6 "gender wealth gap." Leta Hong Fincher, *Leftover Women: The Resurgence of Gender Inequality in China* (London: Zed, 2014).

p. 8 "'extreme' political positions." Emily Rauhala, "Chinese State Media Attacks Taiwan's President for Being a Single Woman," *Washington Post*, May 25, 2016, washingtonpost.com.

p. 8 "leaked censorship directive." Anne Henochowicz, "Minitrue: Delete Op-Ed on Tsai Ing-wen," *China Digital Times*, May 25, 2016, chinadigitaltimes.net.

p. 9 "enacted in 2016." Fincher, *Leftover Women*.

p. 13 "reproductive tools to realize the nation's development goals." Susan Greenhalgh, "Fresh Winds in Beijing: Chinese Feminists Speak Out on the One-Child Policy and Women's Lives," *Signs* 26, no. 3 (2001): 847–86.

Chapter 1. China's Feminist Five

p. 16 "Prison Notes," Wei Tingting, "What Happened on March 7," *Yuzhong zhaji*, Prison Notes (3).

p. 16 "singing songs," The essay posted on WeChat has since been deleted. Here is a scholarly essay she wrote, which refers to her detention: Tingting Wei, "A Look at the Beijing Conference Through Lesbian Eyes," *Asian Journal of Women's Studies* 21, no. 3 (2015): 316–25.

p. 19 "to protect the national interest." Didi Kirsten Tatlow, "Women in China Face Rising University Entry Barriers," *New York Times*, October 7, 2012, nytimes.com.

p. 19 "while taking the subway." Xinhua, "Chinese Public Calls for Harsher Sexual Harassment Penalties," *XinhuaNet*, August 22, 2017, xinhuanet.com.

p. 23 "do farm work." Viola Zhou, "How One of China's 'Feminist Five' is Fighting for Women's Rights, Even After Jail," *Inkstone*, March 8, 2018, inkstonenews.com.

p. 23 "each day was meaningful" ... "show my face in the village" ... "fruit knife for self-defense" Wu Rongrong, "How I Became a Women's Rights Advocate," *China Change*, April 27, 2015, chinachange.org.

p. 23 "Beijing Aizhixing Institute," Aizhixing meaning "love, knowledge and action," a play on the Chinese name for AIDS "ai zi bing."

p. 24 "wad of cash." Sophie Beach, "Deng Yujiao Tells Her Story; Protesters Express Support," *China Digital Times*, May 25, 2009, chinadigitaltimes.net.

p. 24 "threatened with rape," Cai Ke, "Waitress Who Killed Official Spared Jail," *China Daily*, June 17, 2009, Document5chinadaily.com. cn.

p. 24 "embezzled money?" Bob Chen, "China: Netizens Stand with the Waitress Who Killed an Ofiicial," *GlobalVoices*, May 17, 2009, globalvoices.org. The original Chinese blog post has been deleted.

p. 24 "for your dignity," Raymond Li, "Mixed Opinions on Deng Yujiao Verdict," *South China Morning Post*, June 17, 2009, scmp.com.

p. 30 "a huge revelation!" Wang Man spoke to Didi Kirsten Tatlow of the *New York Times* in 2013 about the limitations of the "leftover" woman label. "Rejecting the 'Leftover Women' Label," *New York Times*, April 23, 2013, nytimes.com.

Chapter 2. The Internet and Feminist Awakening

p. 16 "Wang Man." Eric Fish, "Interview: Masked Chinese Activists 'Show Solidarity' with Detained Feminists," Asia Society blog, April 7, 2015, asiasociety.org/blog.

p. 34 "by the police." Rebecca Mackinnon, *Consent of the Networked: The Worldwide Struggle for Internet Freedom* (New York: Basic Books, 2012).

p. 35 "Libcom.org." Wei Zhili, "Free the Women's Day Five! – Statements from Chinese workers and students," Nao's blog, March 13, 2015, libcom.org.

p. 35 "All-China Women's Federation." Didi Kirsten Tatlow, "Supporters of Detained Feminists in China Petition for Their Release," *New York Times* Sinosphere blog, April 1, 2015, sinosphere.blogs.nytimes.com.

p. 36 "more than a thousand." Edward Wong, "China Locks Down Restive Region After Deadly Clashes," *New York Times*, July 6, 2009, nytimes.com.

p. 37 "and pounced." Gady Epstein, "Sina Weibo," *Forbes*, March 3, 2011, forbes.com.

p. 37 "around the world." CIW Team, "Weibo's Monthly Active Users Reached 392 Million in 2017," *China Internet Watch*, March 19, 2018, chinainternetwatch.com.

p. 39 "into marriage." Leta Hong Fincher, "China's 'Leftover' Women," *Ms.* magazine blog, November 12, 2011, msmagazine.com/blog.

p. 40 "Who Are China's Weibo Superstars?" by Helier Cheung, *BBC News*, November 29, 2013, bbc.com.

p. 42 "wealth of China's top leaders." Tania Branigan, "China Blocks Bloomberg for Exposing Financial Affairs of Xi Jinping's Family," *Guardian*, June 29, 2012, theguardian.com; Tania Branigan, "New York Times Blocked by China After Report on Wealth of Wen Jiabao's Family," *Guardian*, October 26, 2012, theguardian.com.

p. 45 "a divorce." Li Ying, "*Wo kan hunyinfa sifa jieshi san*" [My view of the Marriage Law, judicial interpretation (3)], August 8, 2011, lady.163.com.

p. 45 "burgeoning interest in feminist ideas" See Lü Pin's online essay, "*Xingbie geming buhui shi tanhua yi xian*" [The Gender Revolution Is Not Just a Flash in the Pan] available at lady.163.com.

p. 46 "passionate student." Sun Yat-sen petition (translation originally by Wei Zhili, with some polishing by me): Wei Zhili, "Free the Women's Day Five! – Statements from Chinese workers and students," Nao's blog, March 13, 2015, libcom.org.

p. 49 "too weak in their political work," Viola Zhou, "Chinese Universities Encourage Professors, Students to Post Online Content That Promotes 'Socialist Values,'" *South China Morning Post*, September 21, 2017, scmp.com.

p. 50 "with the Han Chinese." Séagh Kehoe, "Plateau Redness and the Politics of Beauty in Contemporary Tibet," Kehoe's website, March 24, 2016, seaghkehoe.com.

p. 51 "were shut down." Dilnur Reyhan, "'Mothers Who Educate': Uyghur Women's Activities in Digital Space," Women and Gender in China, September 25, 2017, wagic.org.

p. 52 "lax security and customer service." Joanna Chiu, "For Chinese Victims of Sexual Assault, 'Going Viral' Is Best Revenge," *Foreign Policy*, April 15, 2018, foreignpolicy.com.

p. 53 "text messages to women." Zhang Liping, "Bank Investigates Allegations of Suggestive Texts to Interns," *Sixth Tone*, May 27, 2017, sixthtone.com.

p. 53 "too tightly controlled." Lü Pin, "Will China Have Its #MeToo Moment?" Amnesty International, November 24, 2017, amnesty.org.

p. 53 "conducting similar investigations." Jodi Kantor and Megan Twohey, "Harvey Weinstein Paid Off Sexual Harassment Accusers for Decades," *New York Times*, October 5, 2017, nytimes.com; Ronan Farrow, "From Aggressive Overtures to Sexual Assault: Harvey Weinstein's Accusers Tell Their Stories," *New Yorker*, October 23, 2017, newyorker.com.

p. 53 "China's all-male rulers." Leta Hong Fincher, "China Is Attempting To Muzzle #MeToo," NPR, February 1, 2018, npr.org.

p. 53 "gender inequality and repression," Lü Pin, "What is the significance of China's #MeToo Movement?" *China File*, March 20, 2018, chinafile.com.

p. 54 "hostile foreign forces." Xiao Meili, "Who Are the Young Women Behind the '#MeToo in China' Campaign? An Organizer Explains," *China Change*, March 27, 2018.

p. 54 "We call for more men to pay attention to the situation of their sisters." English translation of the factory woman's essay by Jiayun Feng, "I am a Woman Worker at Foxconn and I Demand a System that Opposes Sexual Harassment," *SupChina*, January 26, 2018, supchina.com.

p. 54 "evade the internet monitors." Maura Elizabeth Cunningham and Jeffrey Wasserstrom, "Want Insight into China's Political Situation? Keep an Eye on New Animal Memes," *Los Angeles Times*, March 8, 2018, latimes.com.

p. 55 "deprived of medical treatment." Chris Buckley, "Liu Xiaobo, Chinese Dissident Who Won Nobel While Jailed, Dies at 61," *New York Times*, July 13, 2017, nytimes.com.

p. 55 "digital dictatorship." Li Yuan, "Stranger Than Science Fiction: The Future for Digital Dictatorships," *Wall Street Journal*, March 1, 2018, wsj.com.

p. 56 "from my phone and computer," Samuel Wade, "Translation: Open Letter on PKU #MeToo Case," *China Digital Times*, April 23, 2018, chinadigitaltimes.net.

p. 56 "foreign forces." Samuel Wade, Josh Rudolph, Sandra Severdia and Ya Ke Xi, "Translation: Yue Xin 'On the Week Since My Open Letter' (Full Text)," *China Digital Times*, May 1, 2018, chinadigitaltimes.net.

p. 56 "what are you actually afraid of?" Yanan Wang, "Outrage in China Over Pressure on Student to Stop Activism," *Associated Press*, April 25, 2018, ap.org.

p. 56 "surveillance cameras" "Peking University installs new surveillance cameras to monitor bulletin boards where anonymous #metoo poster was found two days ago." @ShawnWZhang, tweet, 9:48am, April 26, 2018.

p. 56 "social media accounts," Samuel Wade, "Minitrue: Do Not Report on PKU Open Letter," *China Digital Times*, April 25, 2018, chinadigitaltimes.net.

Chapter 3. Detention and Release

p. 60 "human rights review." Didi Kirsten Tatlow, "Activist's Death Questioned as U.N. Considers Chinese Rights Report," *New York Times* Sinosphere blog, March 19, 2014, sinosphere.blogs.nytimes.com.

p. 62 "detain Wang Man," Human Rights in China, "Supporting Women's Rights in China," April 14, 2016, hrichina.org.

Chapter 4. Your Body Is a Battleground

p. 79 "expose private parts," Qian Jinghua, "1 in 3 Chinese College Students Sexually Harassed, Survey Says," *Sixth Tone*, September 26, 2016, sixthtone.com.

p. 79 "from a manager or co-worker." Jiayun Feng, "More Than 80 Percent of Female Journalists in China Face Sexual Harassment in the Workplace," *SupChina*, March 7, 2018, supchina.com.

p. 79 "had been sexually harassed," China Labour Bulletin, "Up to 70 Percent of Women Factory Workers in Guangzhou Sexually Harassed," December 6, 2013, clb.org.hk.

p. 80 "*Wei Ping* (Equality)" Equality-Beijing NGO observation of two-year implementation of the anti-domestic violence law, March 6, 2018.

p. 87 "suffering prolonged abuse." Didi Kirsten Tatlow, "Chinese Courts Turn a Blind Eye to Abuse," *New York Times*, January 29, 2013, nytimes.com.

p. 87 "try to 'bear it.'" Didi Kirsten Tatlow, "China, in Suspending Woman's Death Sentence, Acknowledges Domestic Abuse," *New York Times*, April 24, 2014, nytimes.com.

p. 88 "Painful Words," Dan Avery, "Gays and Lesbians Wear Their Tormentors' Words on Their Bodies in Emotional Photography Exhibit," *Logo*, November 10, 2015, newnownext.com.

p. 92 "People's Liberation Army generals." Lynn Elber, "Bai Ling Reveals Dark Memories of Chinese Army," *San Diego Union-Tribune*, July 1, 2011, sandiegouniontribune.com.

p. 92 "delegation visiting China." Rachel Leung, "#MeToo Movement Unearths Heartbreaking Reality of Sexual Assault in Hong Kong," *South China Morning Post*, December 8, 2017, scmp.com.

p. 92 "on a business trip" … "destroying their careers" Catherine Lai, "No #MeToo in China? Female Journalists Face Sexual Harassment, But Remain Silent," *Hong Kong Free Press*, December 5, 2017, hongkongfp.com.

p. 94 "in their lifetime." United Nations Secretary-General's Campaign to End Violence Against Women, "About UNITE: Human Rights Violation," available at un.org/en/women/endviolence/situation. shtml.

p. 95 "an intimate partner." Emma Fulu, Xian Warner, Stephanie Miedma, Rachel Jewkes, Tim Roselli and James Lang, "Why Do Some Men Use Violence Against Women and How Can We Prevent It?" Partners for Prevention, report, September 2013, partners4prevention.org.

p. 95 "economic reforms of the 1980s and 90s." For recent books on the lifestyles of young people, see Zak Dychtwald, *Young China: How the Restless Generation will Change their Country and the World* (New York: St. Martin's Press, 2018); Alec Ash, *Wish Lanterns: Young Lives in New China* (London: Picador, 2017); Jemimah Steinfeld, *Little Emperors and Material Girls: Youth and Sex in Modern China* (London: I.B. Tauris, 2015); Eric Fish, *China's Millennials: The Want Generation* (London: Rowman & Littlefield, 2015).

p. 96 "agree with sex before marriage." Xinhua, "Over 70 pct Chinese University Students Agree with Sex Before Marriage: Survey," *XinhuaNet*, September 26, 2016, xinhuanet.com.

p. 97 "I began to see clearly" … "long-distance walks across China," Xiao Meili, "China's Feminist Awakening," *New York Times*, May 13, 2015, nytimes.com.

p. 102 "and then surveilling them." Human Rights Watch, "China: Police 'Big-Data' Systems Violate Privacy, Target Dissent," press release, November 19, 2017, hrw.org.

p. 104 "why the Feminist Five were arrested?" Parts of her original Chinese account were later translated and posted here (but the translation differs from mine): translation by Peng X, "Drinking Tea with China's 'National Treasure': Five Questions," August 28, 2017, chuangcn.org.

p. 105 "Leads protesters to prison under escort." Pussy Riot, "Punk Prayer," English translation via Genius.com, n.d., accessed February 4, 2018, available at genius.com/1001369.

Chapter 5. Jingwei Fills the Sea

p. 107 "Gina (a pseudonym)," Gina requested a pseudonym because she works full-time as a feminist activist and continues to face frequent persecution from Chinese state security.

p. 108 "prose and sung poetry" "Excerpts from *Stones of the Jingwei Bird*," in *Writing Women in Modern China*, edited by Dooling and Torgeson, 41.

p. 108 "capsized her boat and drowned her." Xin Ran, *Message From an Unknown Chinese Mother: Stories of Loss and Love*, translated by Nicky Harman (New York: Scribner, 2010), 163–4.

p. 109 "Chinese women, arise!" ... "they reconsolidate the nation." "Excerpts from *Stones of the Jingwei Bird*," in *Writing Women in Modern China*, edited by Dooling and Torgeson, 45.

p. 109 "*Stones of the Jingwei Bird*." Also see Louise Edwards, *Gender, Politics and Democracy: Women's Suffrage in China* (Palo Alto: Stanford University Press, 2008).

p. 109 "a bold feminist heroine," Amy Qin, "Qiu Jin: A Feminist Poet and Revolutionary Who Became a Martyr Known as China's 'Joan of Arc,'" *New York Times*, January 20, 2018.

pp. 110–11 "*The Birth of Chinese Feminism*" ... "save the motherland" ... "critical to the household economy." Lydia H. Liu, Rebecca E. Karl, and Dorothy Ko, eds., *The Birth of Chinese Feminism: Essential Texts in Transnational Theory* (New York: Columbia University Press, 2013), 29–30, 78, 31.

p. 111 "historians Dorothy Ko and Wang Zheng." Dorothy Ko and Zheng Wang, eds., *Translating Feminisms in China* (Hoboken, NJ: Wiley-Blackwell, 2007), 4.

p. 112 "modernizing Qing Dynasty institutions." Mizuyo Sudo, "Concepts of Women's Rights in Modern China," *Gender and History* 18, no. 3 (November 2006): 472–89.

p. 112 "in civilized nations" ... "Such happiness and ease!" ... "with feminism?" Translated by Michael Gibbs Hill, edited by Tze-lan D. Sang, in Liu, Karl, and Ko, *Birth of Chinese Feminism*, 208, 2.

p. 113 "hyphenated name of He-Yin." Rebecca E. Karl, "Feminism and Reconceptualizing History: A Brief Comment," *WAGIC: Women and Gender in China*, March 14, 2018, wagic.org.

p. 113 "brief run of their journal" ... "women as private property." Liu, Karl, and Ko, *Birth of Chinese Feminism*, 51, 2.

p. 113 "would no longer be necessary." He-Yin Zhen, "The Feminist Manifesto," translation by Meng Fan and Cynthia M. Roe, in *Birth of Chinese Feminism*, edited by Liu, Karl, and Ko, 184.

p. 114 "China's traumatized self-consciousness." Rey Chow, *Woman and Chinese Modernity: The Politics of Reading Between West and East* (Minneapolis: University of Minnesota Press, 1991), 170.

p. 114 "urban and middle class." Ko and Wang, *Translating Feminisms in China*, 8.

p. 114 "Nora's slamming door." Susan L. Glosser, *Chinese Visions of Family and State, 1915–1953* (Berkeley: University of California Press, 2003), 9.

p. 115 "equal rights in society." This translation of Lu Xun's "What Happens After Nora Leaves Home?" is from *Women in Republican China: A Sourcebook*, edited by Hua R. Lan and Vanessa L. Fong (Oxon: Routledge, 2015), 178–9.

p. 115 "free will in death by suicide" ... "sprouting of small Communist groups across China," Rebecca E. Karl, *Mao Zedong and China in the Twentieth-Century World* (Durham, NC: Duke University Press, 2010).

pp. 116–17 "secret meetings in 1921" ... "to extract themselves" ... "Shanghai Federation of Women's Circles." Christina Kelley Gilmartin, *Engendering the Chinese Revolution: Radical Women, Communist Politics, and Mass Movements in the 1920s* (Berkeley: University of California Press, 1995), 50–2.

p. 117 "than as a political institution," Ibid., 101.

p. 117 "the word 'proletariat' in Chinese." Ibid., 57.

p. 117 "a more important position than her husband." Ibid., 68.

p. 118 "May Thirtieth Incident," Ibid., 133.

p. 118 "primacy of economic class oppression over gender exploitation" ... "avoid antagonizing the heavily patriarchal male peasants." Ibid., 215.

p. 119 "'women's liberation' (*funü jiefang*)." Ko and Wang, *Translating Feminisms in China*, 6.

p. 119 "wouldn't hurt anybody." Ding Ling, "Miss Sophia's Diary," in

I Myself am a Woman: Selected Writings of Ding Ling, edited by Tani Barlow with Gary J. Bjorge (Boston: Beacon Press, 1989), 55.

pp. 119–20 "associating it with lips (labia)" … "equal opportunity to participate in public labor." Lydia H. Liu, "Invention and Intervention: The Female Tradition in Modern Chinese Literature," in *Chinese Femininities, Chinese Masculinities*, edited by Susan Brownell and Jeffrey N. Wasserstrom (Berkeley: University of California Press, 2002), 155–56, 150.

p. 121 "revolutionary masses." See also Tani E. Barlow, *The Question of Women in Chinese Feminism* (Durham: Duke University Press, 2004).

p. 121 "whether he's an artist or a supervisor." This version of Ding Ling's essay can be found under the post "Thoughts on 8 March (Women's Day)," posted December 16, 2009, on libcom.org.

p. 122 "struggle with household chores." Karl, *Mao Zedong and China*.

p. 122 "one's self, one's community, and one's past" … "cities of pre-1949 China" … "liberated little by little." Gail Hershatter, *The Gender of Memory: Rural Women and China's Collective Past* (Berkeley: University of California Press, 2014), 3, 105, 101.

p. 123 "a politics of concealment" … "Even men said, now women are a big deal." Wang Zheng, *Finding Women in the State: A Socialist Feminist Revolution in the People's Republic of China, 1949–1964* (Berkeley: University of California Press, 2016), 18, 33.

p. 124 "commitment to female 'liberation through labor.'" Karl, *Mao Zedong and China*.

p. 124 "work in state-run enterprises" … "normal part of the social economy." Jiang Yongping, "Employment and Chinese Urban Women Under Two Systems," in *Holding Up Half the Sky: Chinese Women Past, Present, and Future*, edited by Tao Jie, Zheng Bijun, and Shirley L. Mow (New York: Feminist Press, 2004), 207, 208.

p. 124 "was not true liberation." Guo Yuhua, "Collectivization of the Soul: Women's Memories of the Agricultural Cooperative Movement in the Village of Ji in North Shaanxi," *Chinese Social Science* 4 (2003).

p. 125 "women are missing from official Party history," Guo Yuhua, speaking at "Contemporary Research on Chinese Women," workshop in Beijing, organized by CEFC, May 11, 2013.

p. 125 "The rationale behind differential retirement ages …" For more on the history of China's different retirement ages for women and men, see Martin King Whyte and William L. Parish, *Urban Life in Contemporary China* (Chicago: The University of Chicago Press, 1984), 195–228.

p. 125 "the last to be rehired later," Liu Jieyu, *Gender and Work in Urban China: Women Workers of the Unlucky Generation* (New York: Routledge, 2007).

p. 126 "gender discrimination in hiring" Human Rights Watch, "'Only Men Need Apply,'" report, April 23, 2018, hrw.org.

p. 127 "inspiring a new group of young feminists." Zeng Jinyan, "Zhongguo nüquan zhuyi sanshi nian" [Thirty Years of Chinese Feminism], *Initium*, September 24, 2015, theinitium.com.

p. 127 "China's National Bureau of Statistics." Yang Yao, "Pay Gap Still Wide Between Men and Women Despite Improvements," *China Daily USA*, March 13, 2015, usa.chinadaily.com.cn.

p. 128 "ranked China 100 out of 144 countries," World Economic Forum, "The Global Gender Gap Report 2017," report, November 2, 2017, weforum.org.

p. 128 "at the end of 2017." According to an analysis of figures provided by HSBC Bank. See Fincher, *Leftover Women*.

p. 130 "national strength." "*Zhonggong zhongyang guowuyuan guanyu quanmian jiaqiang renkou he jihua shengyu gongzuo tongchou jiejue renkou wenti de jueding*" [State Council Decision on Fully Enhancing the Population and Family Planning Program and Comprehensively Addressing Population Issues], *People's Daily*, January 22, 2007, cpc.people.com.cn.

p. 130 "'upgrading population quality [*suzhi*]' was a key goal." For more on *suzhi* see Ellen Judd, *The Chinese Women's Movement Between State and Market* (Palo Alto: Stanford University Press, 2002).

p. 130 "babies for the good of the nation." For more on the role of eugenics in population planning, see Susan Greenhalgh, *Cultivating Global Citizens: Population in the Rise of China* (Cambridge: Harvard University Press, 2010) and Harriet Evans, "Past, Perfect or Imperfect: Changing Images of the Ideal Wife," in *Chinese Femininities/Chinese Masculinities*, edited by Susan Brownell and Jeffrey N. Wasserstrom (Berkeley: University of California Press, 2002).

Chapter 6. Feminists, Lawyers and Workers

p. 138 "violent to a small woman like me?" Wang Yu, "My Endless Nightmare," in *The People's Republic of the Disappeared: Stories from Inside China's System for Enforced Disappearances*, edited by Michael Caster (Safeguard Defenders, 2017).

p. 139 "accept the Chinese government's leadership." James Podgers, "Chinese Lawyer Wang Yu Given ABA International Human Rights Award in Absentia," *ABA Journal*, August 6, 2016, abajournal.com.

p. 139 "thanking her supporters." @YaxueCao, tweet, 9:17 a.m., July 22, 2017. My translation of her Chinese statement.

p. 141 "abuse of girls in schools." See documentary film by Nanfu Wang, *Hooligan Sparrow*, 2016.

pp. 141–2 "guilty of sexually assaulting sixteen young girls" Jiang Aitao, "Teacher Detained for Sexual Abuse in Rural School," *China Plus*, May 27, 2013, english.cri.cn. Liu says the teacher was originally found guilty of sexually assaulting twenty girls, but four girls from two families dropped out of the lawsuit.

p. 143 "vast majority of whom were girls." Xinhua Insight, "Underage Victims of Sexual Assault Struggle to be Heard in China," *XinhuaNet*, May 31, 2016, xinhuanet.com.

p. 143 "between the fall of 2011 and spring of 2015." Robin McDowell, Reese Dunklin, Emily Schmall, and Justin Pritchard, "Hidden Horror of School Sex Assaults Revealed by AP," *Associated Press*, May 1, 2017, ap.org.

p. 144 "unidentified pills." Xinhua, "Police Investigate Child Abuse at Beijing Kindergarten," *XinhuaNet*, November 23, 2017, xinhuanet. com.

p. 144 "Beijing's Chaoyang district," Samuel Wade, "Minitrue: Don't Report on Kindergarten Abuse," *China Digital Times*, November 24, 2017, chinadigitaltimes.net.

p. 145 "first case of its kind in China's history." Tania Branigan, "China: Woman Settles in First Gender Discrimination Lawsuit," *Guardian*, January 28, 2014, theguardian.com.

p. 146 "worried about the small sum." She went by a different pseudonym for the lawsuit.

p. 149 "demanding access to their jailed husbands," Chris Buckley and Didi Kirsten Tatlow, "In China, Wives Fight Back After Their Activist Husbands Are Jailed," *New York Times*, May 18, 2017, nytimes.com.

p. 149 "the tip of the iceberg." China Labour Bulletin, "Strikes and Protests by China's Workers Soar to Record Heights in 2015," January 7, 2016, clb.org.hk.

p. 149 "uphold women's rights and interests." Thank you to Jeffrey Wasserstrom for this observation.

p. 149 "countries with cheaper labor." See also Ching Kwan Lee, *Against the Law: Labor Protests in China's Rustbelt and Sunbelt* (Berkeley: University of California Press, 2007).

p. 151 "she refused to comply," China Labour Bulletin, "Pregnant Woman Takes Employer to Arbitration for Unfair Dismissal," June 1, 2017, clb.org.hk.

p. 152 "pay one woman 10,000 renminbi," Echo Huang, "A Chinese Firm Is Facing a Rare Joint Complaint from Women Workers Fired When Pregnant," *Quartz*, December 11, 2017, qz.com.

p. 152 "settlement from Hitachi of 230,000 renminbi," China Labour Bulletin, "Sacked Labour Activist Continues to Push for Workers' Trade Unions," September 21, 2015, clb.org.hk.

p. 153 "video of the collective action," Video posted on *China Labour Bulletin* website, then taken down. Accessed April 2017.

p. 153 "taking over the cleaning contract," China Labour Bulletin, "Unity Is Strength: The Story of the Guangzhou University Town Sanitation Workers' Strike," October 16, 2014, clb.org.hk.

p. 154 "their role in these serious violations." China Labour Bulletin, "Global Brands Have to Live up to Their Commitments to Chinese Workers," April 28, 2017, clb.org.hk.

p. 155 "causing his head to bleed," Erika Kinetz, "Making Ivanka Trump Shoes: Long Hours, Low Pay and Abuse," *Houson Chronicle*, June 27, 2017, houstonchronicle.com.

p. 155 "such as China, Cambodia and Vietnam." China Labour Bulletin, "Guangdong Workers Show Once Again How Collective Bargaining Should Be Done," March 13, 2018, clb.org.hk.

pp. 155–6 "These Are Women with Strength and Power," Zheng Churan, *"Zhe shi yi qun chongman liliang de nüren/ Guangzhou*

Daxuecheng huanweigong weiquan bagong zhi jishi" [These Are Women with Strength and Power: A Record of Guangzhou University Town Sanitation Workers' Strike to Protect Rights], August 21, 2014, worldlabour.org.

Chapter 7. China's Patriarchal Authoritarianism

p. 159 "one of China's most wanted social activists." Josh Chin, "Meet Lu Jun, One of China's Most Wanted Social Activists," *Wall Street Journal*, September 6, 2015, wsj.com.

p. 160 "had just been arrested." Barbara Demick, "China Lawyer Who Fought Unfair Arrest Is Arrested," *Los Angeles Times*, August 7, 2009, latimes.com.

p. 162 "China's strongman ruler for life." Some of these passages appeared in a different form in Leta Hong Fincher, "Xi Jinping's Authoritarian Rise in China Has Been Powered by Sexism," *Washington Post*, March 1, 2018, washingtonpost.com.

p. 162 "China's authoritarian control of its population." Some other authors who have written about China's patriarchal authoritarianism include Edward Friedman, *National Identity and Democratic Prospects in Socialist China* (Oxon, ME: Sharpe/Routledge, 1995) and Susan L. Glosser, *Chinese Visions of Family and State, 1915–1953* (Berkeley: University of California Press, 2003). See also Tani E. Barlow, "Theorizing Woman: Funü, Guojia, Jiating," *Genders* 10 (Spring 1991): 132–60.

p. 163 "breach in the field of women's issues," Song Xiuyan, *"Ba jiang zhengzhi guanchuan yu Fulian gaige he gongzuo quan guocheng"* [Speaking Politics Should be Integrated throughout the Whole Process of Reform and Work in the Women's Federation], *People's Daily*, May 19, 2017, cpc.people.com.cn. Translated by the author.

p. 164 "collapse of the Soviet Union!" Gao Yu, "Beijing Observation: Xi Jinping the Man," *China Change*, January 2013.

p. 164 "dangerous views from the West." Chris Buckley, "China Takes Aim at Western Ideas," *New York Times*, August 19, 2013, nytimes.com.

p. 164 "family-state under heaven (*jiaguo tianxia*)." Yangshi wei shipin,

"Jiaguo Tianxia" [Family-State Under Heaven], CCTV mini-video, February 18, 2018.

p. 166 "of double-digit growth rates is now over." Michael Forsythe and Jonathan Ansfield, "Fading Economy and Graft Crackdown Rattle China's Leaders," *New York Times*, August 22, 2015, nytimes.com.

p. 166 "economy is widely expected to cool." "China's Economy Set to Slow to 6.5 Percent in 2018 as Government Turns Off Cheap Money," Reuters, January 16, 2018, reuters.com.

p. 166 "after the Tiananmen massacre." John Ruwitch and Yawen Chen, "Moody's Downgrades China, Warns of Fading Financial Strength As Debt Mounts," Reuters, May 23, 2017, reuters.com.

p. 166 "beginning to cannibalize itself." Carl Minzner, *End of an Era: How China's Authoritarian Revival is Undermining Its Rise* (New York: Oxford University Press, 2018), xviii.

p. 167 "defining norms of womanhood," *Women and Confucian Cultures in Premodern China, Korea and Japan*, edited by Dorothy Ko, JaHyun Kim Haboush, and Joan R. Piggott (Berkeley: University of California Press, 2003), 2.

pp. 167–8 "this is *yi* [righteousness]" … "state is well governed." Fangqin Du and Susan Mann, "Competing Claims on Womanly Virtue in Late Imperial China," in *Women and Confucian Cultures*, edited by Ko, Haboush, and Piggott, 225–26, 237.

p. 168 "Ever Since the Eighteenth Party Congress, Xi Jinping Has Talked This Way about Family Values," [*Shibada yilai, Xi Jinping zheyang tan "jiafeng"*], *People's Daily*, March 29, 2017, politics.people.com.cn. Translation by the author.

p. 169 "traditional culture." "*Zhenjiang chengli xinshidai nüzi xuetang guifan nüxing zuozi*" [Zhenjiang establishes New Era Women's Schools on Standards for Women's Posture and Appearance], *Tengxun News*, March 26, 2018.

p. 170 "video posted online in November 2017." Yi-Ling Liu, "Chinese Activists Decry So-Called 'Female Morality Schools,'" February 2, 2018, csmonitor.com.

p. 170 "thirty-one provincial administrations in 2017," Cheng Li, "Status of China's Women Leaders on the Eve of 19th Party Congress," Brookings Institution, March 30, 2017, brookings.edu.

p. 171 *"One Child."* Mei Fong, *One Child: The Story of China's Most Radical Experiment* (Boston: Houghton Mifflin Harcourt, 2016). See also Wang Feng, Baochang Gu and Yong Cai, "The End of China's One-Child Policy," *Studies in Family Planning* 47, no. 1 (March 2016): 83–6; Susan Greenhalgh and Edwin W. Winckler, *Governing China's Population: From Leninist to Neoliberal Biopolitics* (Palo Alto: Stanford University Press, 2005).

p. 171 "population-replacement rate of 2.1." World Bank, "Fertility rate, total (births per woman) – China," accessed March 27, 2018, at data.worldbank.org.

p. 171 "to reproduce for China." Some of these passages appear in a different form in my op-ed, Leta Hong Fincher, "China Dropped Its One-Child Policy. So Why Aren't Chinese Women Having More Babies?" *New York Times*, February 20, 2018, nytimes.com.

p. 171 "over sixty years old by 2030." "China Sees Gray Generation as Quarter of Population by 2013," *Bloomberg News*, January 26, 2017, bloombergquint.com.

p. 171 "were already over sixty," Xinhua, "Elders Make Up One-Third of Shanghai's Population," *XinhuaNet*, March 28, 2017, xinhuanet. com.

p. 171 "to 69.7 percent in 2050," China Power Team, "Does China have an aging problem?" China Power, February 15, 2016, chinapower. csis.org.

p. 171 "113 boys born for every 100 girls in 2015," Xinhua, "*Zhongguo weilai 30 nian nei jiang you yue sanqianwan shihun nanxing zhaobudao duixiang*" [30 Million Marriage-Age Men Won't Find Partners in the Next 30 Years], *XinhuaNet*, February 13, 2017, xinhuanet.com.

p. 172 *"Leftover Women."* See also Mara Hvistendahl, *Unnatural Selection: Choosing Boys Over Girls, and the Consequences of a World Full of Men* (New York: Public Affairs, 2012).

p. 172 "China's Two-Child Policy Results in Largest Number of Newborns since 2000," Xinhua, March 11, 2017, xinhuanet.com.

p. 172 "falling far short of expectations," Wang Xiaoyu, "NBS: Birthrate Dropped, But More Chinese Couples Had Second Child," *China Daily*, January 30, 2018, chinadaily.com.cn.

p. 172 "have one more" Shan Juan, "Incentives for Second Child

Considered," *China Daily*, February 28, 2017, chinadaily.com.cn.

p. 172 "as the nation grows old." "Chinese Lawmaker Proposes Cutting Nation's High Marriage Age," *Bloomberg News*, March 12, 2017, bloomberg.com.

p. 172 "post shared thousands of times on Weibo," Sui-Lee Wee, "After One-Child Policy, Outrage at China's Offer to Remove IUDs," *New York Times*, January 7, 2017, nytimes.com.

p. 173 "forced to have children?" Lü Pin, "*Kaifang er tai, huibuhui rang nüren zaici shou shanghai?*" [Will opening up the two-child policy cause further harm to women?], *Feminist Voices*, October 30, 2015. Translation by the author.

p. 174 "beware birth defects." "*Bie buxin! 30 sui zhiqian shi nüxing zuijia shengyu nianling*" [Don't think it's a lie! Younger than 30 is a woman's best child-bearing age], *People's Daily*, October 24, 2017, health, people.com.cn.

p. 174 "in her arms." "'*Yiyu' cheng jiuye ji youshi/zaixiao beiyun nü daxuesheng zengduo*" ["Already had a baby" becomes a sought-after quality in the job-hunting season—more female university students prepare for pregnancy], December 4, 2015, sohu.com. Translation by the author.

p. 175 "more female university students prepare for pregnancy." "*Beijing yi xueyuan 10 yu ming nü daxuesheng huaiyun shengzi: qiuzhi you youshi*" [University in Beijing has over 10 female student mothers: Bright job prospects], *People's Daily*, December 4, 2015, edu.people.com.cn.

p. 175 "Female University Student's Joyful Love: Freshman Year—Live Together, Sophomore Year—Get Pregnant, Junior Year—Have Baby." "*Nü daxuesheng xingfu ai: dayi tongju, daer huaiyun, dasan shengzi*," April 8, 2017, sohu.com.

p. 175 "for love and marriage." Du Xiaofei, "Communist Youth League Vows to Help Unmarried Young People," *People's Daily*, May 18, 2017, en.people.cn.

p. 175 "if they refused to go." Zhao Yusha, "Staff Complains About Obligatory Blind Dates as China Sees Single People As Problem," *Global Times*, May 21, 2017, globaltimes.cn.

p. 176 "or will marry women," Song Jingyi, "Wives In Sham Marriages

Hidden in the Shadows," *China Daily*, April 22, 2016,chinadaily.com. cn.

p. 177 "child-bearing and child-rearing." Shulamith Firestone, *The Dialectic of Sex: The Case for Feminist Revolution* (London: Verso, 2015 [1970]), 11.

p. 178 "do not want to have babies at all." Zhaopin Limited, "Zhaopin Report Found China's Working Women Less Keen on Childbearing," Cision PR Newswire, May 11, 2017, prnewswire.com.

p. 178 "upper-middle-income or high-income brackets," "China's High-Earning Consumers to Surge by 2030: Report," *XinhuaNet*, November 5, 2016, xinhuanet.com.

p. 178 "eight consecutive years since 2008," Ministry of Civil Affairs of the People's Republic of China, "2016 Social Service Development Statistical Communique"; also see Xuan Li, "China's Marriage Rate Is Plummeting – And It's Because of Gender Inequality," *The Conversation*, October 11, 2016, theconversation.com.

p. 179 "to tell if marriage rates will continue to fall," See also *Wives, Husbands and Lovers: Marriage and Sexuality in Hong Kong, Taiwan and Urban China*, edited by Deborah S. Davis and Sara L. Friedman (Palo Alto: Stanford University Press, 2014).

p. 180 "freeze her eggs." Emily Rauhala, "Why China Stops Single Women From Freezing Their Eggs," *Washington Post*, August 4, 2015, washingtonpost.com.

p. 180 "worryingly high birthrates" "Xinjiang Official Calls for Fewer Births, Later Marriage in Rural South," *Global Times*, January 23, 2015, globaltimes.cn.

p. 180 "efforts to fight terrorism." "Remote Control: The Government in Xianjiang is Trying to Limit Muslim Births," *The Economist*, November 7, 2015, economist.com.

p. 181 "dilute the Uyghur population," Edward Wong, "To Temper Unrest in Western China, Officials Offer Money for Interethnic Marriage," *New York Times*, September 2, 2014, nytimes.com.

p. 181 "for all newborns." Benjamin Hass, "China Bans Religious Names for Muslim Babies in Xianjiang," *Guardian*, April 24, 2017, theguardian.com.

p. 181 "public health deficiency." "Xinjiang Sets New Child Policy,"

Global Times, August 1, 2017, pressreader.com/china/global-times.

p. 184 "comments in class and on social media," Nectar Gan, "Chinese Communist Party Targets University Known For Global Outlook," *South China Morning Post*, March 28, 2017, scmp.com.

p. 184 "have not been properly implemented," Equality-Beijing NGO observation of two-year implementation of the anti-domestic violence law, March 6, 2018. unpublished report, translation by Equality-Beijing.

Conclusion: A Song for All Women

p. 191 "largest single-day protest in US history." Erica Chenowith and Jeremy Pressman, "This Is What We Learned By Counting the Women's Marches," *Washington Post*, February 7, 2017,washingtonpost.com.

p. 192 "Feminism is immortal!" See Free Chinese Feminists Facebook and @FeministChina Twitter site for video and photos.

p. 193 "Go home and live well." Sophie Richardson, "China Tells Women to 'Go Home and Live Well,'" *Human Rights Watch*, August 28, 2017, hrw.org.

p. 194 "lives of bisexuals in China." Wei Tingting, director, *Bi China*, 2017.

p. 195 "America's clean air and democracy." Simon Denyer and Congcong Zhang, "A Chinese Student Praised the 'Fresh Air of Free Speech' at a U.S. College: Then Came the Backlash," *Washington Post*, May 23, 2017, washingtonpost.com.

p. 195 "Chinese Student at University of Maryland Slammed for Biased Commencement Speech." Jiang Jie, "Chinese Student at University of Maryland Slammed for Biased Commencement Speech," *People's Daily*, May 22, 2017, en.people.cn.

p. 196 "brand ambassador for Diesel." Melanie Wilkinson, "Li Yuchun: Meet the Pop Star Taking Gender Neutral Style to China," *Guardian*, October 15, 2017, theguardian.com.

p. 197 "want to sing like men." Benjamin Haas, "Acrush: The Boyband of Girls Winning Hearts in China," *Guardian*, April 30, 2017, theguardian.com.

p. 198 "or gender expression." Di Wang, "What is the Significance of China's #MeToo Movement?" *China File*, March 16, 2018, chinafile. com.

p. 198 "wrestling champions." Amy Qin, "China Fears India May Be Edging It Out in Culture Battle," *New York Times*, September 30, 2017, nytimes.com.

p. 199 "Wanda Pictures also invested in the film," Rob Cain, "'Wonder Woman' Winds Up June In China With Super $89 Million," *Forbes*, June 29, 2017, forbes.com.

p. 199 "reaction to *Wonder Woman*." Da Tu (Giant Rabbit), "*Shenqi nüxia' jiujing shibushi yibu nüquan zhuyi dianying?*" [Is Wonder Woman Actually a Feminist Film?], *Feminist Voices*, June 5, 2017. Translation by the author.

p. 200 "interrogated by police." Tanya Lokshina, "Authorities in Southern Russia Scared of Feminism," Human Rights Watch, August 14, 2017, hrw.org.

p. 200 "retaliation for their advocacy." Nina Lakhani, "Mexico City Murders Put Defenders of Women's Rights on High Alert," *Guardian*, August 20, 2015, theguardian.com.

p. 200 "reinvigorated the women's movement." Traci Tong, "The Dangers of Reporting on Femicide in Argentina," PRI's The World, November 3, 2017, pri.org.

p. 200 "in Rio de Janeiro in March 2018." Suyin Haynes, "The Assassination of Brazilian Politician Marielle Franco Turned Her Into a Global Icon," *TIME*, March 22, 2018, time.com. See also *The Unfinished Revolution: Voices from the Global Fight for Women's Rights*, edited by Minky Worden (New York: Seven Stories Press, 2012).

p. 200 "feminist Mona Eltahawy," Mona Eltahawy, *Headscarves and Hymens: Why the Middle East Needs a Sexual Revolution* (New York: Farrar, Straus and Giroux, 2015).

p. 202 "most serious crisis in decades in 2017" Freedom House, "Freedom in the World 2018 – Democracy in Crisis," report, freedomhouse. org.

p. 203 "holding her sandals in her hands." Jing Xiong, "China Feminist Five – 'Do You Hear the Women Sing,'" YouTube, video, September 21, 2015, youtube.com.

Acknowledgments

p. 208 "Feminism, Chinese" Leta Hong Fincher, "Feminism, Chinese," in *The Wiley Blackwell Encyclopedia of Gender and Sexuality Studies*, edited by Nancy Naples, Renee C. Hoogland, Maithree Wickramasinghe and Wai Ching Angela Wong (Hoboken, NJ: John Wiley & Sons, 2016).

Index

E